Risk and Food Safety in China and Japan

Around the world, food has probably never been as safe as it is today. However, periodic crises have aroused consumer anxiety and contributed to a general lack of confidence in the agro-industrial system. The diverse nature of these crises increases governments' and industry difficulties in predicting and tackling them. This book addresses the relations between risk and food theoretically and empirically through case studies from Japan and China.

Part I of the book examines the interaction between theoretical aspects and decision-making. The book theorizes the links between food and risk and analyses the decision-making process in light of risks and governance. The relationship between food risks, governance systems and economic decisions is assessed to explore ideas such as the "pact of nutrition" and the theory of weak signals. Part II examines case studies from China and Japan in the aftermaths of recent crises such as the milk powder scandal in China and food safety following the Fukushima nuclear accident and tsunami in Japan.

This book will be an important resource for scholars, academics and policymakers in the fields of sociology, economics, food studies, Chinese studies and Japanese studies and theories of risks and safety.

Louis Augustin-Jean is a Research Fellow at the Centre for Economic Research, the University of Paris-Nord (CEPN), France.

Jean-Pierre Poulain is a Professor at Toulouse University Jean Jaurès, France, and at Taylor's University, Malaysia.

Routledge Studies in Food, Society and the Environment

For further details please visit the series page on the Routledge website: www.routledge.com/books/series/RSFSE/

Risk and Food Safety in China and Japan

Theoretical Perspectives and Empirical Insights

Edited by Louis Augustin-Jean and Jean-Pierre Poulain

Routledge
Taylor & Francis Group

LONDON AND NEW YORK

First published 2019
by Routledge

2 Park Square, Milton Park, Abingdon, Oxfordshire OX14 4RN

52 Vanderbilt Avenue, New York, NY 10017

Routledge is an imprint of the Taylor & Francis Group, an informa business

First issued in paperback 2020

British Library Cataloguing-in-Publication Data
A catalogue record for this book is available from the British Library

Library of Congress Cataloging-in-Publication Data
A catalog record has been requested for this book

ISBN: 978-1-138-89765-6 (hbk)
ISBN: 978-0-367-66549-4 (pbk)

Typeset in Goudy
by Wearset Ltd, Boldon, Tyne and Wear

Contents

Figures

Tables

Contributors

Yongkang An is a postdoctoral researcher at the Guanghua Law School, Zhe-jiang University, China. She has obtained her PhD degree at University College Dublin, Ireland. Her main research interests include regulation and governance, food safety regulation and public law.

Louis Augustin-Jean is a research fellow associated to the University of Paris 13, Centre d'Economie de l'Université de Paris-Nord (CEPN), France. He specializes in the fields of economic sociology, sociology of risks and the soci-ology of food. He has lived for over twenty years in Asia, both in Hong Kong and in Japan, where he worked as Associate Professor at the University of Tsukuba. He co-edited *The Political Economy of Agro-food Markets in China* (2015).

Florent Champy is a sociologist and research professor in the National Centre for Scientific Research (University of Toulouse, National Centre for Scient-ific Research, LISST-CERS, Toulouse, France). His main fields of research are professional work, risks and health. His research focuses on the obstacles to practical wisdom in modern societies.

David Kurt Herold taught and researched in China for over nine years, before joining the Hong Kong Polytechnic University in 2007. His research focuses on the everyday use of information and communication technologies (ICTs). In particular, he studies the Chinese internet, encounters between Chinese and non-Chinese online, the impact of the Internet on offline society, and online education. His recent publications include "Xi Jinping's Internet: Faster, Truer, More Positive and More Chinese" (*China: An International Journal*, in press); "Layers of Racism: ChinaSMACK and the Failure of Cross-Cultural Communication" (in A. B. Buccitelli, *Race and Ethnicity in Digital Culture: Our Changing Traditions, Impressions, and Expressions in a Mediated World*, 2017); and "Whisper Campaigns: Market Risks through Online Rumours on the Chinese Internet" (*Chinese Journal of Social Work*, 2015).

Shuji Hisano is a professor of international political economy of agriculture in the Graduate School of Economics at Kyoto University, Japan. He holds a doctoral degree in agricultural economics at Hokkaido University (2001).

His research interests include global governance of food security, industrialization of agricultural biotechnology, social responsibility and regulation of agribusiness corporations, and international comparative study of agrarian and rural development.

Jinghan Ke is a PhD candidate in the International Graduate Programme for East Asia Sustainable Economic Development Studies at the Graduate School of Economics, Kyoto University, Japan. She holds a master's degree in agricultural economics from the Graduate School of Agriculture at Kyoto University (2014). She is researching the alternative food networks of China and investigating the emerging food initiatives in vegetable provisioning system in a Chinese *san nong* context.

Yoko Niiyama is a professor at the College of Economics, Ritsumeikan University and emeritus professor of Kyoto University, Japan. She graduated from the Faculty of Agriculture, Kyoto University and holds a PhD from Kyoto University. Her main research field is food system and food safety. Her publications include *Theories of Food-Safety-System Practices* (2004) and *The Beef Food System: Comparative Analysis of Japan and US/EU* (2001).

Jean-Pierre Poulain is a professor in sociology and anthropology at the University of Toulouse, France. He conducts research in the sociology of food, focusing on the changes of eating patterns, their links with health and food crises under the CERTOP UMR-CNRS 5044. He currently holds the Chair of Food Studies, jointly created by the University of Toulouse and Taylor's University (Kuala Lumpur, Malaysia) and co-directs the International Associated Laboratory (LIA-CNRS) "Food, Cultures and Health". Among his many publications are *The Sociology of Food: Eating and the Place of Food in Society* (2017) and *Dictionnaire des cultures alimentaires* (2018).

Vincent Simoulin is a researcher at CERTOP (Centre of research on work, organizations and public policies), University of Toulouse, France. His main fields of studies are organizational change, governance and research policies. His publications include "An Instrument Can Hide Many Others, Or How Multiple Instruments Grow into a Polymorphic Instrumentation" (*Social Science Information*, 2017), "The Synchrotron Generations: Communities and Facilities at the Crossroads between the National and the International" (*Revue française de sociologie*, 2016) and *La gouvernance territoriale. Pratiques, discours et théories* (with Romain Pasquier and Julien Weisbein, 2013).

Michitoshi Yamaguchi is a lecturer in food safety economics at the Department of Agri-food System, Faculty of Agriculture, Ryukoku University, Japan. His main research interests are animal health economics, (human) health economics and behavioural aspects of food safety. He was the recipient of several academic awards including the 2015 annual award of The Association for Regional Agricultural and Forestry Economics for his book *Economic Analysis of Contagious Animal Diseases* (in Japanese).

Abbreviations

AFSCA	Federal Agency for the Security of the Food Chain, Belgium
AFSSA	French Food Safety Agency
ANIA	French National Association of Food Industries
AOC	appellation d'origine contrôlée
BSE	bovine spongiform encephalopathy
CFDA	China Food and Drug Administration
EFSA	European Food Safety Authority
FSA	Food Standards Agency, UK
FSL	Food Safety Law 2009, China
GMO	genetically modified organism
GMP	good manufacturing practice
HACCP	hazard analysis and critical control point
HPAI	highly pathogenic avian influenza
IBD	infectious bursal disease
MoH	Ministry of Health, China
OIE	World Organization for Animal Health
SFDA	State Food and Drug Administration, China
SPA	French Society for the Protection of Animals
SPCA	Society for the Prevention of Cruelty to Animals
SPS	Sanitary and Phytosanitary
WTO	World Trade Organization

Introduction

Louis Augustin-Jean and Jean-Pierre Poulain

Following the end of the Second World War, providing cheap food in sufficient quantity became a major political issue. In East Asia, the reconstruction of domestic agricultures, the implementation of the "green revolution" and the import of American surpluses – all elements of what Philip McMichael (2000: 410) defined as "a food regime centered on a food import complex" – were important parameters for fulfilling this objective. The strong economic growth enjoyed by the region, which started in Japan and the "four little dragons", ensured the success of these policies and the development of the agro-industrial system. With the political and economic risks regarding food security easing, food issues gradually took a lesser place in the political agenda. In China, the pattern followed a different timeframe, but the final results were mostly similar. In the first stage, the Maoist period of isolation and semi-autarky did not create the conditions for this "East Asian model" to blossom. However, after the launch of the reform period, hundreds of millions of people were lifted out of poverty – thanks to the strong economic growth. The agricultural output was boosted to impressive levels, and Lester Brown's pessimistic predictions in his bestseller, *Who Will Feed China* (1995), were relegated to a distant future (Veeck 2014).

Thus, many shared the optimism that the agro-industrial complex is the answer to food security and food safety concerns so that the existing risks could be minimized. They did not mean that food would be available in sufficient quality and quantity, or that contamination and poisoning will become non-existent, but they generally agree that science and technology could resolve most of these issues.

However, this optimistic perspective did not last. Gradually, fears over quality replaced concerns over quantities. In the 1990s, these concerns mushroomed, boosted by a succession of crises, sowing doubts that the industrialization of production and distribution, with its quality management features, was the solution to tackle food safety. The acceleration of the internationalization of markets also made it difficult to reduce the differences between national legal and cultural frameworks despite the efforts made by the international organizations in charge of that matter.

Such worries over food safety and quality were first shared by a tiny minority of people who had developed a particular sensitivity to certain food issues.

These individuals played an important role in framing the issues at stake, establishing their parameters, and building up the "social problem" by using available scientific and technical data. The main points raised by these people were then discussed by "activists–experts" who shared similar interests and met in small groups, before they were adopted by civil society movements. In some instances, the issues remained almost confidential. In others, however, they were diffused and mediated, to finally become mainstream and debated in the mass media. This pattern, which forms the bedrock of the theory of weak signals, postulates that certain crises can be identified and managed by listening to the messages sent by "activists–experts" when it is still in the setup phase (see Jean-Pierre Poulain in this volume).

This model fits the experience of Japan where the concern for food safety was already voiced in the early 1960s by social movements such as the Japan Consumers' Association (Nihon Shohisha Kyôkai) and the New Japan Women's Association (Shin Nihon Fujin no Kai). "Interestingly, while none of these organizations was founded as a response to a perceived food crisis, many later came to be involved in food and agricultural issues" (Jussaume *et al.* 2000: 217). They were quick to react to the crises, which became more and more visible from the mid-1950s onward. Two events in particular contributed to the rise in Japanese people's awareness of the existence of food safety problems within the domestic agro-industrial complex. The first was the Morinaga milk incident in 1955 when arsenic contamination in milk led to 12,000 cases of poisoning and 138 deaths (ibid.: 218). This crisis was followed by a legal and political battle which extended well into the 1970s, as the company tried to escape its responsibilities (Shoji and Sugai 1992). At about the same time, in 1956, one of the largest industrial scandals in Japanese history erupted with the discovery of the "Minamata disease". After two years of research, it was found that the disease was caused by the dumping of methyl mercury into the seawaters in the vicinity of Minamata city – the methyl mercury was ingested by fishes and other sea animals. But it was not until a similar incident happened in Niigata, in 1965, that strong governmental and legal measures were finally put in place (Ui 1992).[1] In both cases, the protection that industrial ventures enjoyed from the government and their action during the crisis strengthened mistrust for food manufactures – a phenomenon which became ubiquitous in other parts of the world after the bovine spongiform encephalopathy (BSE) crisis erupted in the 1990s.

In China, consumers have experienced the same mistrust about their food industry as their Japanese counterparts did, but this phenomenon started much later. If food shortages were a real concern during the Great Leap Forward and the Cultural Revolution, food safety crises were then virtually non-existent. The reasons have been attributed to low interprovincial trade and the limited industrial transformation of agriculture at that time (Bian 2004; Augustin-Jean 2014). However, when food and agro-food products started to experience a general decline in quality from the mid-1990s (Alpermann and Augustin-Jean 2014), consumers' suspicion of the industrial food system also grew quickly. Among the most prominent reasons were the reorganization of the food chains during the reform period, and the growth of the food industry in a weak legal and institutional environment. The partial economic liberalization created opportunities for the actors, but also loopholes and instabilities. For example, in the wool and cashmere industries, farmers have lost the incentives to produce good quality raw materials because the premium for quality products was captured by middlemen, while the farmers only bore additional costs and work (Brown *et al.* 2014; Waldron *et al.* 2014) – a characteristic that is also prominent in the production of vegetables analysed by Ke and Hisano in this book.

Therefore, it is no surprise that the "weak signals" have considerably strengthened, and that worries concerning food safety – and even food security – have drawn more attention than they have had for years. This was further reinforced by a series of events that occurred at the global level, including in China and in Japan. The first was the dramatic increase in prices of agricultural products worldwide in 2008–2010. Coupled with the 2008 financial crisis, it was an indication to many people that beyond the neoclassical paradigm, the promises of the liberalization of international trade remain elusive: agricultural specialization, which was promoted under the banner of the comparative advantage theory, did not benefit everyone. On the contrary, it placed certain categories of population at risk, especially at times of low (global) reserves and high international prices. During the period 2008–2010, the situation evolved from an economic crisis to a social and political one: following the drastic increase in food prices, protests and riots occurred in more than 50 countries including Indonesia, Malaysia and the Philippines. Thus, the risks associated with food access (Sen 1981) have not been eliminated by the development of international trade – quite the contrary. The reality and the intensity of the 2008–2010 price hikes pushed some traditional rice importers like the Philippines to revert to their former reliance on international trade and stimulate their domestic production with the stated aim to achieve self-sufficiency – a target that the Philippines nearly reached in 2015 (Diaz 2015).

Second, in the same year, 2008, another major incident erupted in China. The addition of melamine to milk (powder) to boost its apparent protein content in tests was far from novel in that country, but it reached a new scale that year due to the worsening of the market conditions. The ensuing poisoning caused the death of six children, while 300,000 others fell ill (Delman and Yang 2012; Augustin-Jean 2014; among others). The situation evolved from a simple public health issue to a major social and economic crisis, further fuelling Chinese people's mistrust against not just locally produced milk powder but also the entire country's food system. The addition of melamine is often understood as the result of unscrupulous behaviour of agents, but this perception is too straitjacketed. In fact, this fraud should be analysed as the consequence of the reconfiguration of market structures, which is affecting the profitability in, and within, the value chain and therefore is not solely the consequence of the fraud committed by these agents – which of course is not an excuse for the poor decision-making and unethical behaviour of some of these agents (see Delman and Yang 2012). The resulting instability has similarities with the food safety crises in nineteenth-century Europe, when changes in market structures and scientific progress created uncertainties and instabilities (Stanziani 2005). It is worth noting that despite efforts to reorganize the value chain of milk, the melamine fraud still remains endemic.

In comparison, the Fukushima nuclear accident in 2011 and its consequences for food safety, analysed in detail by Augustin-Jean in this volume, were of a different nature. On one hand, the food safety crisis that followed the accident was not a by-product of the food system itself, like in the melamine fraud, but the consequence of an industrial disaster which was external to the food system itself. The food crisis, then, is only but one of the sequels that have been damaging to the environment and modifying the social life. The Fukushima crisis can thus be seen as the perfect case that reifies the "risk society" theorized by Ulrich Beck (1992, 1999). For Beck, in the "risk society", risks are generated by technology – they are invisible, difficult to control and difficult to evaluate, among others. Since they permeate the whole society, these risks make it difficult for people to avoid them (even though the lower economic strata of society are generally more affected by them).

An interesting insight to be noted is the differences in these three food crises, which pinpoint that crises may arise at any point along the food chains and develop in unpredictable fashion. Thus, the diversity of the crises reinforces the feeling that the industrial agro-food system is not really safe – even though the risks it generates are generally small in comparison to the size of the market (Champy, in this volume). This feeling of insecurity and, related to it, the lack of trust over the food system in general, are further supported by the fact that the three above-mentioned crises are just the tip of the iceberg. In Asia alone, many incidents involving food safety have multiplied in recent years: the tainted oil from Taiwan, the recurrent avian flu crisis (see Yamaguchi in this volume), the fruits and vegetables containing a high level of pesticide in China (see Ke and Hisano in this volume), the import of contaminated dumplings from China to Japan, just to name a few. Extensive media coverage of these events led to the public questioning further food safety.

Under such circumstances, governments have to provide responses to the increasing concerns of their citizens-cum-consumers – the weak signals of the 1970s are now distant memories. However, the plural answers provided by governments to ease these worries – creation of ad hoc food safety centres, reinforcement of legislation, increased controls, creation and implementation of standards – point more to the complexity of the phenomenon, which cannot anymore be only tackled within national borders, than easing consumer worries. Along with the growth of the international trade of agricultural products, the value chains have lengthened and risks have been globalized, which calls for more international coordination. General guidelines and risk analysis principles have been developed (FAO 2009; Godefroy and Clarke 2016; see Niiyama in this volume), but they are bounded by cultural practices and commercial interests, which limit their implementation and their scope (Ilbert *et al.* 2014). With the liberalization of the agricultural trade and signing of free trade agreements, including in the Asia-Pacific Region, the contradiction between the necessity to, on the one hand, guarantee the freedom of trade and, on the other hand, implement international regulations (which operate a separation between what is allowed to be traded and what is not) in the respect of cultural specificities will become even more crucial.

Thus, as seen from the above, despite their voluntary nature, these government actions (at both the national and international levels) have not been able to fully prevent food safety crises. The efficiency of the different measures put in place by governments, from regulations to the creation of ad hoc food safety centres, is put into question by consumers. To some extent, and paradoxically, it seems that the more government and industry reinforce their system to tackle food safety issues, the more people worry. In short, the number of food safety crises, the diversity and the unpredictability of their origin, their media coverage and the apparent inability of governments to prevent them are all elements that increase people's concerns.

This diversity of risks – which can originate within or outside the food chain, arise from anywhere, concern any type of food, and be spread locally or globally – as well as the way crises are covered by the media, have not only increased people's anxiety, but also have led to diverging evaluations of, and thus, to differentiated ways to react to, these risks. It then becomes crucial to analyse theoretically these two following points: the evaluation or risks; and decision-making in a situation or risks. At least five propositions can be made to answer these two points. First, appreciation of risks and decision-making in a situation of (real or perceived – which does not make any significant difference, as we will see later) risk should not be appreciated (solely) through the lens of the rational choice. On the contrary, the evaluation of risk involves making a judgement that differs greatly from the "calculation" of the rational choice (Callon 1998; Karpik 2010). The classic differentiation between risks and uncertainties (Knight 1921) should be introduced at this stage, but it must already be clear that the distinction between the two notions is mostly a question of degree rather than of nature. Second, in a "risk-free"[2] situation, the operation of judgement (on quality, for example) usually relies on focal points (Boltanski and Thévenot 2006) or judgement devices (Karpik 2010). However, and this is the third point, in a situation of risks, the lack of trust resulting from these risks makes the focal points or devices unable to fulfil their role. The analytical shift from risks analysis to judgements and decision-making implies that the distinction between perceived and real risks loses some of its significance. Fourth, food safety and environmental risks should not be analysed separately from economic risks: when food safety risks are present, economic ones are never very far away. Lastly, food risks should not be analysed as any type of risks. The simple act of ingestion involves a specific relationship between the eater and the food s/he eats, not only physiologically but also culturally and psychologically. As we will see below, this has been conceptualized as the "principle of incorporation". For example, new foods are often regarded with suspicion: more explicitly, eaters perform a specific evaluation of risks, which is not only related to health, but also to social, cultural and symbolic factors. In other words, food contamination is also symbolic, leading to another evaluation of rationality that has to take into account the links that people maintain with their food. These five points are discussed in detail below.

First, the intricate task of defining risks is at times tweaked to just contrasting them in a binary system between, for instance, "local and global, individual and collective, natural and technological, real and constructed, calculable and incalculable, visible and invisible, voluntary and involuntary and actual and perceived risks" (Ekberg 2007: 353). This binary system seems to extend the older tradition that can be traced back to Frank Knight and his classical differentiation between risks and uncertainty: a probability can be attached to a risky event, but not to an uncertain one. But in fact, the Knightian framework is much more sophisticated than this type of binary opposition suggests, and, at this point, a more direct reference to Knight should be introduced to explain the shift from calculation to judgements. For Knight, the opposition between risks and uncertainties was not so straightforward and there was no clear-cut distinction between these two notions. In fact, Knight imagined a continuum based on the construction and the interpretation of probabilities. Situations of "pure risks" are rare, while a certain level of uncertainty remains in most events – which makes life more unpredictable, but at the same time, more bearable. In other words, the probability attached to a given risk often incorporates a certain level of uncertainty which, by definition, is impossible to delimit (Knight 1921; see more on this point in Augustin-Jean in this volume).

Therefore, substituting the Knightian uncertainty with the concept of "incalculable risks", as mentioned above, operates a theoretical displacement, but leaves unresolved the problematic evaluation of the "calculable risks": despite their increasing sophistication, the risk analysis and risk assessment are performed through a series of assumptions that allow room for interpretation. This is completely in line with the seminal work of Knight: the evaluation of (calculable) risks includes a certain degree of uncertainty (which, by definition, cannot be specified). This uncertainty is to be found at every level, from the construction of (statistical) categories, to the calculation and the interpretation of the risk assessment and/or probabilities.[3] Concretely, it means that people's decisions cannot be *solely* based on the reading of probabilities (even when they are available) or the risk assessment; they must also rely on judgements – at least to "evaluate" the degree of reliability of these probabilities and assessments. People have to decide "how much" they should trust "numbers". Therefore, the evaluation of risks is a complex *process*, which involves a series of judgements, and not a simple calculation. This statement still leaves aside the intricate issue of the elaboration of judgements. But before moving on to that point, we still have to discuss how this framework, based on a different level of trust in probabilities and scientific evaluation, is useful in differentiating the two types of judgements carried out by "experts" and "laymen" and, beyond, two different modes of rationality.

In more detail, the trust granted to "numbers" (and probabilities) and the reliability of scientific procedures are understood differently by "experts" and "laymen". As data producers, experts tend to have more trust in "numbers" than ordinary people; however, it cannot be inferred from that phenomenon that "experts" are more rational than "laymen", but only that their ways to evaluate risks are different (Slovic 2000a; Kahneman 2011). From the experts' point of view, if laymen do not judge in the same way as they do, it is mainly because they do not share the same level of knowledge (what economists would call an asymmetry of information). Thus, experts tend to believe that a simple transfer of knowledge and information would necessarily lead to a convergence of judgements. For them, it is then sufficient to evaluate people's knowledge to determine the type of information the "neophytes" have to digest to adopt the same point of view as them. In a slightly more sophisticated version of this paradigm, an interaction between laymen and experts allows the experts to better understand why people think the way they do and to prepare more targeted information to be disseminated to the laymen. This interaction then becomes a tool for the experts to influence the laymen (see Niiyama in this volume).

This perspective highlights the role of information and cognitive perception of the agents in forming judgements; however, a major limitation is to ignore, or even discredit, the laypeople's mode of rationality and to turn a blind eye to the deficiencies in the experts' mode of rationality. Indeed, the experts' judgements are not as rational as they seem. On the one hand, experts tend to discard uncertainties arising from the construction of risk assessments (see above). On the other hand, it has been shown that they tend to grant a prominent importance to *some* numbers and information while ignoring, or minimizing, other, and potentially more important data. There are two reasons for this. First, the process of classification performed by individuals (laypeople as well as experts) tends to eliminate data that do not match with their (preconceived) judgement. Again, this often involves the technical and scientific construction of risks (Slovic 2000b: 393–394). Thus, even for experts, risk assessment often remains subjective, as illustrated by Kraus *et al.* (2000) in the case of toxicology.[4] Second, and related to it, experts, in framing risks scientifically, have to eliminate a certain number of parameters. This simplification, which is part of the scientific process, has important consequences for the evaluation of risks. In other words, in searching for general rules, valid everywhere and anytime, specialists have the tendency to brush aside small differences (this is an issue related to the construction of categories, as presented above), which are often part of local cultures (Wynne 1996).

The resulting confusion, further aggravated by divergent expert opinions, inevitably affects the way laymen form their judgements. As a consequence, people (whether they are experts or not) cannot make a rational calculation since the information they receive is blurred, partial and contradictory. This point, which can be categorized as a case of "bounded rationality" (Simon 1997), is often, and wrongly, neglected by experts and economists. It is nonetheless sufficient to obliterate the vain hope of experts to provide the "right" information to laymen.

Furthermore, there are also differences in the way these two categories of people process and analyse information. On the one hand, experts tend to rely on risk assessments, procedures and probabilities – even though, as seen above, their judgements are also biased and influenced by non-scientific considerations. For ordinary people, on the contrary, probabilities and risk assessments are only some of the elements, amongst others, that are taken into consideration to judge a situation. For example, the expected consequences if an event occurs, and the possibility to reverse the negative impact of this event, are also important elements laymen bear in mind before making a judgement. Laymen also take into account many micro-data and cultural elements that are often ignored by experts (Wynne 1996). Finally, even if the probability of a given risk is considered low by the experts, ordinary people have the tendency to reject it when the consequences are potentially huge and the reversibility low. This explains the negative judgement of ordinary people against nuclear energy, despite the fact that many experts emphasize the negligible risks.

Differently stated, experts and laypeople have two distinct forms of rationality, based on two modes of judgement, with different principles of justification (Poulain, in this volume). Both are rational, but involve what Herbert Simon called "procedural rationality":

> Behavior is procedurally rational when it is the outcome of appropriate deliberation. Its procedural rationality depends on the process that generated it.... Hence, procedural rationality is usually studied in problem situations – situations in which the subject must gather information of various kinds and process it in different ways in order to arrive at a reasonable course of action.
>
> (1976: 65–67)

To put it more radically, while rationality can be understood as procedural, in this case, it cannot be substantive in the sense of the rational choice. Furthermore, the procedural rationality is affected by the incompleteness of the information (because part of it is unknown, not available and, by nature, infinite) and also because it is impossible to know with certainty the result of any decision (bounded rationality; Simon 1997) – the future is, by nature, uncertain, as claimed by Knight.

The consequences of these divergences concern not only the acceptance or rejection of specific technologies (such as genetically modified food and nuclear energy) but also economic decisions. For a consumer (in the sense of both a *buyer* and an *eater*), the existence of risks and uncertainties implies an indeterminacy over quality. In such a situation, the laws of supply and demand can no longer apply, and prices cease to carry signals: the uncertainty regarding food safety/quality translates into an economic indeterminacy. In other words, when there is doubt over the quality of a product, the decision based on rational choice (an operation of calculation) is replaced, or at least completed, by a decision-making *process* based on judgement (which can be called an "operation of judgment") (Karpik 2010: chapter 4).

To sum up, in a situation of risks and uncertainty, the rationality of the economists is replaced (or completed) by a procedural rationality, and the operation of "calculation" is changed into a decision-making process. The point is then to analyse how judgements are made. Two steps have to be considered. In the first one, the uncertainty will be only over quality (i.e. there will be indeterminacy over the quality of the food), while the situation itself will remain free of risks and uncertainty (a theoretical situation). In the second step, it will be analysed how the existence of risks changed the way the evaluation over the quality of goods is performed. These two steps form the second and third propositions, respectively.

The first step leads us back to Lucien Karpik (2010), whose main concern was not the formulation of a theory of action in a situation of risk and uncertainty, but to understand how people select a "unique" product or services. For these types of goods (whether they are a painting, a "good" doctor, a "good" wine and so on), prices do not give suitable information and the consumer's choice requires an act of judgement. Since every one of us, Karpik told us, may have a different definition of the adjective "good", a certain form of coordination of judgements is necessary for (market) exchanges to occur. This function is performed by "judgement devices", which create a type of social relation between the objects (or services) and the consumers (Karpik 2010: 46–47). Karpik further carries out a classification of these devices and separates personal (e.g. networks) and impersonal devices (e.g. guides, experts, rankings, prizes and standards). In practice, these devices function as mediators, which reduce the possibilities of judgements (and choices) of the consumer or the individual. They help to bridge (at least partially) the expectations of the individuals and the properties of the object or service. For example, the choice of a specific guidebook has a strong impact on the experience of a tourist (or, in other words, different guidebooks cater to different types of tourists).

The final important element for our purpose is to note that the social relation operated by the devices is a relation of delegation: "in order to act, ... I voluntarily decide to rely on a device ...; I renounce direct exercise of my freedom on behalf of a representative whose action I hope, think, or am certain will not disappoint me" (Karpik 2010: 46). "Delegation is intimately bound with trust" (ibid.: 47). Differently stated, the judgement over the quality of a good is replaced by a reliance on a "judgement device" that the individual trusts.

But it is exactly at this point that the judgement over the quality of a unique product differs from the judgement over uncertainties – this is the third proposition. In a situation of uncertainty, the indeterminacy cannot be lifted by the reliance on a "judgement device" because the uncertainty extends to these devices themselves. In these situations, judgement devices are powerless in helping consumers to make a choice. The market is then unable to fulfil its role because consumers have no possibility left to assess the quality and the safety of the goods that they find in the shops. For example, after the Fukushima accident, the indeterminacy over quality prompted many people to stop buying agricultural products from the region despite lower prices.

Thus, the food safety crisis may have long-term consequences on people's consumption. If it only concerns a single product, consumers just shift to substitutable goods, leaving the industry or the value chain with economic problems (the archetype being the situation after the milk powder crisis in China in 2008). But if the crisis encompasses the whole production system or the whole environment (like after the Fukushima disaster), a different set of solutions must be found, since everybody has to eat. This may include, for example, the (re)construction of new "judgement devices".

Therefore, the existence of risks and uncertainty (perceived or real – see below) modifies the course of action. In a similar way to the "framing effect" theorized by Tversky and Kahneman (1981), the decision-making process is dependent on the way individuals judge any given situation. Risks and uncertainty modify their cognitive perception of the situation, which means, as seen above, that they can no longer rely on focal points such as "judgement devices" and delegate their decision. The link between cognition and action should therefore be (re)evaluated – which implies that the distinction between "perceived" and "real" risks is, by definition, greatly reduced by the fact that the analysis is situated at the cognitive level. When this framework is applied to the evaluation of food safety in particular, the decision-making process is especially difficult for individuals, especially if the whole food system is (perceived) risky/uncertain. This can create a certain anxiety for some consumers.

For this reason, and this is the fourth proposition, the distinction between economic risks and other types of risks (health and environmental risks, for example) should be re-examined because, in most cases, they are not independent. When a food crisis erupts, economic risks are never very distant, either *ex ante* (economic factors may be one cause of the crisis – see Yamaguchi, as well as Ke and Hisano, in this volume), *ex post* or both. In addition, the link between decision-making and cognition also calls for an evaluation of the forms of governance and market regulation: as food safety risks and economic risks are embedded, there are contradictions in ensuring the development of free markets and regulating them as to ensure the relative safety of food, and prevent the eruption of a food safety crisis (Ilbert *et al.* 2014). With rapid globalization, these different objectives are getting even more difficult to conciliate, since the governance system has partly slipped out of the government's hands. At the international (but also the domestic) level, decision-making (and regulations) comes from four different sources: government and its agencies, international organizations, companies/multinational corporations, and civil society (and consumers).[5] The decentralization of decision centres in the governance system is also, in itself, a source of added risks that are difficult to assess: the recent "horsegate" crisis showed how the fragmentation of the governance system also created loopholes in the responsibility system – markets are getting increasingly difficult to regulate (Simoulin, in this volume).

Finally, this framework should be understood in the context of the "incorporation principle" (Fischler 1990; Rozin 1994; Poulain 2017). The way rationality manifests itself as well as the way judgements are made by individuals cannot be separated from the relationship these individuals have with the food they consume. Concretely, it means that food is not a simple product of consumption (Mennell *et al.* 1992; Poulain 2017). The eater ingests it and, by this action, s/he becomes what s/he is eating. More specifically, the "principle of incorporation" developed by both Rozin and Fischler has a double meaning. On the physiological level, the eater becomes what s/he consumes; s/he incorporates and adopts the qualities of the ingested food. This is true from the objective scientific point of view: part of the food becomes nutrients, especially amino acids, and is absorbed into the body. On the other hand, the process can also be seen psychologically. From a subjective or perhaps symbolic standpoint, the eater may believe or fear what s/he considers the "magical" properties of the food, appropriating its symbolic qualities according to the "I become what I eat" principle. Works of many anthropologists have demonstrated this mental process.

In addition, on the psycho-sociological level, eating is an act in a cultural space. Food, cooking and table manners, which are culturally defined, put the eater in a particular social world and cultural order. The act of eating forges a collective identity and operates as an identification and distinction marker. Barthes (1961), Aron (1973), Bourdieu (1979) and Fischler (1990), as well as numerous works from different theoretical perspectives, acknowledge this function of the act of eating.

Finally, all technological procedures – handling, culinary transformations and operations that come with marketing and all the professionals who provide them – have symbolic consequences on the identity of food and should therefore be studied. With eating, food gets involved in our intimate personal life. It crosses the border between us and the world. It rebuilds us and transforms us, or can transform us. This is why the diet gives us the feeling that it "controls our lives". We understand better why the uncertainties and fears about food may exacerbate, echoing the uncertainty over the future of the eater himself.

To conclude, the relations between food and risks can be analysed through at least three interconnected elements: rationality and the incorporation principle; the decision-making process and judgements; and governance (which are also three of the most debated topics in social sciences). These three elements constitute the backbone of this volume. In the first part of this book, theoretical issues will be presented (Chapters 1–3). The issue of rationality/decision-making will then be examined not only in an analytical way, but also in a prescriptive way, with the objective to make propositions for a better type of governance, and/or for upgrading the linkages between consumers and producers.

In Chapter 1, Jean-Pierre Poulain introduces several paradigms in relation to food crises, and show their respective contributions and limits. Then, starting from the paradox that "the more the industry shows its efforts in controlling the products' quality, the more consumers are sceptical of this quality", the author shows how the consumer information management, the sociology of risk and, finally, food sociology can be used to explain contemporary food crises. These various perspectives lead to a critical analysis of risk management systems based on conferences and hybrid forums that facilitate dialogues between different stakeholders, but can also be interpreted as occasions where people (or public opinion) can be manipulated by the administrative and political authorities.

Chapter 2, by Florent Champy, develops further the relationship between rationality and risks. Completing a theme that was developed in this introduction, Champy denies that laypeople are not rational and emphasizes that the symbolic dimension of food has to be taken seriously. He then discusses how the sociology of health can help us understand the type of rationality at work in the consumers' perception of risks. The original insight of the author is to try to adapt the concept of "pact of care", elaborated by Paul Ricœur to develop the notion of "pact of nutrition". However, at this point such a "pact" should be understood as a theoretical tool only, as, even though its implementation would make sense, it would be, in practice, unreachable: on the one hand, the "pact of nutrition", like the pact of care, would help tackle the asymmetry of information between consumers and producers. But, on the other hand, the lack of direct relation between producers and consumers would make it difficult to assign responsibilities. The author shows that the efforts undertaken by the industry to create the pact did not lead to a significant result as the relationship between producers/distributors and consumers remained imbalanced.

In Chapter 3, Vincent Simoulin analyses the governance of food crises. Like Champy, Simoulin aims to give a greater role to consumers in the management of crises. Thus, he emphasizes what, in the food field, governance would ideally mean: a greater say by consumers' associations and producers, a better spread of information, a greater relevance of rules and regulations, a share of the decision-making cost and finally, greater democratic rights. However, for the author, the issue is not one-sided, and he wonders whether governance is not becoming part of the problem, as new governance makes it more difficult to track responsibilities and understand how some decisions have been adopted. Media pressure, because of the intimate nature of food, also makes it more difficult than other policies to make governance work.

In the second part (Chapters 4–9), case studies from Japan and China will be presented in depth. The reasons for this choice have been explained above: in these two countries, recent events have transformed latent risks into fully fledged crises. Other parts of the world, of course, have not been immune from crises, but by their scale, those occurring in these two countries have resulted in strong reactions from their governments, the industry (including farmers) and people alike. In Chapter 4, Louis Augustin-Jean analyses how, facing an unknown situation after the Fukushima nuclear disaster of 2011, Japanese people modified the way they buy and eat their food. The existence of numerous uncertainties, which were further enlarged by contradictory information provided by the experts in the media, created a sense of insecurity. Many consumers could no longer rely on existing judgement devices, such as labels and standards, cooperatives that link producers to consumers, etc. Similarly, the information provided by the government was systematically questioned. Since everybody needs to eat, consumers started to rebuild their own judgement devices, which may have not been more objective, but which gave them a higher sense of security in the face of existing scientific uncertainty. Interestingly, some of these devices were adopted by the industry (against the opinion of government's officials), giving them more legitimacy.

Analysing the same crisis, Yoko Niiyama, in Chapter 5, takes a very different approach. Taking into account the point of view of the experts and the government (and not of the consumers, as has been done in the previous chapter), she wonders what type of scientific information and communication needs to be provided to the public to ease palpable anxiety. Based on the results of experimentations of an interactive risk communication model, she shows that the following elements have to be incorporated: public questions are probed; full scientific information that addresses those questions is prepared by a team of experts; and the occasions of elaborate information processing for the public are provided. All in all, from the same case study, Chapters 4 and 5 illustrate how procedural rationality is at work to construct an "interactive communication model" or new "judgement devices". It is clear that these two patterns should be more complementary and less exclusive of each other.

In Chapter 6, Michitoshi Yamaguchi analyses the behaviour of egg producers in Japan in the face of the risks generated by avian influenza. He considers two separate but related schemes – the first is the compensation provided by the government for the disposal of the eggs, while the other has been organized by producers to protect themselves from the loss of business, which is not covered by the government scheme. An interesting conclusion of the chapter is that while these two mechanisms have been developed to address economic risks, they also have the unintended consequence of increasing the protection for consumers.

Finally, the last three chapters are devoted to China. Chapter 7, authored by Yongkang An, explores an issue that has been raised by both Niiyama (risk communication and government action) and Simoulin (governance), but from a legal perspective. The author analyses the development of a regulatory framework by the China Food and Drug Administration. Based on a comparison with the relevant practice in the UK, she points out some critical issues concerning risk assessment, the coverage of the risk-based approach, and the contribution of private assurance schemes in China. She concludes with some suggestions for improving the current risk-based approach to implementing food safety law.

Chapter 8, by Jinghan Ke and Shuji Hisano, also echoes the analysis of Yamaguchi, as the authors link food production and risks. However, instead of concentrating on large producers, like Yamaguchi, the two authors centre on the behaviour of small farmers. Returning to the question of rationality, they wonder why these farmers are over-using pesticides, which seems detrimental to their health, the quality of the food and even the profitability of their activity. The answer, they claim, lies in the weak position of these farmers in the three value chains they introduce, which pushes them to use sub-standard input and to favour appearance over quality.

Finally, the last chapter of the book, by David Kurt Herold, ends with a paradox – which may open the door for future research. Also tacking the rationality issue, the author shows that there is a difference between the perception of food safety in China – online comments indicate that consumers have a great awareness of food safety issues – and the behaviour of these same consumers who, most of the time, do not adjust their eating habits at home and in restaurants, with their self-claimed worries. Herold highlights this disconnect by means of anthropological data and observations.

Notes

1 In economic terms, both companies benefited from non-compensated social (and/or environmental) costs.
2 The quote marks here indicate that the point is only theoretical; in practice, there is of course no risk-free situation.
3 On a more general presentation of the different meanings of statistics as well as the construction of categories (statistical classes), see also Desrosières (2002). For the role of successive assumptions in simplifying original hypotheses and in assessing risks, see Callon *et al.* (2001).
4 Quoting Lynn (1987), the authors even noted that "attitudes of occupation health specialists toward fundamental issues in risks assessment were strongly related to whether they worked in the industry, government or academia or whether they voted Democratic or Republican in the previous presidential election" (Kraus *et al.* 2000: 286).
5 On the international regulation of food markets in relation to risks, see Petit (2015). This article is part of a special section edited by Steiner and Augustin-Jean (2015) on "Risks, Markets and New Actors" (in the *China Journal of Social Work*), which specifically analyses food issues.

References

Alpermann, B. and L. Augustin-Jean (2014) "Conclusion: Economic Sociology and the Political Economy of China's Agro-Food Markets", in L. Augustin-Jean and B. Alpermann (eds), *The Political Economy of Agro-Food Markets in China: The Social Construction of the Markets in an Era of Globalization*, Houndmills, Basingstoke: Palgrave Macmillan, 307–320.

Aron, J.-P. (1973) *Le Mangeur du xixe siècle*, Paris: Robert Laffont.

Augustin-Jean, L. (2014) "An Approach to Food Quality in China: An Agenda for Future Research", in L. Augustin-Jean and B. Alpermann (eds), *The Political Economy of Agro-Food Markets in China: The Social Construction of the Markets in an Era of Globalization*, Houndmills, Basingstoke: Palgrave Macmillan, 47–74.

Beck, U. (1992) *Risk Society: Towards a New Modernity*, New Delhi: Sage.

Beck, U. (1999) *World Risk Society*, Cambridge: Polity Press.

Bian, Y. M. (2004) "The Challenge for Food Safety in China: Current Legislation is Unable to Protect Consumers from the Consequences of Unscrupulous Food Production", *China Perspectives*, 53: 4–13.

Boltanski, L. and L. Thévenot (2006) *On Justification: Economies of Worth*, Princeton, NJ: Princeton University Press.

Bourdieu, P. (1979) *Distinction: A Social Critique of the Judgement of Taste*, London: Routledge.

Brown, C. G., A. S. Waldron and J. W. Longworth (2014) "Drivers and Dynamics of the Chinese Wool Market", in L. Augustin-Jean and B. Alpermann (eds), *The Political Economy of Agro-Food Markets in China: The Social Construction of the Markets in an Era of Globalization*, Houndmills, Basingstoke: Palgrave Macmillan, 210–235.

Brown, L. (1995) *Who Will Feed China? Wake-up Call for a Small Planet*, London: Earthscan.

Callon, M. (1998) "Introduction: The Embeddedness of Economic Market in Economics", in M. Callon (ed.), *The Laws of the Market*, Oxford: Blackwell Publishers/The Sociological Review, 1–57.

Callon, M., P. Lascoumes and Y. Barthe (2001) *Agir dans un monde incertain. Essai sur la démocratie technique*, Paris: Le Seuil.

Delman, J. and M. H. Yang (2012) "A Value Chain Gone Awry: Implications of the 'Tainted Milk Scandal' in 2008 for Political and Social Organization in Rural China", in A. Bislev, S. Thogersen and J. Unger (eds), *Organizing Rural China – Rural China Organizing*, Lanham, MD: Lexington Books.

Desrosières, A. (2002) *The Politics of Large Numbers: A History of Statistical Reasoning*, Cambridge, MA: Harvard University Press.

Diaz, J. (2015) "Philippines 96% Self-sufficient in Rice – DA Chief", *The Philippine Star*, 26 August, www.philstar.com/headlines/2015/08/26/1492318/philippines-96-self-sufficent-rice-da-chief, accessed 27 November 2015.

Ekberg, M. (2007) "The Parameters of the Risk Society: A Review and Exploration", *Current Sociology*, 55(3): 343–366.

Fischler, C. (1990), *L'homnivore: le goût, la cuisine et le corps*, Paris: Odile Jacob.

Food and Agricultural Organization (FAO) (2009) *Food Safety Risk Analysis: A Guide for National Food Safety Authorities*, FAO Food and Nutrition Paper 87, Rome: FAO/WHO.

Godefroy, B. S. and R. Clarke (2016) "Development and Application of International Food Safety Standards – Challenges and Opportunities", *Asian Journal of WTO & Int'l Health Law & Policy*, 11(2): 273–287.

Ilbert, H., M. Petit and L. Augustin-Jean (2014) "Le respect des normes de sûreté sanitaire des aliments et des spécificités culturelles de l'alimentation: une double injonction contradictoire?", International Conference: Renouveler les Approches Institutionnalistes sur l'Agriculture et l'Alimentation: la "Grande Transformation" 20 ans après.

Jussaume, R. A., S. Hisano and Y. Taniguchi (2000) "Food Safety in Modern Japan", *Contemporary Japan*, 12: 211–228.

Kahneman, D. (2011) *Thinking, Fast and Slow*, London: Penguin.

Karpik, L. (2010) *Valuing the Unique: The Economics of Singularities*, Princeton, NJ: Princeton University Press.

Knight, F. H. (1921) *Risks, Uncertainty and Profit*, Reprints of Economic Classic, New York: Augustus M. Kelley (1964), http://mises.org/sites/default/files/Risk%2C%20Uncertainty%2C%20and%20Profit_4.pdf, accessed 8 June 2018..

Kraus, N., T. Malmfors and P. Slovic (2000) "Intuitive Toxicology: Experts and Lay Judgments of Chemical Risks", in P. Slovic (ed.), *The Perception of Risks*, London: Earthscan, 285–315.

Lynn, F. M. (1987) "OSHA's Carcinogens Standard: Round One on Risk Assessment Models and Assumptions", in B. B. Johnson and V. T. Covello (eds), The Social and Cultural Construction of Risk, Dordrecht, The Netherlands: Reidel, 345–358.

McMichael, P. (2000) "A Global Interpretation of the Rise of the East Asian Food Import Complex", *World Development*, 28(3): 409–424.

Mennell, S., A. Murcott and A. Van Otterloo (1992) *The Sociology of Food: Eating, Diet and Culture*, London: Sage.

Petit, P. (2015) "Regulating Product Markets: A Growing Challenge for Open Economies – with Special References to Agro-Food Product Markets", *China Journal of Social Work*, 8(3): 217–230.

Poulain, J. P. (2017) *Sociology of Food*, London: Bloomsbury.

Rozin, P. (1994) "La magie sympathique", *Autrement*, 149: 22–37.

Sen, A. (1981) *Poverty and Famines: An Essay on Entitlement and Deprivation*, Oxford: Clarendon Press.

Shoji, K. and M. Sugai (1992) "The Arsenic Milk Poisoning Incident", in J. Ui (ed.), *Industrial Pollution in Japan*, Tokyo: The United Nation University Press, 77–102, http://d-arch.ide.go.jp/je_archive/pdf/book/jes5_d04.pdf, accessed 28 November 2015.

Simon, H. A. (1976) "From Substantive to Procedural Rationality", in T. J. Kastelein, S. K. Kuipers, W. A. Nijenhuis and R. G. Wagenaar (eds), *25 Years of Economic Theory: Retrospect and Prospect*, New York: Springer, 65–86.

Simon, H. A. (1997) *Administrative Behavior: A Study of Decision-Making Processes in Administrative Organizations* (4th edn), New York: Free Press.

Slovic, P., ed. (2000a) *The Perception of Risks*, London: Earthscan.

Slovic, P. (2000b) "Trust, Emotion, Sex, Politics and Science: Surveying the Risk-Assessment Battlefield", in P. Slovic (ed.), *The Perception of Risks*, London: Earthscan, 390–412.

Stanziani, A. (2005) *Histoire de la qualité alimentaire, XIXe–XXe siècle*, Paris: Seuil.

Steiner, P. and L. Augustin-Jean (2015) "Editorial: Markets, Risks and New Actors", Special Issue, *China Journal of Social Work*, 8(3): 201–203.

Tversky, A. and D. Kahneman (1981) "The Framing of Decisions and the Psychology of Choice", *Science*, 211(4481): 453–458.

Ui, J. (1992) "Minamata Disease", in J. Ui (ed.), *Industrial Pollution in Japan*, Tokyo: The United Nation University Press, 103–132, http://d-arch.ide.go.jp/je_archive/pdf/book/jes5_d05.pdf, accessed 28 November 2015.

Veeck, G. (2014) "Post-Reform Grain Markets and Prices in China", in L. Augustin-Jean and B. Alpermann (eds), *The Political Economy of Agro-Food Markets in China: The Social Construction of the Markets in an Era of Globalization*, Houndmills, Basingstoke: Palgrave Macmillan, 77–102.

Waldron, S. A., C. G. Brown and A. M. Komarek (2014) "Growth, Globalization and Upgrading of the Chinese Cashmere Industry", in L. Augustin-Jean and B. Alpermann (eds), *The Political Economy of Agro-Food Markets in China: The Social Construction of the Markets in an Era of Globalization*, Houndmills, Basingstoke: Palgrave Macmillan, 257–278.

Wynne, B. (1996) "May the Sheep Safely Graze? A Reflexive View of the Expert–Lay Knowledge Divide", in S. Lash, B. Szerszynski and B. Wynne (eds), *Risk, Environment and Modernity: Towards a New Ecology*, London: Sage.

Part I

Theoretical and regulatory framework

1 Beyond weak signals listening theory

From risk analysis to the management of alimentary concerns

Jean-Pierre Poulain

As societies modernized, the topic of food became a subject of debates and controversies. The classical food safety and food security concerns have given way to more controversial issues like "genetically modified products", animal "cruelty", raw milk cheese, junk food and its supposed connections with obesity and Non-Communicable Diseases (NCD). Nothing seems self-evident any more. Food industries are targeted; even the farmers, who once had the confidence of the city dwellers, are now attacked on various fronts. Lobby groups are accused of manipulating scientists, the media, politicians and consumers for their own benefit. The system is not running as smoothly as before. A certain tension is rising within the "food social space" over concerns extending from intergenerational responsibility, "What kind of planet are we leaving for our children?", to intra-generational issues, "How can we divide resources between Global North and South, and, within more developed societies, between rich and poor?"

Different interpretations may be deployed to understand current Western consumers' relationship with food. We have explored in previous publications (Poulain 2007, 2012b) trends in modern societies, such as the medicalization of food, its judiciarization, development of environmental concerns, notions of heritage or the transformation of human–animal relationships, which are challenging the hitherto dominant "feeding model" of food. So, it is imperative for the authorities in charge of food policies, as well as all agents along the agro-food chain, to listen to and understand the reactions of consumers and citizens. Monitoring the crisis is the purpose of the "weak signals theory". Different listening and interpretation methodologies are available, but how can they be relevant in the Asian context?

In most Asian countries that have experienced rapid modernization, a "compacted modernization" in Kyung-Sup Chang's (2010a) words, this context is exacerbated. What Europe and North America have lived through in one-and-a-half centuries, Asia is experiencing in fewer than fifty years. In two generations, some Asian societies have faced rapid structural transformations in the domains of economy, housing and urbanization. The transition from concern for food security to food safety that characterizes the evolution of public awareness about food in the Western context – in other words, less concern for famine and more for the quality of food – did not happen in Asia; in fact, in a compacted modernity, food safety and food security coexist at the same time. So we can speak of a double burden of food concerns as, for instance, in the field of malnutrition, where a coexistence of under-nutrition and over-nutrition can be observed in certain countries (Gillespie and Haddad 2003).

Since the 1990s, following various food crises in Western countries, food issues have come to be organized around the concept of "risk" and the theory of strategic "early warning signals". Food issues (safety and food security) have now gained a place on political and media agendas. Henceforth, discussions on these topics are delivered by official agencies where experts scientifically evaluate risks and try to understand the more or less rational perceptions of consumers in order to manage and communicate these risks. "Assessment" (by experts), "perception" (by the customers or citizens) and "management" (by the authorities – in economic and political institutions) are the three keywords in risk monitoring.

Within the social sciences, research has been developed which sometimes supports, justifies or validates these theoretical frameworks and thus has helped to organize and legitimize the vision of administrative risk management (Slovic 1987). Sometimes these research projects also delineate and challenge the rational asymmetry on which they were based – on the one hand, the "experts" who are supposedly presenting the "truth", and on the other, the "laymen" who are more or less "wrong" – by claiming the necessity to articulate the understanding of experts and citizens (Beck 1999). They point out that the diverging understanding of the citizens cannot be reduced to perception bias since they perceive dimensions that are beyond the probabilistic calculation of the risk of mortality and morbidity (Beck 1999; Poulain 2017).

Some anthropological works show that as all human cultures proceed to an orderly organization of the world, they all encounter the same problem. This concerns the definition of a remainder, i.e. what must remain "outside the scope". Mary Douglas and Aaron Wildavsky (1982) have pointed out the existence of this "twilight zone". This concept has mainly been used to analyse the variation in what is included and what is excluded in the public perception of risks in different societies. I aim to show here that, from an epistemological perspective, it is worthwhile to study what factors the contemporary framework of risk maintains "out of the field" and to see how these risks, when they emerge, may be undervalued, overvalued or idealized.

Risk and modernized societies

In the past few years, European sociologists have pointed to risk as one of the characteristics of modern societies (Giddens 1991; Duclos 1994; Le Breton 1995; Beck 1999; Fischler 2002; Godard et al. 2002; Gilbert 2003; Roeser et al. 2012). These analyses do not explicitly address food problems, but may contribute to our understanding of some of the issues facing them. For Ulrich Beck, the concept of risk emerges in modern societies when one ceases to explain the events that affect humans by fate, whims of the gods or by nature. Beck dates its emergence from the time of the great discoveries and the development of the technological mastery of nature by man. Risk accompanies the great expeditions and the growth of international maritime trade. We seek to control the future by calculating the risks, by producing statistics on outcomes. This new grid of information, which attempts to read the future, facilitates the transformation of the chain of causality. Thus, any unfortunate event appears to be the result of a series of inadequate decisions. Human responsibility takes precedence over fate. The notion of risk accompanies the discovery of the world, whether geographical or scientific. We proceed from the revealed or traditional model of truth to a truth constructed in the experience of reality. Risk arises when nature and tradition lose their hold, and man has to decide on his own (Beck 1999).

In the first stage in the evolution of the dominance of the risk paradigm in modern societies, it is the risk's victim who appears to be responsible, as it is he/she who made bad decisions. Then, in the second phase, we look for human responsibilities beyond the victims themselves. For example, victims of an industrial accident were originally considered to be victims of fate. Then, they were seen as personally responsible for what was happening to them, their responsibility was articulated in a moralistic way, and they were considered to be at fault, as the cause of their own misfortune. Lastly, we have come to look for more distant agency, such as officials, on the side of the company and its organization, in the context of seeking a monetized compensation for the damage. The causes and responsibility of an accident are thus dissociated. It becomes the subject of a number of social norms and negotiations aimed at fixing the compensation for injury. These social mechanisms reflect and contribute to the establishment of a process of the judiciarization of society. The emergence of large transnational companies, at both the agro-supply and agro-industry levels, creates the conditions for insolvent liability on a large scale and thus for risk-taking.

At the same time, scientific advances in the identification and analysis of risks allow the setting up of increasingly sensitive surveillance mechanisms. However, the pace of knowledge development, and the awareness of the unknown factors accompanying it, contributes to a growing sense of insecurity. But, above all, they allow the attribution of responsibilities and the identification of culprits, which in some cases may turn into "the designation of scapegoats" (Champagne 2000). Thus, in the first step, the victim of the risk appears to be responsible; he/she made the wrong decisions.

However, these analyses, which have resulted from research carried out on environmental or nuclear risks, do not fully exhaust the issues associated with food risk. While the sociology of risk, founded on the work of Ulrich Beck, poses the risk as one of the characteristics of modernity, if we investigate the "archaeology" of this notion – in the sense that Michel Foucault (1969) gives to it in *The Archaeology of Knowledge* – it points out risk as resulting from a process of rationalization. For instance, the sociology and anthropology of food studies show food anxiety to be an anthropological invariant of the relationship of people to food in society (Fischler 1988; Beardsworth 1995; Warde 2016;

Poulain 2017). Only the way this anxiety is expressed varies according to different social and historical contexts. Some historians have shown, for instance, that since the beginning of the twentieth century in the United States, food anxiety has been exacerbated by the process of the industrialization of the food supply chain (Gaudillière 2002).

On a short historical scale, food crises in Europe seem to have started with the case of Bovine Spongiform Encephalopathy (BSE), also known as "mad cow" disease. If this event is indeed a decisive moment in which the risk takes on a new form, in both symbolic and real dimensions, while a deeper historical analysis shows stories of poisoning and other food crises that go far beyond what we have experienced, mad cow disease stimulates us to follow the evolution in the technical and social contexts which have preceded the contemporary crisis, in order to grasp its characteristics and the extent of its impact.

The speed with which modernization has taken place in certain Asian countries led the Korean sociologist Kyung-Sup Chang (2010b) to propose the concept of compressed modernity. It corresponds to a "civilizational context in which economic, political, cultural and social changes occur in an extremely condensed manner both in space and in time" (p. 33). Moreover, in compressed modernity, disparate historical and social elements coexist, contributing to the construction and reconstruction of a complex social system characterized by fluidity (Chang 2017). The phenomenon of the compression of time and space was described in the 1980s by geographer David Harvey (1990). It would be the result of technological innovations developed in the sectors of communication (telegraph, telephone, fax, internet, etc.), transportation and travel (high speed trains and democratization of air transport), which would reduce or sometimes even cancel out spatial and temporal distances. These technological innovations were to be at the heart of economic development and would help to open up new markets, shift spatial barriers, accelerate production cycles and help reduce turnover time. By now we can see that all these things have come to pass.

Beck and Grande (2010) articulate theories of compressed modernity based on Chang's concept, in terms of "first" and "second" modernity (Beck), and have described it as a situation in which the processes of urbanization, industrialization and liberalization of economic conditions are carried out with such rapidity that the transition from "first" modernity to the "second" stage is almost simultaneous. Beck defines the first modernity as the rise in rationality and the "de-traditionalization" of societies, and the second as a weakening of the legitimacy of the "normative system", leading to an "individualization of lifestyles" (Beck and Lau 2005). The second modernity would correspond to post-traditional societies, not in the sense that there would be no intergenerational transmission, but in the sense that the normative models would have lost part of their strength and legitimacy. South Korea, Malaysia and China fit more or less well into this framework, but not so Japan, which has undergone a much longer process of modernization.

For Malaysia, Poulain *et al.* (2014) have empirically shown how the practices related to lunch and dinner are largely individualized, while the social norms for these meals (i.e. what constitutes a "proper meal") are still collective. This lag between norms and practices shows the weakening of traditional social norms and creates a context conducive to anxiety, which increases the perception of risk. The analysis of the modalities of the socialization of a meal supports the idea proposed by Han Sang-Jin (2015) that we will find original forms of individualization in societies with compressed modernity.

The second modernity is accompanied by the intertwining of various types of risk that take place in particular historical contexts. For example, the coexistence of risks associated with food security and food safety in China, together with a high level of fraud in the society, creates a specific context. The compressed modernity present in some Asian countries corresponds to the colliding of these two forms of modernity. Chang describes two sub-phenomena that have an impact on both the time and space dimensions: "condensation" and "compression". Condensation "refers to the phenomenon that the physical process required for the movement or change to take place between two time points (eras) or between two locations (places) is abridged or compacted" (2010b: 33–34). Compression is a "phenomenon that diverse components of multiple civilizations that have existed in different areas and/or places coexist in a certain delimited time-space and influence and change each other" (2010b: 34). Reduction of distance in space increases the mobility of food and populations, at the national level (between regions and between rural and urban areas), as well as at an international level (between countries). Through this mobility the interlinking, or crossover, of food cultures – and in certain contexts, the hybridizing or the creolization of cultures – developed (Tibère 2016). This mobility also encompasses a mobility of microorganisms and diseases, and affects the genetic and epigenetic characteristics of populations. The reduction of time pushes the process of designating food cultures as heritage and, more broadly, ways of life, and it promotes the development of cosmopolitan cultures. The compression superimposes different cultures and, in the context of food, the entire food social space is of concern.

It is possible to add another category to the traditional distinction between "food security" and "food safety", namely, "controversial risks". This concept covers the problems generated by hazards linked either to technological innovations (such as the application of genetic engineering or molecular engineering, and nanotechnologies) to food, or to the evolution of knowledge, which in itself elucidates and makes visible new dimensions of an issue. These risks are not based on the same body of knowledge and their management is not safeguarded by the same scientific, administrative and political actors. Moreover, conditions that are conducive to the traditional issue of fraud are found in societies that have been rapidly modernized. On the one hand the state services in charge of combating frauds are weakly developed and on the other hand technological progress offers new possibilities.

So, we can identify four main categories of crises (see Table 1.1):

- **Food security crisis** due to a shortage of food or accessibility issues for a certain segment of the population.

Table 1.1 Food risks and crises

	Food security crises	Food fraud crises	Food safety crises	Controversies crises
Examples of crisis	Famines: Lack/shortage of food for some parts of population due to availability or accessibility issues.	Fake food products: fake eggs, shrimps, melamine milk, etc.; Disrespect of the characteristics of the products.	Health problems related to long-term or short-term poisoning. The origin may be microbiological or chemical.	Controversies over the consequences of using a technology for food production or processing.
Nature of knowledge	Important body of agronomic knowledge + Economic and socio-cultural knowledge of food models and food systems.	Intentional incongruity between what is promised and what is delivered. Technological race between fraudsters and controlling bodies.	Important body of knowledge in microbiology and toxicology + Some socio-cultural knowledge.	Knowledge not yet stabilized or subject to controversy.
Political management	Steering is mainly conducted at the international level through interactions between nation states and the involvement of many NGOs.	National and international political management. Legal and sanitary dimensions mix.	Steering is conducted at the national level, but with interaction with the international level. Management is mainly in technical-scientific areas.	National and international political management. Relationships between science, media and society.

- **Food fraud crisis** where the normal, legal and/or traditional characteristics of the products are not respected. It can be falsified products like melamine milk or totally "fake food" made with technologies that are intended for producing real "artefacts" that simulate food. The food fraud crisis is a legal issue and can be, in addition, a safety issue.
- **Food safety crisis** due to a contamination of either chemical or microbiological origin, which is likely to have adverse health consequences in the short or long term. The issue could also come from the presence of foreign objects in the food.
- **Controversial crisis** due to the impossibility of scientifically adjudicating the problem. This impossibility can be temporary, if scientific advancement gives rise to the possibility of elucidating the nature of the risk, or permanent because the nature of the risk is not scientifically determinable.

This chapter will explore the different methodologies developed in the sociology of risk and the sociology of food to monitor food crises, including listening to weak signals and the management of socio-technical controversies.

The sociologies of risk

The "classical" sociology of risk points to the discrepancies between the ways laypeople approach risk and scientific risk assessment. Experts use statistical tools and reason in probabilistic terms. The "perception" of risks by laypeople is subject to the influence of particular social factors. Thus, risk is perceived more acutely in social groups distant from power and decision-making centres (Douglas and Wildavsky 1982). Moreover, the degree of familiarity with technologies comes into play; a new and unknown technique is to be judged more dangerous than traditional technology; for example, the ionization of food was considered more risky than canned food. The sense of mastery and personal control is also decisive; flying is felt to be more dangerous than driving an automobile, whereas the statistical risk is much lower (Slovic 1987, 1993). Finally, in relation to the food sector, it seems that women "display more anxiety than men" in countries as diverse as France, Japan, Belgium and Holland (Rozin *et al.* 1999). Furthermore, while scientific risk analysis focuses on measuring the negative consequences of an action, the tendency of a layperson's thinking is to balance the potential benefits and risks in a cost–benefit calculation. Because of these profound differences, dialogue between quality and safety specialists and consumers is often difficult, as the former have the perception that the latter are irrational and reject progress. In such situations, the experts are tempted to either take refuge in authority-based arguments or to educate "the good people" to make them understand the scientific truth. To overcome this deadlock, we must take into account the strategic conflicts around risk and accept seeing these discrepancies as a confrontation of rationalities and interests (Beck 1999). Beck invites us to focus on the qualitative dimensions of the analysis of risk by the public. While the experts focus on the probability of an adverse event and measure its consequences in quantitative terms – almost exclusively in terms of mortality – laypeople include in their definition of risk more qualitative criteria, that is, they are more interested in the nature of the consequences rather than their probability. They also attach a particular importance to the circumstances surrounding the exposure to the risk and to the kinds of people concerned. The common perception is structured, it can be quantified – according to the psychometric paradigm, for example – and, to some extent, predicted. It is therefore not irrational, but more complex than that of experts. Considering public perception is then justified by its ability to bring some light to certain aspects of the problem left in the shadows by scientific evaluation. Strictly science-based analyses exclude certain social dimensions of risk (identity issues, social choices, etc.), which are precisely at the centre of conflicts and social controversies.

The psychometric model can be used to understand, if not the abruptness, at least the acceleration of the sense of a food crisis. The profound transformations in the organization of the agro-food sector, its widening and its clustering in increasingly large companies, keep the food consumers away from the natural origin of food products, thus cutting off their traditionally natural and social environment. In this way, the very nature of the food risk would have been transformed. It would have seemed "sudden" that culinary activity was partly taken over by industry. The concentration of production in increasingly large units would make it likely to affect a very large number of people. The acuity of assessment tools and policies for monitoring and assessing health risks would point to food as a source of new and immediate threats, such as collective food poisoning, or delayed threats, as with the cumulative effects of heavy metals, or prion diseases. The peak of this transformation is reached in the context of school catering, where children consumers are the real sanctuary of the nation, and are considered to be incapable of producing choices.

But some social scientists, such as the group of British researchers from the Economic and Social Research Council, who worked on genetically modified organism (GMO) risk, consider that the public is not stupid and ignorant in its approach to risk, but rather has an elaborate understanding of the main issues. They conclude that taking into account laypersons' perceptions is essential in risk assessment processes, because it helps explain and question the knowledge and implicit assumptions of scientists, as well as their reductionist results (Adam *et al.* 1999). Thus, the analysis of risks under certain conditions can give profane thought a "nobility" and democratic debate a legitimacy. Other trends in the sociology of risk, particularly in France, promote the idea that certain actors, depending on their position in the social space and their personal trajectory, can become *lanceur d'alerte*[1] and reveal dimensions of the problem that were invisible, either because they have been deliberately concealed, or they did not have a place in the reference framework of dominant positions (Chateauray-naud and Torny 1999, 2005).

It is therefore possible to identify two main perspectives in the sociology of risk. The first, based on a positivist reading, considers the experts as capable of analysing the objective causes of the crisis, and the laypersons as individuals subject to perception bias. To manage crises in this perspective, after "assessing" the risk (by the experts) in terms of mortality and morbidity, it is necessary to take into account the "perceptions" of the public, to build communication with them and often to educate and reassure them.

The second perspective considers laypeople as capable of identifying problems that experts do not perceive, either because these risks are outside the scope of science, or because their interests (scientific, or concerning their relationships with industrial or political actors) do not allow them to be seen. We are dealing here with inverse symmetrical conceptions.

One can parody this, saying that the first perspective adopts an objectivist attitude and "idealizes" the capacity of the experts and points out the "biased" character of the understanding of laypeople. The second, assuming a constructivist point of view, "idealizes" the foresight of citizens and their ability to identify risks and points to experts as "partial" and more or less "biased". Between these two poles, different positions are possible. The positioning could be more or less close to an objectivist or constructivist reading, depending on the nature of the risks and of certain characteristics of the populations and of the scientific and political actors.

The crisis without risks: the epistemological "lasagna" fracture

In February 2013, it was reported that packages of lasagna, Bolognese spaghetti and meatballs labelled as beef turned out to contain a mixture of horsemeat and beef, leading to recalls and investigations across both retail and food service markets in the European Union (EU). The so-called "lasagna crisis" in the EU disrupted indirectly the fragile balance on which the conceptual framework of risk management was based. Did here the crisis come without risk to health? Yet we had an economic, a trust and a political crisis. The food security services had done their job, as they were the ones who uncovered the case. However, the key issue is elsewhere. It was a case of what might wrongfully be considered the irrationality of the eater. Subsequently, the climate worsened, and it was as if this crisis management system, which was efficient on health topics, had more and more trouble understanding the underlying social and political issues. The most serious media broadcast documentaries uncovered the "behind the scenes" of the food industry, such as in viticulture, livestock or fish farming. No sector was spared from their determination to "unveil" a world that wanted to "hide from us". The tone of these documentaries was purposely inquisitive.

Food risk is a risk like no other. The lasagna crisis that occurred in the spring of 2013 is an almost textbook demonstration of this. First, it came as a reminder that a commercial transaction belongs within an ethical framework. What we call in law the "good will" of a commercial transaction reflects the fact that the seller must provide the buyer with a good or service that complies with the commitments that have been made. Horsemeat is not beef and thus to represent it as such is a fraud of dishonesty. It was also discovered that a cascade of subcontractors and raw materials change multiple times in space across their journey. Yet all of this is only one of the explanations to this crisis and not sufficient in explaining the scale of emotion and outrage which it provoked.

Horses are not the equivalent of beef cattle as edible goods. Certainly, the same cuts of meat are found in horses and beef cattle. Certainly, they can be prepared and cooked in the same way. Certainly, in the lasagna, horsemeat can be mistaken for beef. Despite this functional equivalence between horsemeat and beef, there is no symbolic equivalence. The product containing horsemeat that had been prepared for consumers was, from their point of view, inedible. It was shocking to say the least. This is where "the betrayal" was, and it was not only in the broken promise. If, for example, wild boar was replaced with pork, the shock would not be the same: both are taboo foods for certain populations, but for those who are willing to eat boar meat, substituting it with pork, which is cheaper, will not create the same emotion, as both belong to the same family and especially to the same category of edibles. From a strict sanitary point of view, there was no risk in consuming these lasagna meals containing horsemeat. This "case" reveals that the quality of food is not limited to its sanitary dimension but extends to a symbolic level.

In Christianity, there is practically no forbidden food. However, there is a distinction between days when you can eat meat, days when you cannot and fasting periods. The only prohibited food is the horse. It started in the eighth century, when the Popes Gregory III and Zachary banned its consumption to mark the difference between civilized people and barbarians, who eat their mounts. However, this ban was not absolute: it was acceptable to consume horseflesh during famines and wars.

In the mid-nineteenth century, four elements converged in favour of hippophagy in France. First, surprisingly, the demand was from the animal's advocates. At that time, cities and countryside were full of horses used for pulling carts. Yet people did not know what to do with the animals in their old age and they were forced to work to the limit of their strength. The spectacle of horses falling down dead under the plough unsettled sensitivities even back then. The French Society for the Protection of Animals (SPA, the French equivalent of the Royal Society for the Prevention of Cruelty to Animals – RSPCA), newly created in 1845, advocated allowing the trade of horsemeat in order to alleviate their suffering. The second argument was economic: the flow of animals generated cheap meat, which would be a shame to waste. A third element was the rise in veterinary schools in France, which positively promoted the nutritional value of horsemeat: lean meat, rich in iron, etc. The final factor was the rise of anti-clericalism. At that time, eating horsemeat was seen as an act of distancing oneself from Christian taboos and values. Horsemeat consumption reached a peak in 1960. After the Second World War, the mechanization of agriculture and the development of the automobile meant that the livestock were no longer renewed and a large stock of horsemeat made its way to the market – this is currently happening in Eastern Europe. This high availability of raw materials, combined with the rise of nutritional discourse, contributed to its success on the plates of diners. Since the 1970s, a strong decline has been caused by the fact that horses were considered almost as pets. Kids learned to ride on ponies, and a strong affectionate relationship between horses and humans began. The horse is not an anthropomorphic object, but one sees it as intelligent, sensitive, etc. Even though the horsemeat was in the lasagna, for certain eaters, it was no longer in the edible category. And here it was as if the "symbolic" element that was once sent back to the museum of curiosities of the discipline by the "modern" sociology of risk was now making a return. With the lasagna, "no risk" was evaluated more than perceived, yet a crisis still occurred. Therefore, this was not a sanitary risk, but a crisis of trust. A crisis that taught us that the edible cannot be reduced to just sanitary or nutritional categories. There was a classical fraud, horsemeat instead of beef, and there was a symbolic dimension that amplified the breach of trust.

By highlighting all that goes beyond the framing of risk and what is essential, the beef lasagna crisis puts the framing of food risk, although dominant, in jeopardy. With this "crisis" we can see that a food "problem" cannot be reduced to health or safety issues. While risk assessment in morbidity and mortality terms is essential, it does not exhaust the "problem". There are other perfectly legitimate issues, which, until then, had had an ambiguous status, in that they were sometimes considered to be biased perceptions, reducible to the irrationality of eaters, and sometimes were more or less idealized within the stance of the *lanceur d'alerte*. Framing the issue through the concept of "concern" calls upon us to consider the "outlook" of the eaters seriously, that is, to take into account their worries and concerns, or the arguments used to justify their choices. In other words, it is to re-establish a dialogue between food industry actors, experts and the consumers/eaters/citizens.

Food crises have contributed to the thematization of an object hitherto in the shadows: food. Although most conferences, where participants share the same view, and even mixed opinion forums, focused on specific food issues (GMO, mad cow, prions, etc.), they have also boosted other topics such as risk and socio-technical controversies (Callon *et al.* 2001). Powerful, elaborate models developed in the studies of industrial risk in the wake of Ulrich Beck's work on the sociology of risk, which did for a time occupy the centre stage. Several dominant schools of thought clashed over the articulation of perceptions and the assessment of risk, the *fabrique du risque* (Gilbert *et al.* 2007; Gilbert 2013), and the *lanceur d'alerte* citizen (Chateauraynaud and Torny 1999, 2005). The first school considers that the layperson's view is capable of including dimensions that are excluded from quantitative evaluation, which emphasizes morbidity and mortality criteria. Yet at the same time, it was considered that the layperson's understanding is marred by perception bias that prevents him or her from grasping the "true nature" of the risk.

The second school rejects the idea of consumer "perceptions" that are supposed to "impair" the consumers themselves who are designated as irrational. And in doing so, they accuse this theoretical perspective of playing the game of manufacturers who try to impose more or less controversial products on the market. On the contrary, it considers that certain social actors have developed a particular sensitivity to certain subjects and can become *lanceurs d'alerte*. Some theoretical advances in these positions have shown that the experts, along with the citizen consumers, not only did not grasp the same dimensions of the risk, but both were driven by their own social determinants and interests. To this day, strong splits have divided this field to the point that some have moderated their conclusions. For its part, the sociology of food reminds us of certain symbolic characteristics of food consumption itself and the risks that accompany it.

The horsemeat lasagna crisis reduced the hegemony of the problematizing in terms of risk. This weakening allowed the rise of food concerns, which were until then hidden in the shadow of sanitary risks – concerns that fall under social, political and symbolic dimensions of what makes a society.

The theoretical framework of early warning signals

The 1990s and the 2000s were marked in Europe by food crises in multiple forms: for instance, the emergence of "new" pathologies such as prion diseases and avian flu, which affect consumed animal species and are likely to be transmitted to humans. They have taken root in scientific issues that were not well established or were in the midst of being constituted. This has led, on the one hand, to wide variability in the assessment of the level of severity by experts, and sometimes to controversies.

The emergence of new pathologies also led to critical reflection on methods of production and distribution, on the organization of food chains and on the mechanisms of their technical and political management at large.

The dynamic of crises

The analysis of the development of a crisis shows its evolution in five principal steps (see Figure 1.1). The first is the latency phase and may last for a long time. In this phase, certain constitutive elements of the crisis are known, but the issue does not garner public interest, for the time being only certain population groups that have developed a sensitivity to, and for others, an expertise on, the issue. These individuals are often "activists", social actors who consider themselves to be ahead of the times in the construction of an issue and whose intention is to promote a new vision with the purpose of making a difference to society. They can also be "scholars", more or less recognized as "experts", acting on the margins of scientific circles. These activists or scholars participate in the construction and thematization of the issue, namely its conceptual organization, to the defining of the risk and to the explanation of its sanitary, social and political consequences. They may sometimes adopt an attitude of exposure, showing or pretending to show that the hazard was, willingly or not, underestimated, or that there were some management mistakes along the way, or that vested interests have manipulated the situation to their advantage.

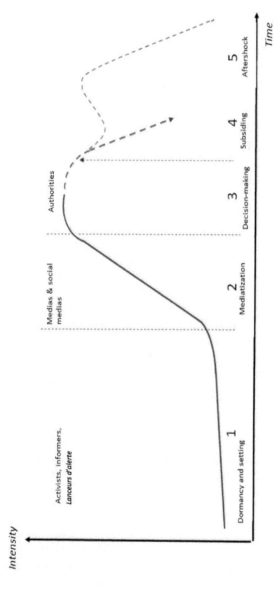

Figure 1.1 Dynamics of a crisis.
Source: Poulain (2012b).

Francis Chateauraynaud and Didier Torny (1999) have proposed the use of the expression "lanceur d'alerte", instead of "activist" or "informer", with the purpose of making this phenomenon more neutral and descriptive. This phase is long and may last, in some cases, for a few decades.

During the second phase, the issue enters the media's agenda with a growing importance. Media includes written media, radio, TV channels but also social media on the Internet where it usually starts. The duration of this phase is shorter. Mediatization can be measured by the intensity of the presence and reiteration of the topic on the various media. This phase is sometimes accompanied by a high level of social emotion or indignation exacerbated by the discovery of the problem, which now tends to reach more and more people.

The third step is the decision-making phase. Administrative and political authorities come into the picture to make often urgent decisions supposedly to "manage the crisis" and bring the situation back to normal. Their decisions may translate into banning, temporary withdrawal from the markets, changes in the legal framework, and so on. Decision-making actors vary according to context: spatial scale (local, regional, national, international); and activity area (private, public, mixed). The duration of this phase is very short and the decisions are taken in the heat of the moment, under the scrutiny of the media and sometimes in a very tense climate.

The fourth step of the cycle is the subsiding of the crisis. The decisions taken, whether they were banning, withdrawal, setting up stricter controls or offering health and psychological care, and compensating victims, have their expected effects and bring down the pressure. The situation returns to normal, more or less rapidly. The issue leaves the political and media centre stage. However, more or less intense aftershocks may occur and reinstate the crisis, forming a fifth step. The decision-makers sometimes have to round off the older decisions with new policies (Table 1.2).

The dynamics of crises make it possible to consider the setting up of several plans of hearing and anticipation in the service of their management. Plans can be developed at two specific levels of the cycle with complementary roles.

Table 1.2 The five phases of a crisis

Phases	Actors	Processes
1 Dormancy and setting	Activists, informers, lanceur d'alerte	Issue setting
2 Mediatization	Various media	Thematization and appearance on the media agenda
3 Decision-making	Politicians and administrators	Appearance on the political agenda and the planning of decisions
4 Subsiding	Public or private administrators	Evaluation of policies in place
5 Aftershock	All of the above	Rectification

During the phase of dormancy, it is possible to hear the "early warning signals", and during mediatization, it is the social thematization of the crisis (namely how it is conceptually constructed as a social problem) that emerges.

The theory of early warning signs appeared during the 1970s. This theory postulates that warning signs of low visibility are detectable before a major event occurs (Ansoff 1975). It would then be possible, for crises managers who detect and interpret weak signals, to see the crisis coming, sufficiently early and so prepare decisions that can be used when the time comes, thus avoiding the need to work under conditions of urgency and media pressure. This theory was developed in the framework of strategic management and has resulted in the concept of "economic intelligence". It then spread to other sectors such as public health or political decision-making. It has evolved along with risk theories.

The concept of listening to known, recurrent and spreading phenomena based on an epidemic mindset has proved to be relevant. Hence, surveillance systems have been developed to anticipate the occurrence of a problem. For health surveillance, the network "Sentinelles", which maps general practitioners within the French Territories, and follows the arrival and spread of epidemics, is an example of one such success.

The application of this model to crisis management is an extension of the initial scope of this theory. However, emerging risks present particular difficulties because the issue has not yet become completely problematic. From this perspective, the main problems to solve are the identification and interpretation of weak signs, since they coexist alongside strong information and signs and the task is more difficult as it is not clear what we are trying to listen to.

Once a potential crisis is identified, two main approaches are possible: population analysis and thematic analysis.

The first one identifies concerned populations and studies their numeric evolution in time (see Figures 1.2 and 1.3). Are there inbound and outbound groups

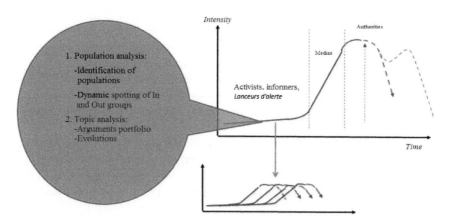

Figure 1.2 Listening to weak signals: to identify populations and arguments.
Source: Poulain (2012b).

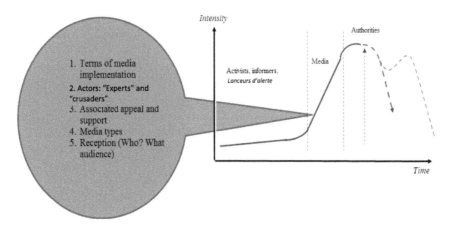

Figure 1.3 Phases of mediatization.
Source: Poulain (2012b).

in the population in relation to the crisis? The second one identifies the portfolio of arguments surrounding the crisis and their evolution. It is then possible to span both dimensions to know which population is susceptible to which type of argument.

One of the least understood aspects of crises is their entry into the various media. For instance, how and why does a potential crisis go from a dormant state to a media issue? The study of mediatization can partly be done with the agenda-setting theory (McCombs 2005). Who are the actors, "crusaders" and experts who contribute to establishing the issue in the media? Who are the gatekeepers (journalists but also publicists, public relations functionaries) who facilitate media access? What are the modalities of the media releases? What types of media are involved in the beginning of the process? Are they social media, or traditional media, such as radio, news channels or general-purpose television? How does the issue spread to other media? For example, does it start on social media and then spread to more official media such as TV? Whose interests are at stake? What are the relations of interest between the different actors ("crusaders",[2] experts), the different gatekeepers (journalists, media)? Who makes up the audience in quantitative and qualitative terms?

Taking into account the dynamics of crises and using the approach of focusing on weak signals are also ways of viewing crises compatible with a constructivist conception. In this case (see Figure 1.4), they also serve to identify the controversies and conduct the analysis (Brante 1993; Chateauraynaud and Torny 2005).

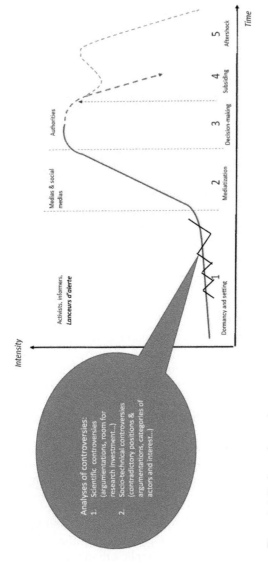

Figure 1.4 Early analyses of controversies.

Concern as an invariant of the eater

One of the contributions of the sociology of food is that it shows that food risk is linked to the process of incorporation that accompanies food consumption and participates in the construction of social identities. By triggering the forms of rationality and levels of analysis mobilized by eaters, food risk facilitates their realization of their common perception. Eaters implement an intellectual style of functioning that anthropologists have called "magical thinking", which was believed in the early days of their discipline to be a characteristic of primitive societies. Today we know that primitives do not exist and this famous magical thinking is present at the heart of the reasoning of the contemporary eater and cohabits along with other forms of rationality. The laws of magical thought are simple to formulate: the symbolic qualities of everything that comes into contact with food, whether tools, other natural or non-natural products, packaging, but also the individuals who produce food, handle, cook and sell it. The qualities of all these objects and individuals are transmitted by "symbolic contamination" to the food itself.

Paul Rozin experimentally demonstrated this phenomenon of symbolic contamination. It is enough to place a disinfected dead cockroach, therefore bacteriologically safe, in a glass of milk and then remove it, to render this product inedible, yet consumable from a strictly objective point of view. Worse, if it is suggested to an individual that he writes on a label "Beware! Cyanide danger" and sticks it onto a glass, then fills that glass with a drink of any kind, then for a large number of individuals, those said drinks become inconsumable (Rozin 1976, 1994).

Let us expand the issue to the contemporary food context. All technological interventions: handling, culinary transformations, operations that accompany commercialization, etc., as well as all the professionals who perform them impart symbolic consequences for the identity of the foods. These need to be studied in order that we may fully understand them. By eating, we bring into ourselves an item of food that participates in our intimate carnal life. It crosses the border between the world and us. It rebuilds and transforms us or can potentially transform us. That is why diet gives us a sense of control over our daily life. With this in mind, we understand better then why uncertainties and fears about food exacerbate, and echo, uncertainties about the future of the eater himself.

This notion of concern, with its broad and somewhat imprecise definition, is very present in the sociology of food.

> In a strange boomerang effect, the more security and quality are spread in the discourse of companies or public authorities, the more concern is deployed among consumers. The implicit thinking works in this fashion: "If one takes so many precautions, it is therefore that it is really dangerous!"
>
> (Poulain 2017)

Concern is therefore an old notion within the sociological view of food that pre-dates the one of risk. It has the advantage of being less focused on sanitation and encompasses wider meanings. The spreading of the notion of risk and its penetration to the heart of the production and processing chains have saturated the thematic way of approaching the relationship between producers and consumers, by pulling it out of the concerns for health and placing other important issues of food at the forefront. This diffusion of the objects of concern was necessary to face health crises and ensure security. Making health topical has had the effect of making certain concerns inaudible and communication more difficult between the actors in the sector and the consumers, eaters and citizens.

Crisis monitoring system

Anticipative crisis management can be conducted with two different and complementary approaches during the dormancy phase: the weak signals listening system to explore the concerns of the populations and the monitoring system of controversies (see Table 1.3).

To listen to the food concerns, several methodologies are available:

- **Focus groups**, to study qualitatively the way in which the issue is constructed by different categories of actors, customers, (citizen, eaters) of the agro-food chain and activists.
- **Quantitative approaches** of the "concerns",[3] of the population(s) using representative samples. This approach uses the techniques of idea associations that ask of the different categories of food (meat, seafood, dairy, fruits, vegetables, etc.) what are the concerns that come to mind? That can be part of a "Food Barometer" (Poulain *et al.* 2014; Poulain 2016).
- **Hybrid forums**, that bring together representatives of consumers, of publics, administration, of professional associations of the food chain and scientists from various disciplines. The purpose of this structure is to establish what makes consensus and what makes debate. They enable one to identify what are the arguments and justification of the different stakeholders.

For controversies monitoring, we need to keep in mind that the status of scientific controversies varies with the epistemological framework with which they are

Table 1.3 Crisis monitoring tools

	Methods	*Objectives*
Exploring the concerns of populations	• Internet listening • Focus groups • Second circle • "Concerns" barometers	• Identification of the concern themes • Identification the populations concerned
Controversies management	• Scientific controversies • Socio-technical controversies	• Identification of the topics on which to invest in research • Analyses of thematization

observed. In a positivist posture, they are simple transitions between two theories, quickly forgotten when the more powerful is accepted. With science progressing by overcoming successive contradictions, they appear as stages in the process of development of knowledge, certainly interesting steps, pointing out the breaks and theoretical reframe, but steps all the same. They always fall more or less quickly to the profit and loss account of the history of science. If we adopt constructivist postures, the controversies deserve more attention, because they constitute a place where the interests of the actors concerned are concentrated, from those of the scientific community, to the politicians through the lobbyists, the activists and the media, a place where knowledge is made.

Whatever the posture, the study of controversies offers multiple interests. It indicates where the research effort is to be carried out. It is a counterpoint to the scriptwriting and simplification effect of consensus conferences. It reveals the logic of interests that clash in a given field of science, facilitates their arbitration and prepares political decisions (Brante 1993; Martin and Poulain 2011).

How to and why study controversies? It is necessary, first of all, to give a definition. They are characterized by the existence of contradictory positions supported by "legitimate" scientific arguments, that is, published in scientific conditions validated by the community, most often peer reviewed. There are, however, weakened forms of controversy or even pre-controversies with few or no published arguments, but with clashes of scientific personalities sometimes recognized in related scientific fields.

Controversies are not always easy to study, because first they are sometimes partially masked or even denied by the researchers themselves. This masking can be read as a consequence of the domination relations of the "mandarins" and the "pressure of conformity" which weighs on the lower-ranking academics who aspire to be recognized. But this masking also results from a "natural" movement of scientific organizations to operate logical scenarios of knowledge. In the presence of partially contradictory empirical data, the scenarization consists of favouring some of them, in setting them apart from others, in order to bring out a logical vision of the problem. This logical scriptwriting work takes place during consensus conferences, writing articles or summary reports, or textbooks and extension books. Thus, through these phenomena, the scientific community tends to reduce controversies and to unify positions. In addition to the foregoing, the idea that debates must end with consensual agreement is widespread in the scientific community, regardless of the adopted epistemological postures; for the rationalists, because it is the "essential truth of the world that is grasped", and for the constructivists, it is in the nature of social negotiation to conclude with shared facts (Berthelot 2002; Poulain 2011).

All these tend to reduce the importance of controversies, when they are not denied by them, and to discredit scientifically or morally (at least for a certain time) those who put them forward by designating them as "outsiders", by invoking their "lack of seriousness", the "marginality of their position", or even possible "collusions of interest". More recently, as part of the tobacco controversy, they have been described by some tobacco control advocates as smoke curtains kept by lobbyists to slow down the implementation of public health measures.

The controversies are therefore not always very visible and their study must take place through an empirical material of various origins and which is not reduced to scientific documents in the strict sense of the term. We therefore use:

- classical scientific papers (articles published in peer-reviewed journals, expert reports, summary books written by researchers);
- productions of lobbyists, whether they are economic, consumerist, users (websites, publications with more or less wide distribution, advertisements, etc.);
- press articles (analyses carried out by journalists and interviews of scientists);
- TV shows.

The study of controversies is a counterpoint to the optimism bias that emerges from the consensus analyses. When consensus conferences invite action by showing everything we know and can be backed by decisions, controversy analyses call for caution by identifying areas of uncertainty. This is why their uses complement each other. The limitation of consensus expertise is to erase the points that are debated and the low level of proof of certain knowledge.

If the scientific and political circles do not take up the controversies, they inevitably expose themselves at the time of the return to reality, to serious disappointments. The very critical reading of the general public and the press then takes place on the mode: "we were hiding something". It is the Chernobyl cloud syndrome that was supposed to stop at the border of certain European countries.... This was the case with the H1N1 flu, which has raised suspicion on the part of the experts of the World Health Organization (WHO), and more seriously on the expertise of WHO itself. Risk and crisis management has taught us that risk deniers often turn against their sponsors.

Two complementary families of technique exist:

- Collective expertise and consensus conferences that inventory, rank and prioritize levels of evidence of a scientific issue. This methodology has been in place in the United States since the 1970s as part of the National Institutes of Health (NIH) Office of Medical Application of Research (OMAR).
- Inventory and analysis of the conditions for arbitration of controversies that point out the lines of disagreement and sharing of knowledge, but which also attempt to identify the terms of arbitration and possible overtaking. If the study of controversies is the subject of an important literature (Raynaud 2017), the methodologies have not yet, like those of the consensuses, been the subject of standardization.

At first it could be useful to make the distinction between "scientific controversies" and "socio-technical controversies". The first category can be defined by contradictory readings based on legitimate scientific arguments. That means arguments published under equivalent conditions in peer-reviewed journals (Poulain 2012a). The study of this type of controversy makes it possible to identify where to focus the research effort in order to overcome theoretical conflicts. The second is not based primarily on scientific questions, but rather on technical, social and ethical dimensions. They are part of issues of choice of society and their arbitration is therefore more a political choice. The first category of controversy may, when scientific arbitrations have been made, change in nature and fall into the second category.

From democratic risk management to the social reconstruction of food in the social arena

Since zero risk is non-existent, as scientific discoveries both reduce the fields of uncertainty and create new ones, we collectively negotiate the share of acceptable risk. Since human activities cannot all be based on science, some experiments have been conducted or are underway, in the form of citizen conferences or hybrid forums with experts, politicians and citizens. The first Citizens' Conference was held in Denmark in 1987 and was devoted to "the use of genetic technology in industry and agriculture". Since then, the experience has been repeated a few times here in France and has been replicated in various other Western countries. In France, the first such action was about genetically modified organisms (Joly *et al.* 2000; Marris and Joly 1999); it was extended with the setup of "Etats Généraux de l'Alimentation" [Citizen Conference on Food] in 1999 and repeated in 2017. The aim of these hybrid forums is to set up dialogue between the different categories of social actors, to debate the political choices that surround modern food systems, in order to build or rebuild consensus.

Pierre Lascoumes (1999) proposes three readings of these risk management mechanisms. The first – optimistic – sees increases in participatory democracy. By involving social actors of different categories, hybrid forums contribute to the dissemination of knowledge usually enclosed within small circles of initiates. By exposing experts and political actors to the criticisms of the citizens, they (the hybrid forums) play a part in repositioning issues related to technoscientific progress within a political context. In this way, they have established controversy as a method of managing society along democratic lines.

Second, there are fears that new forms of manipulation by modern states will be installed under the guise of democratic debate. Through this perspective, citizen conferences are seen as simulacra of debates, which are above all, intended to be mediated. Their true function would be to legitimize decisions "whose substance will always be controlled by political and administrative actors" (Lascoumes 1999). The selection of lay actors poses the problem of their representativeness (of which social group's interests are they the representative?) and their adequacy for representation (their cognitive ability, but also what technical, media and political resources do they have?) From this point of view, these mechanisms would only be smoke screens intended to cover up the real stakes and beneficiaries of the decision.

Between the first reading benignly praising the progress of democracy and the second, more pessimistic, articulated around the thesis of "big manipulation" or notions of a generalized conspiracy, a third, intermediary position is possible which considers these tools as elements forming a conception of procedural democracy (Habermas 1984). It is not always possible to build consensus on the issues involved, or to agree on the decisions reached by other means. On the other hand, it is possible to agree on the modalities of the social handling of the decision and of the arbitration between contradicting strategies.

The appeal of democratic risk management mechanisms is that they curtail the perception of food crises as social anomalies and create the conditions to start the process of reciprocal learning by the actors and their respective rationalities. To eat is a common practice for all individuals, it affects society as a whole. A debate on diet is thus more than just a debate on patterns of food consumption; it is also a debate on the organization of society, a debate of civilization. Eating is an act of trust that presupposes a certain social consensus throughout the food chain from farmers or breeders to the eaters themselves. Yet among all those scientists, experts, journalists, politicians, activists, whom Corbeau (1997) calls the actors of the "eating sector", are those who help define and redefine periodically the stakes associated with food. In this reading, to fight food crises, mechanisms should be set up to restore or reconstruct dialogue and achieve a certain minimal level of consensus. The first step is to recognize that behind food issues are not just health risks, but social choices. Granting food concerns their full legitimacy is one of the first steps towards achieving this goal.

Notes

1 The English term "whistle-blowers" does not have exactly the same meaning and is not a proper translation of *lanceur d'alerte*. Whistle-blowers originate from the role of a referee in a football match. That refers to one who knows the rules and has the legitimate position to remind the players of them. The position of a *lanceur d'alerte* is at the intersection of the scientific and technical world and the public one: with enough "insiders" to have access to strategic and relevant information in the former, and enough "outsiders" to be free from the network of interests of the latter.

2 The notion of crusader comes from the agenda-setting theory (McCombs and Shaw 1972) and describes a role of activists who advocate a cause. This role is complementary to the expert one. That is, the "crusader" and "expert" contribute a problem to enter on the agenda.

3 The methodology used for the study of "food concerns" was developed, under the direction of Jean-Pierre Poulain, as part of research funded by the French Ministry of Agriculture, Forestry and Food Grant no. 19276: 2010–2013. It was developed using empirical data from three surveys conducted at different times (2009–2010, 2013 and 2016). It is the result of a partnership between CERTOP (Centre d'Etudes et de Recherche, Travail, Organisations, Pouvoir) UMR-CNRS of the University of Toulouse, CREDOC (Centre de Recherche pour l'Etude des Conditions de Vie) and OCHA (Observatoire CNIEL des Habitudes Alimentaires). This research is characterized by the fact that it:

- works in the general population and not a specific group likely to have developed a particular sensitivity to food (activists, only prescribers, etc.), as is the case in the classical theory of weak signals;
- uses the technique of idea associations that ask of the different categories of food (meat, seafood, dairy, fruit, vegetables, etc.) what are the concerns that come to mind?;
- uses the notion of "concern", instead of "risk", in the writing of questions, in order to get out of the sanitary framework and to collect more widely the respondents' concerns.

References

Adam, B., F. Berkhout, T. Dyson, R. Grove-White, T. Marsden, T. O'Riordan, I. Scoones, A. Scott, A. Stirling, C. Williams and B. Wynne (1999) "The Politics of GM Food: Risk, Science and Public Trust", ESRC Global Environmental Change Programme, Special Briefing 5, Brighton, Sussex: University of Sussex.

Ansoff, H. I. (1975) "Managing Strategic Surprise by Response to Weak Signals", *California Management Review*, XVIII(2): 21–33.

Beardsworth, A. (1995) "The Management of Food Ambivalence: Erosion and Reconstruction?", in D. Maurer and J. Sobal (eds), *Eating Agendas: Food and Nutrition as Social Problems*, New York: Aldine de Gruyter.

Beck, U. (1999) *World Risk Society*, Cambridge: Polity.

Beck, U. and E. Grande (2010) "Varieties of Second Modernity: Extra-European and European Experiences and Perspectives", *British Journal of Sociology*, 61(3): 409–443.

Beck, U. and Lau, C. (2005) "Second Modernity as a Research Agenda: Theoretical and Empirical Explorations in the 'Meta-Change' of Modern Society", *The British Journal of Sociology*, 56(4): 525–557.

Berthelot, J.-M. (2002) "Pour un programme sociologique non réductionniste en étude des sciences", *Revue Européenne des Sciences Sociales*, XL(124): 233–252.

Brante, T. (1993) "Reasons for Studying Scientific and Science Based Controversies", in T. Brante, S. Fuller and W. Lynch (eds), *Controversial Science: From Content to Contention*, Albany, NY: SUNY Press.

Callon, M., P. Lascoumes and Y. Barthe (2001) *Agir dans un monde incertain. Essai sur la démocratie représentative*, Paris: Le Seuil.

Champagne, P. (2000) "L'affaire de la 'vache folle' (ESB): les nouveaux risques de santé publique et leur gestion", in A. Garrigou (ed.), *La santé dans tous ses états*, Biarritz, Atlantica.

Chang, Kyung-Sup (2010a) "The Second Modern Condition? Compressed Modernity as Internalized Reflexive Cosmopolitization", *The British Journal of Sociology*, 61(3): 444–464.

Chang, Kyung-Sup (2010b) "Compressed Modernity in Perspective: South Korean Instances and Beyond", 5th World Congress of Korean Studies, 25–28 October 2010, Chinese Culture University, Taipei, Taiwan.

Chang, Kyung-Sup (2017) "Compressed Modernity", in B. Turner, K. Chang, C. Epstein, P. Kivisto, J. Ryan and W. Outhwaite (eds), *The Encyclopedia of Social Theory*, Chichester: Wiley Blackwell.

Chateauraynaud, F. and D. Torny (1999) *Les Sombres précurseurs: une Sociologie pragmatique de l'alerte et du risque de Paris*, Paris: Editions de l'EHESS.

Chateauraynaud, F. and D. Torny (2005) "Mobiliser autour d'un risque. Des lanceurs aux porteurs d'alerte", in Cécile Lahellec (ed.), *Risques et crises alimentaires*, Paris: Tec & Doc.

Corbeau, J.-P. (1997) "Pour une représentation sociologique du mangeur", *Économies et sociétés*, Développement agroalimentaire, 23: 147–162.

Douglas, M. and A. Wildavsky (1982) *Risk and Culture: An Essay on the Selection of Technical and Environmental Dangers*, Berkeley, CA: University of California Press, 1982.

Duclos, D. (1994) "Quand la tribu des modernes sacrifie au dieu risque", *Déviance et société*, 18(3): 345–364.

Fischler, C. (1988) "Food, Self and Identity", *Information* (International Social Science Council), 27(2): 275–292.

Fischler, C. (2002) "Food Selection and Risk Perception", in H. Anderson, J. Blundell and M. Chiva (eds), *Food Selection: From Genes to Culture*, Levallois-Perret: Danone Institute, 135–149.

Foucault, M. (1969) *The Archaeology of Knowledge*, London and New York: Routledge.

Gaudillière, J. P. (2002) "Mettre les savoirs en débat? Expertise biomédicale et mobilisations associatives aux Etats-Unis et en France", *Politix*, 15(57): 103–122.

Giddens, A. (1991) *Modernity and Self-identity*, Cambridge: Polity.

Gilbert, C. (2003) "La fabrique des risques", *Cahiers internationaux de sociologie*, (1), 55–72.

Gilbert, C., R. Amalberti, H. Laroche and J. Paries (2007) "Errors and Failures: Towards a New Safety Paradigm," *Journal of Risk Research*, 10(7), 959–975.

Gillespie, S. and L. Haddad (2003) *The Double Burden of Malnutrition in Asia: Causes, Consequences, and Solutions*, New Delhi: Sage Publications India.

Godard, O., C. Henry, P. Lagadec and E. Michel-Kerjan (2002) *Traité des nouveaux risques: Précaution, crise, assurance*, Paris: Gallimard.

Habermas, J. (1984) *The Theory of Communicative Action*, Vol. I. Boston, MA: Beacon Press.

Han, S. (2015) "Second-modern Transformation in East Asia: An Active Dialogue with Ulrich Beck", *Socio*, 6. https://socio.revues.org/1897, accessed 30 September 2016.

Harvey, D. (1990) *The Condition of Postmodernity: An Enquiry into the Origins of Cultural Change*, Cambridge, MA: Blackwell.

Joly, P.-B., G. Assouline, D. Kréziak, J. Lemarié, C. Marris and A. Roy (2000) *L'innovation controversée: le débat public sur les OGM en France*, Grenoble: INRA.

Kjærnes, U., M. Harvey and A. Warde (2007) *Trust in Food: A Comparative and Institutional Analysis*, London: Palgrave Macmillan.

Lascoumes, P. (1999) *Corruptions*, Paris: Presses de Sciences-Po.

Le Breton, D. (1995) *La sociologie du risque*, Paris: PUF.

Marris, C. and P.-B. Joly (1999) "La gouvernance technocratique par consultation? Interrogation sur la première conférence de citoyens en France", in "Risque et démocratie savoirs, pouvoir participation … vers un nouvel arbitrage?", *Les cahiers de la sécurité intérieure*, 38: 97–124.

Martin, A. and J. P. Poulain, eds. (2011) *La controverse scientifique, Lettre scientifique Fonds français Alimentation & Santé*, Paris: Fonds français Alimentation & Santé.

McCombs, M. (2005) "A Look at Agenda-Setting: Past, Present and Future", *Journalism Studies*, 6(4): 543–557.

McCombs, M. E. and D. L. Shaw (1972) "The Agenda-Setting Function of Mass Media", *Public Opinion Quarterly*, 36(2): 176.

Poulain, J.-P., ed. (2007) *L'homme, le mangeur, l'animal. Qui nourrit l'autre?* Paris: Les cahiers de l'OCHA (Observatoire Cidil des Habitudes Alimentaires).

Poulain, J.-P. (2011) "Controverses scientifiques: Principe de précaution et principe de circonspection", in A. Martin and J. P. Poulain (eds), *La controverse scientifique, Lettre scientifique Fonds français Alimentation & Santé*, Paris: Fonds français Alimentation & Santé, 9–19.

Poulain, J.-P. (2012a) "Risques et crises alimentaires", in J.-P. Poulain (ed.), *Dictionnaire des cultures alimentaires*, Paris: PUF.

Poulain, J.-P. (2012b) "The Affirmation of Personal Dietary Requirements and Changes in Eating Models", in C. Fischler (ed.), *Selective Eating: The Rise, Meaning and Sense of Personal Dietary Requirements*, Paris: Odile Jacob, 253–264.

Poulain, J.-P. (2016) "De la perception des risques à la prise en compte des inquiétudes alimentaires, Première analyse des résultats de l'étude 'Inquiétudes' 2016 (OCHA – Université de Toulouse – CREDOC)", www.lemangeur-ocha.com/wp-content/uploads/2016/12/conference-jean-pierre-poulain-ttem-2016.pdf, accessed 11 June 2018.

Poulain, J.-P. (2017) *Sociology of Food*, London: Bloomsbury; translation of *Sociologies de l'alimentation*, Paris: PUF, 2002.

Poulain, J. P., C. Laporte, L. Tibère and E. Mognard (2014) *Malaysian Food Barometer*, Subang Jaya: Taylor's University Press.

Raynaud, D., ed. (2017) *Scientific Controversies: A Socio-Historical Perspective on the Advancement of Science*, London and New York: Routledge.

Roeser, S., R. Hillerbrand, P. Sandin and M. Peterson, eds. (2012) *Handbook of Risk Theory: Epistemology, Decision Theory, Ethics, and Social Implications of Risk*, Dordrecht and New York: Springer Science & Business Media.

Rozin, P. (1976) "The Selection of Food by Rats, Humans and Other Animals", in J. Rossenblat, R. A. Hide, C. Beer and E. Shaw (eds), *Advances in Study of Behaviour*, vol. 6, New York: Academic Press, 21–76.

Rozin, P. (1994) "La magie sympathique", *Autrement*, 149: 22–37.

Rozin, P., C. Fischler, S. Imada, A. Sarubin and A. Vrzesniewski (1999) "Attitudes to Food and the Role of Food in Life in the USA, Japan, Flemish Belgium and France: Possible Implications for the Diet–Health Debate", *Appetite*, 33(2): 163–180.

Slovic, P. (1987) "Perception of Risk", *Science*, 236: 280–285.

Slovic, P. (1993) "Perceived Risk, Trust and Democracy", *Risk Analysis*, 13(6): 675–682.

Tibère, L. (2016) "Food as a Factor of Collective Identity: The Case of Creolisation", *French Cultural Studies*, 27(1): 85–95.

Warde, A. (2016) *The Practice of Eating*, Cambridge: Polity.

2 Food safety and consumer rationality

Is a "food pact" possible?

Florent Champy

Since Beck's seminal work on risk societies, risk perception has become a significant topic of the research field (Beck 1986). Slovic's work on cognitive biases in risk perception emphasizes the part played by irrationality in attitudes towards natural and industrial dangers or risks (Slovic 1987). In a different way, Douglas and Wildavsky's work on risk cultures also shows that attitudes towards risk do not actually stem from a risk assessment that would seek objectivity (Douglas and Wildavsky 1983). Both cultures and cognitive biases impact these perceptions. In the very case of cognitive biases, Slovic has shown a general tendency to overestimate risks. More recently, other researchers have also argued that general concern about risks has been increasing, while actual risks had never been lower than since the end of the twentieth century.

Research on food safety provides a good illustration of this paradox (Raude and Denizeau 2008). On the one hand, experts agree that the level of food safety has never been so high in developed countries. The use of conservation and sterilization techniques and the normalization of products have reduced short-term health risks (i.e. poisoning) associated with food. Yet, on the other hand, consumers feel more and more concerned with these risks. Food quality has become a public issue, that is to say, a matter of controversy about which government authorities are often questioned and pressured. To explain this paradox, some authors mention cognitive biases, underlining the fertility of Slovic's approach (Raude 2008). Yet there are also limitations to this largely shared analysis, which stems from a narrow conception of rationality, defined mainly in concordance with experts' claims. There is no consideration here as to whether consumers do have good reasons to distrust experts. The conclusion about consumers' irrationality is drawn without enough investigation into the rationale of their attitude towards food. If the level of food safety has actually been increasing for decades, how does one account for the above paradox? Which appropriate analytical frame should be adopted?

The aim of this chapter is to show that consumers' attitudes towards food risks can be seen as rational even though experts are right in that food safety has significantly increased since the second half of the twentieth century. To this end, I will seek to highlight three dimensions of the problem that are usually given too little attention. These are the anthropological specificity of food as consumption, which makes the reasoning consistent for other products irrelevant here; the uncertainties food consumers are facing, concerning both the risk of health incidents and the long-term health consequences of their consumption; and the close relationships between trust and rationality in uncertain contexts. I will also use the evidence paradigm identified by the Italian historian Ginzburg as a reference to a certain form of rationality. The discussion will focus on a presentation of the general evolutions of food industries, notably in France, and the "food pact", a notion used by the food industry, will be investigated as a possible analytical concept.

Food specificities and increasing uncertainties

When addressing food risks, the high specificity of food, as compared to other consumptions, should be taken into account. The specificity is twofold. First, eating brings vulnerability. Indeed, eating what someone else has cooked exposes the eater to the risk of being poisoned, of falling ill and even of dying. Experts, who say that food safety has been increasing, consider that these risks are actually decreasing thanks to standards and conservation techniques. Yet the commercial relationships between food producers and food consumers generate another problem, and this will be my second point. Eating has a strong symbolical dimension, highlighted in Levi-Strauss's study of "magical thinking" and by a standard experiment on food (Levi-Strauss 1962; Nemeroff and Rozin 1989). If one sterilizes a roach and puts it in a glass of milk, the milk remains impossible to drink, even after the roach has been removed. It is biologically pure. Yet, in any ordinary eater's mind, something remains of the contact with an animal perceived as disgusting. The milk is undrinkable because the drinker would symbolically incorporate some undesired qualities of the roach. Something purely symbolical, yet crucial, is at stake beyond the issues of health and life.

Eating something prepared by someone else involves two main concerns: first, that of health and sometimes of death; and second, the feeling that one is being treated as a person worthy of respect, which contributes to self-esteem. When consumers feel they are badly treated, that is enough to bring strong discomfort and undermine trust. This explains why it is so crucial for victims of negligence who suffered health problems to be able to express their suffering by telling their story. This is also why, in addition to financial compensation, moral compensation is so crucial in the case of personal injury. Attentive listening and moral compensation restore their status as a person. How does the current food supply system concretely meet these high expectations of safety and respect?

In a production and distribution system that can be referred to as traditional, in which food is produced close to consumers, even often in the family, these expectations can be met through interpersonal relationships on food markets and in prudential cultures. First, food products follow short and well-known routes of interpersonal exchanges. People who exchange food on the market often have a lasting relation as members of the same family, the same village or the neighbouring villages. This is crucial. When cooperative behaviours are needed in a situation of incomplete information (in this case the eater expects respect but cannot check how the food has been prepared), regular interactions are one of the best ways to guarantee trust (Laurent 2012). Fed by their family or neighbours, eaters know that the food has been prepared for them and that they are being treated as persons. Second, farming and cooking are, or used to be, based on a relationship made up of fear and respect towards nature. This limits experiments. Constant production techniques reduce uncertainties about product quality. Agricultural and culinary knowledge used to be incorporated in customs and cultures ("culinary cultures" is the common phrase but "agricultural cultures" or "breeding cultures" could also be used), thus prohibiting some ways of dealing with food. Practices that have been tried and recognized as safe become norms while dangerous practices are prohibited. Of course, these cultures are not perfect. There are also bad habits, for instance alcoholism or excessive consumption of salt or fermented products, which may cause stomach cancer. Yet these cultures incorporate knowledge and safeguard from dangerous experiments. For a long time, nearby production and prevailing cultural habits have made everyday food easy to be consumed without distrust.

After the Second World War, France and other rich countries experienced major changes that challenged both the previous production and distribution system. Relationships between producers, distributors and consumers changed radically and new concerns emerged (Mendras 1967; Hervieu and Purseigle 2013). First, interpersonal connections between food producers and consumers were broken. Moreover, a new mass distribution system made the identification of producers by consumers difficult or impossible. Consumers do not always know who produced what they eat and where. Second, the highly concentrated distribution system and globalized trade have brought about an increasing geographical distance between producers and consumers. Tomatoes from the south of Spain and lambs from New Zealand have mostly replaced former local productions in supermarkets, even though recent consumer demand has also called for shorter circuits. The food supply chain has become opaque: agricultural techniques, origins of products, transformation techniques, actual conditions of conservation, transportation and storage are largely unknown. How can consumers accept to ingest products without having a clear idea of their production and distribution processes?

The construction of distrust

The increasing distance between food production and consumption on the one hand and the lack of transparency in the production and distribution processes on the other problematize the issue of trust in producers and distributors. Can consumers put enough trust in food suppliers to ingest what they provide without reluctance or hesitation? Trust is a crucial issue for actions in uncertain situations, because it compensates the consequences of uncertainty (Mollering 2001). Trust makes it possible for consumers to eat without knowing everything about how the food has been prepared. Yet as production is more and more distant and as consumers do not always know where the food comes from, trusting the whole food system currently seems to be a prerequisite. This is also why labels are crucial. Standards, registered designation of origin (*appellations d'origine contrôlée* (AOC) in France), and certifications for organic food, for instance, contribute to make a product trustworthy even though there is no precise information about the concrete process of production, provided that consumers see the labels as reliable. In addition, the industrial food supply system questions the extent to which experts' claims on the increasing food safety can be relied on. Statistics are only one of a number of elements in the construction of attitudes towards the food supply system. As a matter of fact, two sets of signals play a significant part in the increasing distrust.

The first one is the financialization of agriculture and of the food sector during the last few decades. It has introduced new logics of decision and tensions between stakeholders' and consumers' interests. Decisions are made on financial criteria, while sanitary and symbolic food issues require special attention to concrete products. In financial capitalism, decision makers are less stable than those in family firms, which tends to free them from their accountability. Short-term decisions become more common (Blondel 2012), which may contribute to increasing distrust.

Food crises as signals

The second set of signals is food crises. I will spend more time on this, as it is both more specific to food and more determining. For about twenty years, food crises have strongly impacted the representation of the food production system. However, their impact is not the sole result of biased and exaggerated representations, as claimed by Jocelyn Raude. They also operate as the signals consumers use to build up their opinion and eventually make their decisions about the opaque production and distribution system. I will explain why using the information provided by these crises in order to get some idea about the system is fully rational.

As food is associated with major personal issues, consumers, when confronted with such an unintelligible food supply system, have to be able to decide what they can trust or what they cannot. They know they cannot reach any certainty about the quality of the food they buy, since they have no global view of the production and distribution chain. In such situations, marked with high uncertainty, rationality does not consist of seeking certainty or blindly trusting statistics. As Carlo Ginzburg has shown, it consists of using any kind of information available (that is to say even tiny pieces of evidence) to build up one's judgement, trying to understand the indications they give about the reality, which cannot be known systematically (Ginzburg 1986). This rationality is a modest one, yet it is much more realistic and wiser than trusting strong assertions meant to deny uncertainty. Several characteristics of these crises help to understand what consumers can learn from them. I will provide a systematic presentation of these characteristics and then illustrate them with three examples.

The first one is their recurrence. Even though fewer people die, as compared to past collective intoxications, repeated crises and scandals reveal the general vulnerability of the food system, whereas experts present it as safer and safer. In addition, the more the food industry and the experts assert that the system is safe, the more each crisis is felt as a misconduct or a failure, the evidence of a broken promise. Food crises then echo the numerous examples, existing in other fields of activities, of the lack of information about the actual dangers created by technology, such as the cases of asbestos and civil nuclear power presented as safe and clean for years. The second characteristic of food crises is their diversity. Causes vary from mere negligence to criminal conduct, and consequences are very different, as we will see. The third characteristic is their ability to capture imagination, as they confront consumers with visions of production techniques that were a priori unthinkable for many people. The fourth characteristic is the plurality of the actors involved: producers, distributors, public authorities in charge of food safety, governments and experts. This makes the process that has led to the crisis often unclear. Finally, the fifth characteristic is the attitude of unaccountability adopted by most actors. When a crisis occurs, the actors involved in the supply chain tend to shift responsibility from one to the other. The large number of actors and the opacity of the system aid unaccountability. This is all the more damaging as accountability is an essential condition for trust.

Thus, one after another, crises provide a disturbing insight into the production system, which consumers see as a sufficient source of information to pass their own judgement. Yet too much secrecy and uncertainty remain for analysts to consider consumers' judgement as rational if one sticks to the narrow definition of rationality commonly used. Under uncertainty, consumers wisely go along with the "evidence paradigm" described by Ginzburg. Food is too sensitive a subject to allow for the only other alternative, blind trust. If one accepts to reconsider what rationality means and rules out the definition given by experts, consumers are fully rational in their judgement. Let us consider three striking examples of recent food crises.

Studying three emblematic crises

At the beginning of the 1980s, the scandal of "adulterated oil" broke out in Spain. During the two months of May and June 1981, the collective food intoxication was front-page news in the country and much commented on in other European countries. This intoxication finally made thousands of people ill and killed hundreds of them. Investigations never fully cleared up the whole case. WHO blamed the intoxication on colza oil, which was made unfit for consumption by being processed for industrial use and sold as olive oil. It revealed, on the one hand, that some actors in the food industry were prepared to ignore health risks out of mere greed and, on the other, how difficult it was to shed light on this kind of scandal.

In 1996 there was the "mad cow" crisis (Raude 2008; Lepiller 2016). Cow meat was infected by bovine spongiform encephalopathy, or mad cow disease, and resulted in the onset of Creutzfeldt-Jakob disease, a fatal degenerative disease due to a prion and affecting the nervous system, for a number of consumers. This crisis was striking for several reasons. The incubation could last for more than fifteen years, which raised the fear of unexpectedly serious consequences. Any cow meat consumer could feel unsafe, and it was impossible to estimate how many people would actually get ill. In addition, this crisis exposed the use of a technique consumers could not even have suspected, feeding cows with fish and bovine bone meal. Indeed, some commentators stressed that this feeding technique was a twofold serious transgression: herbivores eating meat and eating conspecifics (Lepiller 2016).

Besides deaths and the fear of more deaths to come, consumers also felt mistreated. They realized they did not know what they had been given to eat, and they were able to judge that the livestock industry was playing God. That crisis alone revealed three transgressions: nature had not been respected, while the food industry kept using it as a marketing argument, as they knew many consumers value it (Lepiller 2012); consumers' informed consent about what they were eating had not been respected; the demand for prudence, that is required when food preparation is delegated to others, had not been taken into account. These transgressions were all the more devastating for the reputation of the food industry as consumers discovered them all at once, against the backdrop of an unpredictable number of deaths. That is why this crisis reactivated the criticism of industrial food, which had become scarce for about twenty years as a result of new regulations (Lepiller 2016). Public authorities responded by improving consumers' information about the origin of meat in order to allow for an informed choice. Yet, there is no means of being certain which techniques are actually used by the food industry, and even about the nature of the products sold, as shown by the next example.

In 2013, frozen food, mainly lasagna, was withdrawn from sale. It had been discovered that some products were made of horsemeat, while sold as beef. This new crisis may have seemed less serious than the previous ones. It consisted only of substituting one edible product with another. It did not have any serious health consequences, even though doubts about the safety of the products were also raised. Yet, less than ten years after the "mad cow", this new crisis once again evidenced disrespect for consumers' free choice. If product labelling is not reliable, then there is no proper means to choose what one eats. In addition, a pet, the horse, was inevitably provided to some consumers who had a very strong attachment to the animal. A new symbolical barrier had been ignored, while concern for animal welfare has been increasing and the distance between humans and animals decreasing. Finally, as in the case of adulterated oil, accountabilities were difficult to establish. Of course, producers knew they were selling horsemeat for beef, whereas what distributors knew remained uncertain.

Crises, signals and distrust

These three crises revealed the total lack of respect of some actors of the food supply chain for their clients, as they took the risk of poisoning them to increase their profits. Such crooks are a minority, yet they show how vulnerable the system is. These crises have also revealed the lack of caution in agri-food innovation, exemplified by the common practice of feeding herbivores with bone meal without anticipating that pathogens might cross species barriers. And yet, the food industry communication showed that they were not aware of how shocking this innovation could be for consumers, or refused to acknowledge it. What they think should be acceptable to consumers seems to be a long way from what consumers are prepared to accept. This gap increases distrust. Finally, the crises revealed the unreliability of labelling and the loss of credibility of experts whose word should have contributed to restoring public trust. What experts claim may be statistically accurate: considering only the short-term sanitary consequences, food has never been so safe. Yet crises reveal that the word of experts does not guarantee the quality or even the very nature of a given product. Accordingly, it is only natural that consumers see crises as evidence of *general* disrespect towards them.

Particularly after the mad cow crisis, there was a strong demand for food traceability, and the French government created the label "French meat". Debates about labelling improvement also developed. Yet the debates showed that some actors of the food industry still stand in the way of some initiatives. In 2016, an experiment of four nutritional labelling systems in forty supermarkets from three different commercial brands illustrated the difficulties encountered in promoting the readability of nutritional quality. Initiated by the French Ministry for Health and based on an agreement with distributors, this experiment aimed at fighting obesity, diabetes and heart diseases. Yet several members of the scientific board quit, arguing that industrial lobbies were too influential, and the press echoed the difficulties in implementing a reliable experimental programme. This event is very likely to reinforce the widespread conviction that powerful actors of the food supply chain are more concerned about their reputation than about public health issues and that, for this purpose, they are prepared to purposely limit the quality of information.

Crisis after crisis and controversy after controversy, the food industry is backing up the idea that actors do not do what they say, and that their clients' safety matters less than profit. Thus, cognitive biases are not needed to explain why crises bring distrust. If one seriously considers food specificities and examines crises as a source of information for consumers compelled to eat despite uncertainties about food quality, the image that clearly emerges is that of a food system regulation which is not only responsible for a number of deaths or illnesses, but also causes symbolical damage that is never taken into account. Revelations about food production also affront everybody's status as a person and our relation to food. Crises show an agribusiness with neither caution nor respect for consumers, an agribusiness context where secrecy is preserved and where the consumers' free choice is hindered. This cannot generate confidence and is not acceptable for most consumers.

Food crises may seem incidental from the experts' point of view based on epidemiology, as they cause few deaths in industrialized countries, when compared to casualties from car accidents, domestic accidents or criminality. Yet this judgement fails as it is based on a conception of rationality that is inappropriate to food. Aside from deaths or illness statistics, respect should also be an end in itself. In addition, consumers can never be sure that the next crisis will not be far worse than all the previous ones. Experts infer from the low number of deaths that food is safer and safer. However, consumers see the information crises give them as evidence that food production is far from what they could easily accept. The expert logic is a mechanical use of statistics, that is to say, abstract knowledge, whereas consumers use more concrete information to decide how reliable food producers and distributors are. As they cannot avoid eating and are faced with a high degree of uncertainty, their logic is closer to the "evidence paradigm", and they seek to exercise caution. This is totally rational.

The "food pact": from a commercial notion to a concept

Some actors of the food industry are aware of the consumers' distrust, and they are looking for solutions. Several initiatives have been taken as exemplified by some French attempts. Distribution is in direct contact with consumers. For this reason, it pioneered in innovations to seek to bring trust back. The chairman of the commercial brand "System U", Serge Papin, published a work entitled "Pour un nouveau pacte alimentaire" (For a new food pact) (Papin 2012). It aimed at convincing consumers that distributors were prepared to be accountable to the environment, to local producers and to consumers. Yet the question of risk was minored and the difficulty of reconciling the large retail organization with a real "food pact" was not dealt with either. Papin's work is mainly business communication, even though it also shows that the food industry is becoming aware of its negative or fragile image. More significantly, ANIA (the French National Association of Food Industries) also published a manifesto that declared its wish to establish such a pact with its clients (ANIA 2016). This manifesto was written after a questionnaire-based survey of consumers. The number of people who answered the questionnaire between November 2015 and March 2016 totalled 8832. The manifesto mentioned that progress had been made in food safety, nutritional quality, transparency and respect for the environment and that it should be supported and improved. Yet both its approach and its text raise questions. A pact implies a contract involving at least two parties, each of them being a real actor. In that case, ANIA had not invited the consumers' organizations, and consumers were involved only through the individual answers to the survey, in a very fragmented and distant way. In addition, a pact requires a shared diagnosis. Yet the reasons for consumers' distrust were ignored. On the contrary, the manifesto stated that "your food safety … is a duty.… It is in our firms and teams' DNA" (ANIA 2016: 8; my translation), while crises have demonstrated that it is rarely the case. In addition, besides some sweeping statements, no practical solution is put forward to reduce the tension between actual production conditions and the demand for food safety as well as the necessary requirements to achieve consumers' trust. That is why this discourse may be seen as an attempt to convince consumers they should agree with a system that has been conceived neither with them nor for them. One may wonder whether the conditions for a modernization of the food system are emerging, or whether inappropriate communication may once again prompt and strengthen consumers' distrust.

Mass retail has also been taking some concrete initiatives to modify the offer of food products or at least its image. The Carrefour brand claims it wishes consumers to become real subjects of their food choice, thanks to a milk brand named "Who is the boss? The consumer's brand". Thanks to NICTs (New Information and Communication Technologies), a consumer survey was organized. They were asked to express their preference on price and quality: would they be willing to pay more, and how much, for this or that improved product? Some 6000 people answered. Then a product was created to meet the demand expressed by the respondents. It consisted of a milk bottle without GMO and sold for an extra 7 euro cents per litre. The survey respondents may have considered that they actually took part in the definition of the product. This innovation was aimed at restoring, within the frame of mass consumption, conditions of production and consumption similar to those that had allowed for trust before the financialization of the food industry. Yet it only concerns a small section of food production and consumption. It is mostly symbolic.

Such discourses and innovations illustrate the food industry's ability to reuse criticism in their own communication, as Olivier Lepiller has shown by pointing out that the presentation of food as "natural" has become a marketing argument to convince or seduce consumers. The change made is bringing a major sense distortion (Lepiller 2012). Yet one wonders how effective the strategy is. How many consumers will actually be convinced? Is there any real change in commercial relationships? Or are these so-called "innovations" only signals that, once decoded as such, are bound to reinforce distrust towards the food industry communication?

A comparison of the "food pact" with a philosophical concept will be helpful to shed light on what a real "food pact" could be without being trapped by ANIA's discourse. This concept is the "pact of care" (*pacte de soin*) created by Paul Ricœur as part of his philosophical reflection about relations between patients and professional caregivers, notably doctors. So, what makes this comparison fruitful to enlighten the conditions of a real "food pact"?

Ricœur named "pact of care" the result of a process in the doctor–patient relationship (Ricœur 2001). This process is crucial because it contributes to building trust. The asymmetry between doctor and patient makes this pact necessary, as the former knows and the latter suffers. This gap is bridged by a moral promise shared by both parties to faithfully fulfil their respective commitments. Patients are committed to taking an active part in their treatment, and notably to doing their best to respect the cure protocol once they have accepted it. More significant to the comparison with food is the doctor's commitment to helping their patient through the treatments they judge the most appropriate to their case in the current state of medical knowledge; their commitment to considering them a person whose informed consent is required before any medical act. In addition, the Aristotelian concept of "practical wisdom" (or prudence, another translation for the Greek *phronesis*) describes some of the requirements for adequate medical decisions. Doctors must pay attention to the uniqueness and complexity of each patient's situation, avoiding the easy option of one-size-fits-all solutions. They must also take into account all the reasonably predictable good or bad consequences of their decisions, and inform the patient. They may be mistaken, but they must do their best to avoid making a mistake.

According to Ricœur, the "pact of care" must be investigated as it is very vulnerable, often deceptive and precarious once initiated. Ricœur mentions three sources of vulnerability: medical power; the technologization of medicine; and public health concerns. Medical power may lead to paternalistic attitudes, assigning the patient to the status of a minor. Second, biomedicine has established an increasing division of labour on a technical basis. This hinders the direct relationship between doctor and patient. The hospital has become a Kafkaesque place where patients mainly meet eyes focused on their organs or on their medical file without much attention to their suffering. Finally, public health concerns (the management of major epidemics is an example) sometimes hinder the attention doctors should first and foremost pay to the patients they are in therapeutic relation with. These vulnerabilities of the "pact of care" explain why it has been formalized in the Code of Ethics, which grants it a judicial value (Ricœur 2001: 231). For instance, a pact of confidentiality is part of the "pact of care", and it has led to the formal inscription of the medical secret in law.

Besides ANIA's use of the notion of "food pact", two points mentioned above demonstrate how useful the concept of "pact of care" is to enlighten the relations between food producers and consumers. First, the asymmetrical information between the food industry and consumers is quite similar to the asymmetry between doctors and patients: both patients and eaters are faced with uncertainties about the quality of the service or the product they need. Second, the possible dangers to a person's body and life similarly require respect. That is why knowing exactly what the "pact of care" is helps explore what a real "food pact" would be. Better statistics against fatality are very valuable; yet they are not enough. A real "food pact" would require that food producers and distributors only make responsible and legitimate decisions, which also means that they need to be prudential. They must respect their consumers and the preferences they express, allowing them to make their own free choices. The analogy with the "pact of care" helps understand that these conditions are not only tools for better food safety, but also ends in themselves.

To bring the analogy to completion, I will also develop the differences existing between the medical field and the food supply system. These differences have far-reaching implications. They explain why a real "food pact" is more unlikely than a satisfying "pact of care", at least in the context of financialized industrial production. Ricœur has explained how fragile the "pact of care" is. Patients' associations have had to struggle hard to get both patients and their families acknowledged as persons and subjects of their own treatment (Starr 1982). Things are even tougher in the field of food. Consumers are not faced with a professional with whom they could build a trusting service relationship. They are faced with actors who remain anonymous. The interaction is limited to the exchange of goods on a market, often without direct contact. In addition, these actors clearly claim that they work for profit, while doctors often point out their supposed selflessness (Champy 2012). The medical profession has adopted a Code of Ethics and Orders to make sure the code is enforced. Surely, the limits of this presentation of professions are well known (Freidson 1986). Yet in comparison, the food industry has two disadvantages. Relationships on the market are anonymous, as I have already mentioned, and ensuring the compliance of regulation is very hard because of the economic interests and the opacity of the field. There are technical rules about the quality of products; yet no process formalizes the relationship between consumers and producers as the Codes of Ethics do in the medical field.

Does it mean that the concept of "food pact" is useless? I do not think so, as it may guide an in-depth analysis of the different production systems: the industry, local food systems and self-production. To what extent does each of them provide characteristics favourable to an effective "food pact"? The specific conditions to establish a "food pact" should not be studied globally, as I have just done here, for the mere sake of presenting the notion. Each system should be studied separately, as the various methods of production and distribution greatly impact the possibility of fostering such a pact. The concept of "food pact" could provide the basis for some successful innovative research. For instance, the semiotic study of local food systems can demonstrate why this system better meets the requirements for a "food pact" (Champy 2018).

Conclusion

Cognitive biases, that is, a wrong intuitive assessment of risks by consumers, are not the only possible explanation for the gap between their perception of the risks and the experts' claims about decreasing food risks over several decades. As a matter of fact, a mere statistical view of risks ignores one particularly significant aspect of the issue. For consumers, trust not only requires decreasing risks, but also implies actually avoiding easily avoidable risks. It is fully rational for consumers to expect respect, care and caution from food producers and distributors. If this care is too uncertain, their reluctance is understandable.

Using the concept of "pact of care" as a reference, the concept of "food pact" may help to clarify some demands the sociology of food has paid too little attention to, that is, a more cautious attitude from food producers and distributors, as well as respect for consumers, fully considered as subjects capable of choosing what they eat. Respecting this "food pact" is an end in itself. Yet looking at the question through mere statistics both leaves aside the consumers' demand for respect and possible uncertainties about long-term risks, as the mad cow crisis has illustrated. The demand for respect and the concern for long-term risks make each crisis a sensitive signal. It is rational to pay more attention to them than to what statistics alone claim.

References

ANIA (2016) *Pour un nouveau pacte alimentaire*, www.ania.net/wp-content/uploads/2016/05/2016_05-09_ANIA_Pacte-alimentaire_WEB.pdf, accessed 11 June 2018.

Beck, U. (1986) *Risk Society: Towards a New Modernity*, London: Sage.

Blondel, C. (2012) "Investissement à long terme et capitalisme familial", *Revue d'économie financière*, 108: 57–68.

Champy, F. (2012) *La sociologie des professions*, Paris: PUF.

Champy, F. (2018) "Le pacte alimentaire", in J.-P. Poulain (ed.), *Dictionnaire des cultures alimentaires*, 2nd edition, Paris: PUF, 1031–1043.

Douglas, M. and A. Wildavsky (1983) *Risk and Culture: An Essay on the Selection of Technological and Environmental Dangers*, Berkeley, CA: University of California Press.

Freidson, E. (1986) *Professional Powers: A Study of the Institutionalization of Formal Knowledge*, Chicago: Chicago University Press.

Ginzburg, C. (1986) "Clues: Roots of an Evidential Paradigm", in C. Ginzburg, *Clues, Myths and the Historical Method*, Baltimore, MD: Johns Hopkins University Press, 96–125.

Hervieu, B. and F. Purseigle (2013) *Sociologie des mondes agricoles*, Paris: Armand Colin.

Laurent, E. (2012) *Economie de la confiance*, Paris: La Découverte.

Lepiller, O. (2012) *Critiques de l'alimentation industrielle et valorisations du naturel: sociologie historique d'une "digestion" difficile (1968–2010)*, mémoire de thèse de doctorat de Sociologie, Toulouse: Université de Toulouse II-Le Mirail.

Lepiller, O. (2016) "La place des médias dans la relance de la critique de l'alimentation industrielle: Le Nouvel Observateur et l'alimentation après la "vache folle", in E. Doidy and M. Gateau (eds), *Reprendre la terre: Agriculture et critique sociale*, Rennes: PU de Rennes.

Levi-Strauss, C. (1962) *La pensée sauvage*, Paris: Plon.

Mendras, H. (1967) *La fin des paysans*, Paris: Actes Sud.

Mollering, G. (2001) "The Nature of Trust: From Georg Simmel to a Theory of Expectation, Interpretation and Suspension", *Sociology*, 35 (2): 403–420.

Nemeroff, C. and P. Rozin (1989) "You Are What You Eat: Applying the Demand-Free 'Impressions' Technique to an Unacknowledged Belief", *Ethos, the Journal of Psychological Anthropology*, 17: 50–69.

Papin, S. (2012) *Pour un nouveau pacte alimentaire*, Paris: le Cherche Midi.

Raude, J. (2008) *Sociologie d'une crise alimentaire: les consommateurs à l'épreuve de la maladie de la "vache folle"*, Paris: Editions Lavoisier.

Raude, J. and M. Denizeau (2008) "La perception des risques alimentaires: une influence complexe et incertaine sur le comportement des consommateurs", *Economies et sociétés*, 42 (11–12): 2171–2188.

Ricœur, P. (2001) *Le Juste 2*, Paris: Esprit.

Slovic, P. (1987) "Perception of Risks", *Science*, 237: 280–285.

Starr, P. (1982) *The Social Transformation of American Medicine*, New York: Basic Books.

3 Contemporary food crises

When industrial failure meets state impotence

Vincent Simoulin

Food crises are not a contemporary phenomenon. They have for a long time taken the form of crises of scarcity linked to irregular and unpredictable, but nevertheless natural, disturbances within societies subject to malnutrition and famine (Sen 1981; Flandrin 1998). This type of analysis has not disappeared. Today, it takes the form of inquiries into the possibility of redeveloping production in light of the risks of resource depletion and overconsumption, especially of water, and even in view of the foreseeable disorders due to the effects of climate change and global warming (Thompson and Cohen 2012; D'Silva and Webster 2017; Palmer 2017).

Much of the present-day analysis of situations of scarcity also emphasize the systemic character of problems associated with access to food. Market prices indeed make certain products inaccessible to sections of the population, which sometimes include farmers themselves (Janin 2008; Karrer 2010; Heltberg *et al.* 2012; Rosin *et al.* 2012; Saad 2013). From this perspective, technology is both the source of and a possible solution to food crises through agronomic research into new crop varieties (Madramootoo 2015). We also look to solutions from a world organization adapted to the new challenges (Heintzman *et al.* 2005; Charvet 2006; Anseeuw and Wambo 2008; Clapp and Cohen 2009; Lambek 2014).

On the whole, however, the Industrial Revolution changed the nature of food crises, at least in those countries that went through it and became affluent societies. Such societies are certainly still unequal, and problems of access to food remain for certain populations, but obesity and risks linked to the extension of production cycles have become even greater threats. In this context, crises of scarcity have been largely replaced by disturbances to the public order resulting from food or food product scares (whether real, potential or presumed).

For the past thirty years, that is to say at least since the bovine spongiform encephalopathy (BSE) epidemic, popularly known as "mad cow" disease, food crises have consistently maintained a significant place on political agendas and in the media. They have become a major concern for consumers and public authorities, and have caused distrust of food products. Some crises have been brief, affecting only small groups, but others have hit countries and sometimes the whole world, just as what happened with BSE and the crises linked to bird flu.

The necessary conditions for the occurrence of a food crisis in the sense that we understand it in this chapter are: (1) a failure in the quality of a food product or at least uncertainty surrounding this quality; (2) inability of the public authorities to immediately identify the origins of this situation and to remedy it safely and firmly; (3) a denunciation of this situation by whistle-blowers, that is to say consumers, doctors, groups, etc.; and (4) a media campaign to broadcast the situation and denounce the risks to the population.

This definition therefore excludes cases of failure which go unperceived or unpublicized. It implies, above all, that food crises cannot just be explained by considering the characteristics of the food in question. A number of large-scale food crises have indeed had consequences that were totally disproportionate to the risks actually incurred by consumers. This feature appears, in fact, to increase with time, which would furthermore indicate that the models of prevention of crises and reaction to them are relatively effective.

We will attempt to define and characterize these models by showing, first of all, that to understand food crises we must now analyse the links between the practices of government and those of governance. We will then be able to distinguish different types of food crises while claiming that, in the end, all follow a logic of correction and adjustment by governments in a situation which had escaped their control. This will finally lead us to examine the foreseeable consequences of the increasing influence of New Public Management regarding food crises, and public authorities' capacity to prevent and manage them.

Food crises: where government meets governance

Although they vary greatly, food crises do of course have commonalities owing to the characteristics of food (Fischler 1990 and 2011; Poulain 2002; Raymond 2006). On the one hand, food can threaten the way in which our bodies function, and yet it is necessary to our survival, and, on the other hand, it is linked to a number of religious and cultural prohibitions. Food is therefore a field that is controlled to a high degree by public authorities, and many public policies aim to guarantee food safety and manage potential failures.

But, in a context of globalization, governance also plays an increasingly important role. The occurrence of food crises is therefore extremely significant not only for the evolution of food-chain safety procedures, but also for the reconfiguration of the links between practices of government and governance to ensure safety as far as possible.

The (official) pre-eminence of governmental practices

Food crises lead to high demands being put on public officials. This responsibility initially fell to actors at the municipal level, which were for a long time the only ones able to intervene effectively, not only because of difficulties of transport, but also owing to the limits of science and medicine. These limits generally reduced practices of food safety to visual inspections of the apparent quality of products (in terms of freshness), and the enforcement of temporary bans. From the start of the eighteenth century, when royal power began to assert itself in this domain, the implementation of preventive slaughter in the event of an epidemic began (Ferrières 2002).

This historical perspective reminds us first of all that central power has not long had the scientific or material means to intervene in the field of food safety. It then highlights the fact that royal intervention has long been disputed – decisions often going unheeded – and that interventions by police or royal agents provoked a great deal of resistance and sometimes even uprisings.

It was not until the middle of the nineteenth century, and then only in a handful of developed countries, that governments were truly able to enforce their pre-eminence in terms of food safety and the battle against deception linked to food products. Their mission with respect to all citizens became to take the necessary measures to ensure their protection, just as their mission with respect to the nation had already for a long time been to maintain territorial and national sovereignty.

Officially, from this point on, the emphasis was on the prevention and, to an even greater extent, management of food crises. These tasks were part of government practice as embodied, depending on country and product, by administrations in charge of health, agriculture, industry, or the prevention and suppression of fraud. Monitoring and inspection services had to take all necessary and relevant measures to ensure the quality of food products and the safety of consumers. This requirement is not, in theory, called into question by the contemporary dynamics of decentralization and regionalization. Public services must simply adapt to the evolutions of the geographic organization of their country.

This purely governmental approach is therefore recent and perhaps more fragile than we might think. Indeed, it clashes with the trend of globalization, and, in particular, with the separation of spaces of production and consumption. This has posed a challenge when it comes to health inspections of food and products manufactured in countries other than those where they are consumed. Since such foods and products are not intended to be consumed principally by local populations, the priorities of employment, attracting multinational companies, and competition conflict with scrupulous monitoring, which might taint the reputation of national products or increase their cost. Governments thereby face huge problems in regulating markets and controlling the quality of food products.

The rise of governance

Globalization and free trade agreements make it increasingly difficult to maintain the relevance of national regulation standards since government services are left powerless to control every exchange and flow of food products. In the present-day context, the prevention of food crises is therefore also based on vigilance on the part of economic actors (especially farmers and manufacturers), all segments of the food chain and potential whistle-blowers. It thereby involves not only governmental policies but also governance, and we should at this point clarify the meaning of this highly debated and contested term as far as possible.

It is impossible to reach total agreement on a definition of governance (Simoulin 2013), partly since there are so many definitions, and partly because this concept is the subject of passionate scientific and sometimes ideological debates. From our point of view, we will define the term "governance" as fundamentally describing all situations of cooperation that cannot be regulated by structure of authority alone. In other words, governance refers to situations of cooperation and decision in which no actor may claim from the outset to impose its opinion because of its status (Simoulin 2003). This is what distinguishes it from government practice, where, by means of elections or appointments, hierarchies exist, are legitimate and rule debate, which may be interrupted and determined by official "decision makers".

This situation is due either to the way actors are increasingly connected to different sectors (public/private/voluntary) or to distinct geographical levels (local/regional/national/global), or to their increased level of education to the point that they are capable of greater critical distance in response to orders or instructions they are given. In any case, the concept of governance describes this dual situation: one of cooperation that is not purely hierarchical, and one in which traditional borders are blurred and there is an increasing porosity between sectors, geographical levels and different spaces of attachment for an individual.

It is, however, for this very reason that this concept is so often and so heavily criticized. Not only is it accused of vagueness because it reflects a less determinate situation than the hierarchical and governmental structures which previously prevailed, but the term "governance" also contains opposing ideological meanings, referring to both a situation of lesser government advocated by neoliberals, and a requirement of participation and consultation as sought by the alter-globalization movement.

At an even more complex level, the concept of multilevel governance (Hooghe and Marks 2001; Bache and Flinders 2004) refers to the fact that international relations are also less and less governed by intergovernmental negotiations. They involve, above all, multinational companies, international organizations (such as the International Labour Organization and the World Trade Organization), and non-governmental organizations. As such, multilevel governance refers to relations between various locations and various types of governance: local, national, regional (Asian or European, for example) and global. Decisions are increasingly taken and regulations adopted following discussions and negotiations between actors representing these different levels.

Food crises as tests of governments and governance

Like other sectoral policies, food policies face the challenge of reconciling practices of government and governance. This is perhaps even more so in their case,
partly on account of the extremely specific nature – a combination of culture
and biology – of food products, and partly on account of their increasing globalization. Governments must protect populations, but globalization means that
they are less able to act alone, and must increasingly ensure this protection
through supranational negotiations, dealings with private actors, and all under
the pressure of consumers, non-governmental organizations and the media.

We can add to this that food crises, like all social phenomena, are not always
objective. They sometimes stem from the intervention of social actors, which
bring problems to the fore that would otherwise scarcely attract attention: either
in order to discredit a rival producer or even a whole country, or because it is an
opportunity for an administrative service to affirm the need to increase its
resources by denouncing a scandal in the field of food safety, or because an
opposing political party sees an opportunity to denounce the action of the
authorities. The crisis linked to the hospitalization of young consumers of Coca-
Cola in June 1999 in Belgium, and then in France, can thus partly be explained
by the concern of recently implemented institutions wishing to assert their
legitimacy. They challenged dominant actors, causing them problems by spreading information (Besançon *et al.* 2004).

As our definition emphasizes, food crises are not only related to dysfunctions,
but also to the intervention of the actors that denounce them and demand (and
often propose) corrective actions. In most analyses of contemporary food crises,
therefore, they are seen as both a test of food safety policies and a chance to
reinforce them. Food crises very often function as opportunities to develop new
policies, create new public bodies and affirm or influence political and administrative structures. They are "political windows" – moments that allow a read-
justment of the practices of government and governance (Kingdon 1984).

We must at this point distinguish the different types of food crises, which
involve and implement practices of government and governance to better
understand the contemporary links between the two.

Different types of food crises, one form of correction

Food crises vary greatly and are often distinguished according to the contami-
nants concerned (Knowles *et al.* 2007). If we seek to think rather in terms of
the social phenomena involved, even leaving aside scarcity crises, we can
identify at least three different types. The first corresponds to a double failure,
on the one hand in the process of food and food product safety, and on the
other hand in the response of the public authorities to this failure. The second
covers crises that are due to attempts of fraud and deception. The third is
linked to the rationale of optimization pushed so far that it causes unintended
contamination.

Of course, as in all typological distinction, most crises combine elements of these various types. If fraud occurs, it may also be the case, for example, that food safety procedures are flawed and fallible. Furthermore, although the types are different, they all illustrate the difficulties faced by public authorities in truly ensuring their mission of guaranteeing food safety, and their dependence on actors in the sector and whistle-blowers. It is only during the second phase, that of resolving the crisis, that the government dominates the scene while hiding the previous phase of governance.

Accidental crises

Some crises are accidental, such as the one linked to Coca-Cola production mentioned above, or the many alerts raised due to the presence of Salmonella or Listeria in food products that are frequently in the spotlight today in a number of countries. These are essentially due to the first two elements of the definition that we have proposed. They result first and foremost from a failure in the process that is intended to ensure food safety and thus from an error (or a series of errors) on the part of farmers or manufacturers. They are then compounded and prolonged by a certain period of incapacity by the public authorities to identify the causes of the problem and find solutions. The unlikely, accidental and rare nature of the contamination means that the authorities are surprised by its appearance and sometimes struggle to identify its origin with precision.

The "cucumber crisis" (May–June 2011) is a good example of this type since cucumbers were not even the issue in the end. It originated with the outbreak of *Escherichia coli* (*E. coli*) bacterium infection cases in northern Germany and their rapid multiplication in May 2011. Infections and deaths increased over several days – reaching a figure of nearly 4000 people affected in northern Europe, of which 3600 were in Germany, and 48 deaths, nearly all in Germany – while a major scare developed around cucumbers of Spanish origin. The German authorities even publicly identified Spanish cucumbers as the cause on 26 May 2011. It was finally revealed on 10 June 2011 that the contamination did not come from cucumbers but from an organic farm in Lower Saxony that produced sprouted seeds.

In this type of crisis, the goodwill of those involved is not in question. The contamination is due to chance, or more often, as Perrow (1984) shows, to a combination of chance, poor transfer of information, and reactions which do not resolve it and sometimes make it worse, precisely because they are based on incorrect information. Experience shows, nevertheless, that the discovery of contamination is not often disclosed (when possible) by producers to avoid accusations, damages and the compensations that could follow. This was the case in Spain in 1981 when the official explanation for the deaths of around 1000 people and the serious consequences for thousands of others was that unscrupulous importers had been selling industrial oil in place of cooking oil. It is generally agreed today that this massive food poisoning was in fact due to the excessive use of pesticides in tomato cultivation, even though this interpretation is still not enforced.

This type of contamination may be countered by better-informed action by the public authorities, but it has above all given rise to the development of protocols aimed at guaranteeing food safety by agri-food manufacturers (Hazard Analysis Critical Control Point – HACCP – Prerequisite Programmes) and standards (ISO 22000). All stages of the food chain are designed to prevent contamination and accidents as far as possible. This forms part of a system of industrial organization and quality management (Motarjemi and Lelieveld 2017), which the public authorities then complete by establishing specific regulations. This final step now tends to take place at the global level through the adoption of standards and the establishment of regulatory bodies (Hammoudi *et al.* 2015).

The ideal would of course be that political and industrial actors work together at each stage of managing the sector and on the improvement of safety in the food chain. However, as we have mentioned, the risk of blame and payment of financial compensation means that manufacturers try to solve the problems encountered themselves instead, away from the public eye, which leads to these incidents happening again until a more serious or longer-lasting contamination or hazard results in their public disclosure.

Either the safety breach is resolved by action on the part of the producers without consumers ever being made aware, or a whistle-blower or state service denounces the situation and it is put on the agenda until a solution is found. Once protocol and safety regulations have been corrected to take into account the circumstances that led to the contamination, these are in any case enforced on all actors in the sector.

In other words, the state comes relatively late in this respect, even if its media appearances may be more significant. As the goodwill of the actors is not to be blamed in the incident itself, the resolution of the crisis remains mostly within the realms of governance in terms of needing the cooperation of all actors concerned to correct the safety breach. By means of its refining of regulations and monitoring processes, the state simply approves and legitimizes the action of other stakeholders.

Crises arising from fraud and deception

Other crises arise from fraud. In this case, those responsible for the crisis are fully aware from the outset of the illegal nature and negative impact of their actions. The desire to make a profit nevertheless leads them to trade products that do not comply with the law and sometimes pose a proven threat to consumers.

The milk crisis – which broke out in China in July 2008, though there had been multiple warning signals of which in previous years – is a good case study of this. Laboratories discovered and announced that melamine had been added to milk to artificially increase its protein content and thus be able to replace a portion of the milk with water. According to the Chinese authorities, this crisis caused around 300,000 cases of sickness, of which 50,000 involved hospitalizations and six resulted in death. They responded with the trial of twenty-one people in December 2008, which led, most notably, to the sentencing to death and the execution of two people.

Fraud attempts have a long history and historians have, for example, documented the evolution of tampering practices in the wine industry (Stanziani 2005) at the same time as a system of quality labels was gradually being introduced. They corresponded, paradoxically, to a consequence of the implementation of these labelling systems designed to guarantee the quality of the product. Social actors sought to profit from these systems, which involved additional costs, to offer lower-quality or tampered products by taking advantage of consumer confidence.

Such cases of fraud do not always involve a real risk to the consumer, which clearly highlights the disparity that can exist between food risks and food crises. It was discovered, for example, in Europe in 2013 that horsemeat was sometimes secretly used in products supposedly manufactured from beef. This substitution did not present any health risk and did not even have any consequences in terms of taste. In this case, a scandal arose in several countries because of the product deception alone when it was discovered that the manufacturers of food products, as well as the traders and slaughterhouses, had been contributing to this type of fraud for years, at least since 2007, and in several countries, according to the investigations.

While the denunciation of a crisis sometimes relies on whistle-blowers, it nevertheless lies at the heart of government duty. The quality of food safety protocol and regulation is then at issue, as each fraud scandal also stems from a failure in this protocol, as in China, and leads to change to prevent the repetition of similar fraud attempts; government action is primarily repressive in view of deception and manifest fraud.

Crises related to cost-reduction practices

These crises, such as that of "mad cow disease" or the above-mentioned pesticide-contaminated tomatoes in Spain in 1981, are the result of optimization strategies that were fully rational since the risks were potential but not certain. The negative result in this case is not due to a desire to defraud or a failure in rationale, but partly to an attempt at a maximum reduction of production costs, and partly to the irrevocable uncertainty of science and to the difficulties in predicting the future.

The major "mad cow disease" crisis was thus due to an attempt to reduce the cost of cow feed by using animal meal produced from animal carcasses. It caused the slaughter of hundreds of thousands of animals, more than 200 human deaths and a sudden collapse in beef consumption. It also resulted in the adoption of measures prohibiting the export of beef and veal from affected countries, the devastation of thousands of farms and a new way of perceiving our society as one of risk (Lahellec 2005). It is the mother of all crises, one which gave birth to a deep suspicion concerning the methods of the agri-business industry, and to a very high number of scientific and media investigations into the conditions of the production and processing of the food we consume.

In different ways depending on the countries (Ferrari 2016), this major crisis also led to the adoption of the precautionary principle and the establishment of agencies for food safety in several countries and at the European level. We can cite the French Food Safety Agency (AFSSA) (1999), the Federal Agency for the Security of the Food Chain (AFSCA) in Belgium (2000) and the UK's Food Standards Agency, then at the European level the European Food Safety Authority (EFSA) (2003). The following crises (Besançon *et al.* 2004) contributed to strengthening and structuring the institutions that were gradually put in place to prevent these crises.

A single re-normalization model

The circumstances behind food crises are therefore varied. However, they share the common feature of being crises, that is to say, partly the product of failure and partly a moment of "moral panic" (Beardsworth 1990), during which consumers adopt a behaviour of avoidance towards the products in question, and governments must display resolute action and competence. Both consumers and governments essentially overreact when it comes to the real objective risks, which are admittedly undetermined and will remain so until further down the line.

Consumers overreact by stopping buying all products related, whether closely or distantly, to the identified contamination. Governments overreact by suddenly paying disproportionate attention to this product and the conditions of its production. Put under pressure by the media, the public authorities also discover production and distribution conditions previously unknown to them at this level of detail. Like every crisis, food crises are simultaneously opportunities to observe dysfunctions and to re-evaluate systems that were previously enshrined and unassailable. Since the monitoring and inspection services have failed to prevent the crises, it is either whistle-blowers or the producers themselves who make contaminations public. The crises themselves take place in an atmosphere of governance: a number of unclearly ranked actors intervene at any point without first establishing their legitimacy and competence beyond all doubt. Government actors are for their part criticized for failure in prevention and come under pressure to quickly identify the causes of the contamination and solutions to it.

It is only when these causes are identified and solutions begin to be effective that the public authorities can regain control. Fraud prevention services can then establish sanctions in cases of fraud, those dedicated to inspection can work to establish new protocols and regulations in the case of an accident, and health services can strive to analyse the possible consequences of the contamination. Government practice then resumes its rule and the law enshrines a new productive and regulatory framework, which acknowledges the failure and aims to correct it.

We must note again that even during this normalization phase, the situation is nowadays more complicated for government actors. They must take on board a greater requirement of participation by consumers and private actors (Randall 2009). They must also enter a landscape that is now international, in which regional partnerships such as the European Union (Marsden *et al.* 2010; Havinga 2012) or international institutions aspire to play a growing role. The situation has therefore greatly evolved towards a multilevel governance.

More and more, this process is ultimately one of correcting a failing. We touch here on the symbolic aspect of government activity. This certainly consists essentially of preventing fraud, deception and mistakes, but it must equally create conditions for trust. The second phase of a food crisis – that of correction, reorganization of production and regulation by means of initially ineffective activity – can eventually be so successful that the initial failing is forgotten. But in the era of New Public Management, reforms and public sector cuts, how long will public authorities be able to make such corrections and guarantee food safety as far as possible?

Connecting government and governance in the New Public Management era

Connecting practices of government and governance to prevent and manage different and unpredictable food crises must indeed now take place within the framework of New Public Management. The favoured means to connect the two is that of the "steering state", that is to say a central level that concentrates on the tasks of planning and monitoring, while the local and regional levels assume the practical management of crises. But is this approach sustainable? Does the weakening of state actors at the local level lead over time to weaker information feedback, weak operational control and finally to rather superficial and approximate monitoring?

The impact of New Public Management

Like governance, New Public Management has experienced many attempts at definition. The measures and programmes that implement it indeed differ considerably depending on the country and time, and it is not easy to summarize in a few words the revolution it represents. All agree, however, that it appeared principally in the UK, Australia and the US at the end of the 1970s, that it consists of adapting models taken from the private sector to the public sector, and that it has gradually conquered almost all countries and sectors of activities.

New Public Management is an ideal doctrine which postulates that it is possible to simultaneously limit bureaucracy and the administrative load, strengthen elected representatives' oversight of civil servants, and increase the participation of ordinary citizens in public affairs. It is also an ideological initiative conducted by opponents of the rise of the welfare state who wished to reduce the scope of governmental action, lower taxes and increase citizens' freedom of choice, particularly in terms of social services and education.

New Public Management is also reflected in the growth of evaluation and benchmarking. It appeared and spread with globalization, and it is intrinsically linked to a continual process of comparison. This involves defining indicators and a systematic practice of comparing results achieved by a state, territory or company according to these indicators in a given domain. The overriding objective is one of excellence, and a concept of management that is less about controlling employees and more about encouraging them to go to and beyond their limits.

The effects of New Public Management are known and well documented. While it has generally increased consumer choice in many areas and profoundly transformed some sectors, it has also resulted in greater mental pressure on employees and led to practices of fraud and deception in the way indicators are filled in. By its very logic, it increases the need to control private actors, as it means delegating larger and larger sections of activity to them, and hence in fact leads to the growth of evaluation.

The hope of the "steering state"

New Public Management has also had consequences for the relationship between the central and the decentralized state, between practices of government and governance. Keen to reduce public spending, central actors broke with the age-old approach of controlling nations by means of a massive presence of government agents, especially police, tax officials and teachers. The new approach was to govern remotely, to oversee local actors via the introduction of benchmarks and a practice of systematic evaluation.

This logic, wagered on abandoning management tasks in favour of strategy, also corresponded to an attempt by traditionally prevailing actors (such as the finance ministry or home affairs) to reaffirm their pre-eminence and control the spending of sector ministries and local and regional authorities.

The risk of impotence

This evolution towards a steering state raises questions above all. The first concerns the strengthened prominence of central actors and the control of sectoral actors. The need to control public expenditure and the practice of privatizing whole swathes of governmental operations could lead to the delegation of food safety to private actors and to even more limiting public actors' capacity to only reacting to cases of crisis.

The second question concerns the definition of a political strategy. Food policy cannot, indeed, be reduced to simply a matter of cost or even safety. It should also correspond to the definition of sectors, priorities and territorial development strategy. Yet, although the New Public Management approach is aimed at supporting the strategic capacity of the state, this implies maintaining and even strengthening research and investigation services, which is, in reality, incompatible with measures of fiscal contraction.

The reality is one of increased recourse to consultants and a loss of control of the administration on data and information that are the basis of policies and programmes. Studies show that under the guise of a steering state, central actors often retrospectively reconstruct the meaning they wish to give to steps they have taken (Crespy *et al.* 2010). This is the consequence of an approach that aims at replacing the distribution of grants as part of clear and defined multi-year programme frameworks with calls for tender which leave those carrying out projects with the task of defining not only their proposed actions, but also the whole system behind these actions.

The third question relates to the response capabilities themselves. Decentralized public-sector services have in effect lost staff and capacity for action in a number of countries. Such capacity was already fragile and reactive, either because it was in the process of being built in the case of emerging states, or because it has been weakened in the case of states in financial difficulty. Once again, we find that the effect of New Public Management may be to multiply food crises instead of achieving the desired, or in any case proclaimed, goal of building a steering state capable of defining food policy in all its dimensions.

Food crises correspond to a failure of governmental action, which is resolved retrospectively by the adoption of new protocol or regulations. This is not a feature specific to postmodernity, since history shows that public authorities have always had difficulty controlling the food sector.

In a more strictly contemporary sense, the development of practices of governance should theoretically facilitate the prevention of food crises by improving information gathering via consultation with producers, manufacturers, groups and all actors concerned. Governance could from this perspective lead to greater relevance of regulations and greater democracy.

Indeed, while government services now have real legitimacy to intervene, they most often depend on the actions of industry, local authorities or whistle-blowers to learn of the dysfunctions that they are supposed to prevent or correct. We may, however, consider whether public authorities, profoundly transformed by policies of privatization and reforms inspired by New Public Management, are still in a position to really take advantage of crises to become stronger. The steering state approach is certainly not incompatible with government intervention centred on the management of food crises; but can effective intervention take place at times of crises without the benefit of information and skills accumulated via a continued presence?

Like other policies, such as monetary, environmental or anti-terrorism policies, food safety policies question the ability of public authorities to assume contemporary challenges at the national level. This capacity is, of course, uneven: it is known to be weak in some countries, but it is perhaps even over-estimated in others. It is not completely trivial to point out that food crises are frequent in countries such as China and France, two countries with a very powerful, even burdensome, administration.

Finally, while the link between government and governance is a fundamental requirement of postmodernity, it is in no way straightforward since it supposes the combination of actors that seem opposed to one another. Whistle-blowers thus see themselves as necessary precisely because, according to them, the state hides information of interest to populations so as not to threaten economic activity or call jobs into question, or because the whistle-blowers perceive some public representatives as corrupt or at least vulnerable to conflicts of interest.

It is clear, besides, that public policies aimed at food safety are neither linked only to the risks themselves nor to the political, administrative and institutional capacity of governments and administrations. They are also subject to the development of representations of animals (Atkins 2008), their suffering and their rearing conditions, and to the rise of vegetarianism (Beardsworth and Keil 1993), the development of GMOs, and so on. From this point of view, new challenges lie ahead to achieve greater food safety, and progress made in the prevention of accidental contamination in the realm of the food industry will surely soon appear to us as an easy step compared to the impending dangers in a landscape that is more diverse, small-scale and fluid.

References

Anseeuw, W. and A. Wambo (2008) "Le volet agricole du Nouveau partenariat pour le développement de l'Afrique (NEPAD) peut-il répondre à la crise alimentaire du continent?", *Herodote*, 2008/4, 131: 40–57.

Atkins, P. (2008) "Fear of Animal Foods: A Century of Zoonotics", *Appetite*, 51 (1): 18–21.

Bache, I. and M. Flinders, eds. (2004) *Multi-Level Governance*, Oxford: Oxford University Press.

Beardsworth, A. D. (1990) "Trans-science and Moral Panics: Understanding Food Scares", *British Food Journal*, 92 (5): 11–16.

Beardsworth, A. D. and T. Keil (1993) "Contemporary Vegetarianism in the UK: Challenge and Incorporation?", *Appetite*, 20: 229–234.

Besançon, J., O. Borraz and C. Grandclement-Chaffy (2004) *La sécurité alimentaire en crises: Les crises Coca-Cola et Listéria de 1992–2000*, Paris: L'Harmattan.

Charvet, J. P. (2006) *L'alimentation dans le monde: Mieux nourrir la planète*, Paris: Larousse.

Clapp, J. and M. J. Cohen, eds. (2009) *The Global Food Crisis: Governance Challenges and Opportunities*, Centre for International Governance Innovation/Wilfrid Laurier University Press.

Crespy, C. and V. Simoulin (2015) "Le gouvernement à crédit. Tâtonnements des gouvernants, aveuglement des gouvernés?", *L'Année sociologique*, 66 (2): 467–492.

D'Silva, J. and J. Webster, eds. (2017) *The Meat Crisis: Developing More Sustainable and Ethical Production and Consumption*, London: Routledge.

Ferrari, M. (2016) *Risk Perception, Culture, and Legal Change: A Comparative Study on Food Safety in the Wake of the Mad Cow Crisis*, London: Routledge.

Ferrières, M. (2002) *Histoire des peurs alimentaires du Moyen-Âge à l'aube du XXe siècle*, Paris: Seuil.

Fischler, C. (1990) *L'homnivore*, Paris: Odile Jacob.

Fischler, C. (2011) "Les ressorts des paniques alimentaires: Rencontre avec Claude Fischler", *Sciences humaines*, July.

Flandrin, J. L. (1998) "Risques et angoisses alimentaires avant le XIXè siècle", in M. Apfelbaum (ed.), *Risques et peurs alimentaires*, Paris: Odile Jacob, 113–123.

Hammoudi, A., C. Grazia, Y. Surry and J. B. Traversac, eds. (2015) *Food Safety, Market Organization, Trade and Development*, New York: Springer.

Havinga, T. (2012) "Transitions in Food Governance in Europe: From National Towards EU and Global Regulation and from Public Towards ...", *Nijmegen Sociology of Law Working Paper* No. 2012/02.

Heintzman, A., E. Solomon and E. Schlosser, eds. (2005) *Feeding the Future: From Fat to Famine: How to Solve the World's Food Crises*, Toronto: House of Anansi Press.

Heltberg, R., N. Hossain and A. Reva, eds. (2012) *Living Through Crises: How the Food, Fuel, and Financial Shocks Affect the Poor*, Washington, DC: World Bank Publications.

Hooghe, L. and G. Marks, eds. (2001) *Multi-Level Governance and European Integration*, Lanham, MD: Rowman & Littlefield.

Janin, P. (2008) "Crise alimentaire mondiale: Désordres et débats", *Herodote*, 2008/4 (131): 6–13.

Karrer, L. (2010) *Global Food Crisis: A Critical Analysis*, Saarbrücken: VDM Verlag.

Kingdon, J. W. (1984) *Agendas, Alternatives and Public Policies*, Boston, MA: Little, Brown and Company.

Knowles, T., R. Moody and M. G. McEachern (2007) "European Food Scares and Their Impact on EU Food Policy", *British Food Journal*, 109 (1): 43–67.

Lahellec, C. (2005) *Risques et crises alimentaires*, Paris: Lavoisier.

Lambek, N. (2014) *Rethinking Food Systems: Structural Challenges, New Strategies and the Law*, New York: Springer.

Madramootoo, C., ed. (2015) *Emerging Technologies for Promoting Food Security: Overcoming the World Food Crisis*, Cambridge: Woodhead Publishing.

Marsden, T., R. Lee, A. Flynn and S. Thankappan (2010) *The New Regulation and Governance of Food: Beyond the Food Crisis?* London: Routledge.

Motarjemi, Y. and H. Lelieveld, eds. (2017) *Food Safety Management: A Practical Guide for the Food Industry*, Amsterdam: Academic Press.

Palmer, L. (2017) *Hot, Hungry Planet: The Fight to Stop a Global Food Crisis in the Face of Climate Change*, New York: St. Martin's Press.

Perrow, C. (1984) *Normal Accidents – Living with High Risk Technologies*, New York: Basic Books.

Poulain, J. P. (2002) *Sociologies de l'alimentation: Les mangeurs et l'espace social alimentaire*, Paris: PUF.

Randall, E. (2009) *Food, Risk and Politics: Scare, Scandal and Crisis – Insights into the Risk Politics of Food Safety*, Manchester: Manchester University Press.

Raymond, J. (2006) *Comprendre les crises alimentaires*, Paris: L'Harmattan.

Rosin, C., P. Stock and H. Campbell, eds. (2012) *Food Systems Failure: The Global Food Crisis and the Future of Agriculture*, New York: Earthscan.

Saad, M. B. (2013) *The Global Hunger Crisis: Tackling Food Insecurity in Developing Countries*, London: Pluto Press.

Sen, A. (1981) *Poverty and Famines: An Essay on Entitlement and Deprivation*, Oxford: Clarendon Press.

Simoulin, V. (2003) "La gouvernance et l'action publique: le succès d'une forme simmélienne", *Droit et société*, 54 (June): 307–328.

Simoulin, V. (2013) "La gouvernance territoriale près d'une décennie plus tard: retour sur les discours, les stratégies et les cadres théoriques", in R. Pasquier, V. Simoulin and J. Weisbein (eds), *La gouvernance territoriale. Pratiques, discours et theories*, Paris: L'Extenso, 3–25.

Stanziani, A. (2005) *Histoire de la qualité alimentaire (XIXe–XXe siècle)*, Paris: Seuil.

Thompson, B. and M. J. Cohen, eds. (2012) *The Impact of Climate Change and Bioenergy on Nutrition*, New York: Springer.

Part II

Perspectives from Japan and China

4 Revisiting Frank Knight

Risks and uncertainties in the context of food safety in Japan after the Fukushima nuclear accident

Louis Augustin-Jean

Food safety incidents arise everywhere. The 48 food safety incidents listed under the Wikipedia page, "food contamination incidents", since 2001 showed a remarkable heterogeneity of sources (Wikipedia n.d.). The range of products involved in those incidents was so diverse that it encompassed nearly all edible items – vegetables, mushrooms, chickens, eggs, beef, pork, etc. The causes of the incidents were also endless – from counterfeiting to microbiological, chemical, or physical contamination. They occurred at every stage of the value chain from agricultural production to processing and distribution and had different geographical implications from local to worldwide. They originated everywhere and, despite the development of traceability systems, have become increasingly difficult to pinpoint given the growth of international trade. Finally, they were often characterized by terms that were hardly evocative of the general public: "dioxin", "fake Armillarisni A", "malachite green", "melamine", "banned pesticide Aldicarb", "coliform bacteria", etc.

Beyond the meaning of these expressions, this Prévert-style catalogue is informative on at least four accounts. First, it confirms that food safety incidents and crises can pop up anywhere and at any time. Second, it shows that the heavy use of chemicals or medicines in food production, from the agricultural stage (pesticides, fertilizers, vaccinations, etc.) to the processing and distribution stages (food colouring, preservatives, etc.), plays a role in compromising food safety: if handling errors or natural contamination are common, technological causes are also central. Third, this catalogue emphasizes the role of economic factors in food safety issues and at any point in the value chain. For example, adulteration and counterfeiting are not only caused by the greed of certain individuals, but also by the structure of the value chain and economic conditions at the local or national level: China's milk powder contamination is a case in point.[1] Last, the names of the chemical agents that have contaminated food there show clearly that most individuals are unable to assess risks by themselves.

These four points show the pertinence of the "risk society" conceptualized by Ulrich Beck (1992a, 1992b, 1999). For Beck, risks transcend social class and geography to become world phenomena, but, at the same time, individuals have difficulties assessing – not to mention controlling – those risks. While many risks are technologically induced, these same risks can only be tackled by technology. In other words, technology is both the source of, and remedy to, such risks. This is a major aspect of the concept of "reflexive modernity" he developed.

Thus, the concept of a "risk society" provides a macro-context to analyse the multiplication of food safety incidents worldwide – despite the fact that the current food supply is probably the safest ever in human history. However, the concept is too broad to differentiate among different types of risk. For Beck, it would be meaningless to make such a differentiation because risks are embedded in the chains of causality, which impact all of society:

> Risk may be defined as a *systematic way of dealing with hazards and insecurities induced and introduced by modernization itself*. Risks, as opposed to older dangers, are consequences which relate to the threatening force of modernization and to its globalization of doubt. *They are politically reflexive.*
>
> (Beck 1992a: 21; original emphasis)

In other words, whether risks are linked to nuclear contamination, to the presence of a carcinogen in processed food, to the sale of Brazilian rotten meat worldwide, or to the introduction of an alien element like melamine to milk matters little, since they all belong to the "risk society". Similarly, whether the probability of an event's occurrence is high or low is only marginally important to this framework because every risk adds up to comprise the "construction" of a risk society. Indeed, Beck only once uses the word, "probability", in his book, *Risk Society* (1992a).

Therefore, if a "risk society" provides a useful framework, it should be completed by other perspectives, in order to take a differentiated approach to risk. In this respect, the approach developed by Frank Knight (1921) offers a good starting point in part because of the pioneering nature of his work and its influence on subsequent authors. Most of these authors resort to his differentiation of risk and uncertainty (a probability can be attached to a risky event, but not to an uncertain one), but sometimes without quoting him. Additionally, Knight's influence extends well beyond this initial differentiation and incorporates the role of judgements in the construction and interpretation of risk probability. This major result, which is unfortunately and mostly forgotten today, is fundamental for showing that not only are risks socially constructed (and, hence, filled with judgements), but that their assessment is also prone to judgements and interpretations.

In relation to this paradigm, the first section of this chapter will present the major ideas of Knight and show how uncertainty and risk cannot be separated from each other, but, on the contrary, are completely intertwined. The consequence is that most risk assessments and food safety standards are not fully "scientifically based", but include a certain degree of uncertainty and judgements. It is, therefore, necessary to see how judgements are formed.

Based on the theses of Lucien Karpik (2010), this will be the objective of the second section. More specifically, the author will show that people use focal points, such as "judgement devices", to assess food safety and, more generally, the quality of the food they consume. However, when the level of uncertainty increases, the reliance on these devices decreases and other devices are sought.

From these theoretical perspectives, the third section will analyse the specific case of food contamination following the 2011 nuclear disaster in Fukushima. The author selected this example due to a discrepancy that existed between the Japanese government's assurances of food safety, scientific uncertainty and public perceptions. As a result, a significant number of people distrusted the newly created government standards, instead choosing to rely on their own norms. This prompted some retailers and restaurants to also adopt them, which granted them a measure of legitimacy.

From probabilities to judgements: a Knightian approach to risk

"Risk" is inherently difficult to define. There is neither a universal definition nor a unified theory of risk – this book is a definitive proof of that. The concept of risk involves a dimension of time and refers to possible future states of the world and their probabilities of occurrences. However, aside from the way these probabilities are calculated (which is merely a technical issue), this section aims to understand how they can be interpreted beyond the simple reading of the data. This will be done in two steps. In the first one, the author will introduce the probabilistic dimension of risk. In particular, he will show that there is a general agreement among scholars to link risk and probabilities, even if they do not have the same understanding of it. Despite the differences in terminology among authors, most differentiate between what is predictable (at least statistically) and what is not. This differentiation will lead the author to introduce in the second part of this section the main insights of Knight regarding risk and its differentiation with the concept of uncertainty. This will have the effect of displacing the analysis from risk to judgement, which will be explored in depth in the second section.

Risk and probability

To start with, one should be reminded that a quantitative indicator is the perfect tool for food regulators and policymakers, as it provides a compact and easy-to-use signal from which they can anchor their decisions. Probability has been widely used by governmental food safety centres and specialized international organizations such as the FAO to assess risk. For these organizations, risk is commonly defined as the probability of a hazard's occurrence – a hazard being "a factor or agent which may lead to undesirable effects, whereas risk refers to the probability that the effect will occur".[2] In addition, food safety hazards have three origins: biological, chemical and physical (FAO 2009: xi).

The above definition outstrips the field of policymaking and resonates in the academic field, even though most scholars amended it. For example, Mary

Douglas, despite her cultural focus, accepted this probabilistic definition – but at the same time, she pointed out the practical difficulties of calculating these probabilities:[3]

> No person can know more than a fraction of the dangers that abound. To believe otherwise is to believe that we know (or can know) everything. Yet even if we did, it would still be necessary for us to agree on a ranking of risks. In the absence of complete knowledge, and in the presence of disagreement between scientists and laymen alike, how can anyone choose to zero in on any particular set of dangers? How, faced with endless possibilities, can anyone calculate the probabilities of harm (the risks)?
>
> (Douglas and Wildavsky 1982: 5)

Other scholars have also kept this approach, but found the above definition too restrictive; they believe that risk should not only be defined as the probability of an event's occurrence, but should also include the extent of the potential damages. For them, two events with the same probability of occurrence are not equivalent if the spread of damages is different. They consequently defined risk as the double dimension of the probability of a destructive event's occurrence[4] and the potential damages attached to that event (Flanquart 2016: 24).

Thus, both definitions deserve credit, but also have limitations. The first relates to the inclusion of the size of the potential damage and the second to the use of probability when events are rare enough to make it difficult to calculate. Concerning the first type of limitation, Jon Elster noted that when the potential damages trend towards the infinite (as in the case of a nuclear disaster), this definition makes the calculation of probabilities pointless because the risk then also trends towards the infinite independently of its probability:

> If the extinction of mankind is evaluated at minus infinity, then it swamps all disasters of finite size. We must, of course, have some precise probability attached to this event: mere logical possibility is not sufficient. It does not matter, however, if this probability is extremely small, for an infinite number multiplied by any positive number remains infinite.... The weakness of this argument is that it may turn out that most actions have such total disasters associated with them, as an extremely unlikely but still quantifiable probability.
>
> (Elster 1979: 390)

Notwithstanding this objection, food regulators understand the necessity of including the dimension of potential damage so that they associate other indicators with the probabilistic approach to risk. The food safety analysis promoted by the FAO and WHO, for example, is multidimensional and includes an assessment of the number and categories of people most susceptible to specific hazards, while aiming to keep indicators as compact and easy to use as possible (FAO 2009).

The second limitation, which is more fundamental, comes when the negative events are rare or even exceptional (e.g. nuclear accidents). It then becomes impossible to infer a probability. For Flanquart, such events can still be qualified as risks if they can be asserted with certainty that the probability exists and if there are methods to lower this probability. However, the problem is not only one of terminology or classification: whether the probability can be calculated or not, it still incorporates a slice of uncertainty. This is exactly what Knight argued. The next section will present in greater detail the basis of Knight's theory, which implies an analysis of how a judgement can be part of the construction of risk.

The contribution of Knight

Frank H. Knight is known as the forerunner of all these definitions and for the reliance on probability in risk assessments. In anticipation of Herbert Simon (1997), Knight's starting point is the intrinsic indeterminacy over the future. For him, it is this indeterminacy that generates uncertainty, but not only can this uncertainty not be eliminated, it may not be advisable to do so even if it were possible:

> It goes without saying that rational conduct strives to reduce to a minimum the uncertainties involved in adapting means to ends. This does not mean, be it emphasized, that uncertainty as such is abhorrent to the human species, which probably is not true. We should not really prefer to live in a world where everything was "cut and dried", which is merely to say that we should not want our activity to be perfectly rational.... Perhaps it is the manifest impossibility of reaching the end which makes it interesting to strive after it. In any case, we do strive to reduce uncertainty, even though we should not want it eliminated from our lives.
>
> (Knight 1921: 238)

Therefore, the problem is not to eliminate uncertainty, but to be able to deal with and find ways to reduce it. Then, for Knight the right question becomes: how is it possible to make the future more predictable?

To answer this question, he proposed a two-step approach. The first involved classifying objects or events (all Knight termed "things") into categories that have common features. These categories are, in the second step, used to draw evidence and "calculate" probability. It is through this construction that the future can become more predictable: an event to which a probability of occurrence can be attached is then intrinsically similar to a definite one. This analysis is the basis of Knight's main legacy – the differentiation between risk and uncertainty:

> Uncertainty must be taken in a sense radically distinct from the familiar notion of Risk, from which it has never been properly separated.... The

essential fact is that "risk" means, in some cases, a quantity susceptible of measurement, while at other times it is something distinctly not of this character; and there are far-reaching and crucial differences in the bearings of the phenomena depending on which of the two is really present and operating.... It will appear that a measurable uncertainty, or "risk" proper, as we shall use the term, is so far different from an unmeasurable one that it is not in effect an uncertainty at all. We shall accordingly restrict the term "uncertainty" to cases of the non-quantitative type.

(Knight 1921: 19–20)

The author immediately noticed two pitfalls of this differentiation: the first related to the construction of categories and the second to the calculation (and the meaning) of probability. As explained below, both aspects are not free from uncertainty.

The first difficulty arises with the construction of categories because "[w]hen our ignorance of the future is only partial ignorance, incomplete knowledge, and imperfect inference, it becomes impossible to classify instances objectively" (Knight 1921: 259). Thus, Knight pinpointed that the construction of categories is subjective, which gives way to uncertainty and entails judgements.[5] Three examples will help us understand the consequences of this statement.

Analysing the radioactive contamination of sheep in Cumbria (United Kingdom) after the 1986 Chernobyl accident, Wynne (1996) rightly noted that experts were caught several times for making wrong judgements. One of the reasons for this was their refusal to take into account local knowledge. For example, they rejected the discourse of the locals, who ascribed the sheep contamination not only to the Chernobyl disaster, but also to the nearby nuclear plant in Sellafield. These experts also insisted on implementing experiments that were unrealistic in regard to the local conditions (landscape, soil, microclimate, etc.). Thus, for Wynne, "many conflicts between lay farmers and scientists centred on the standardisation built into routine structures of scientific knowledge" (Wynne 1996: 66). Differently stated, in their effort to construct categories, the experts neglected crucial, but more unique, elements, which added to the uncertainty and jeopardized the ability of the experts to tackle the crisis. Thus, Wynne revisited Knight's dry language with a more flowery discourse: "scientific culture starts with what is 'standardisable' as if an industrial mass-product, then attempts to reorganise the world to optimise the production of this standard universal ideal type" (ibid.: 71).

The second example was borrowed from Kahneman and Tversky. While Wynne showed that the building up of categories could discard important information for evaluating risk, the two scholars demonstrated that the way categories are introduced to people has influence on their choices. This forcefully appears in the "framing effect" theory, which they started to develop during the 1970s. The theory states that people make different choices when the probability of an event's occurrence is presented in a positive or negative manner. (For a more recent presentation see, for example, Kahneman 2011.)[6]

Similarly, but from a different perspective, quantitative research has shown that people respond differently depending on how a question is drafted. This remark may not be as trivial as it looks and even experts can be sensitive to this phenomenon, as Marsal showed. This author was interested in understanding why, following the bovine spongiform encephalopathy (BSE) crisis at the end of the 1990s, experts from the European Commission recommended resuming beef sales in Europe, while the French experts from AFSSA (now ANSES – the French Agency for Food, Environmental and Occupational Health & Safety) had a completely opposite opinion. The answer to that question is quite surprising:

> Despite appearances, despite the clear diverging positions regarding the embargo, there was no fundamental divergences in the responses of European and French experts. The scientific bases, the facts that were analysed were the same; the major difference lay in the nature of the questions and in the networks between scientists and decision makers.
>
> (Marsal 2000: 3; my own translation)[7]

These three examples illustrate the existence of biases in the categorizations of risk and, in turn, these biases induce judgements. More surprisingly, perhaps, the same presence of judgements can also be found – not in the categorization, but in the calculation of the probabilities for each "thing" (or state of the world). This is the second pitfall noted by Knight.

To arrive at this conclusion, the author started by differentiating three probability levels that evolved from complete certainty to uncertainty. But the most important one is elsewhere: for Knight, the calculation of probability often incorporates a certain degree of uncertainty, which has the effect of blurring the separation between risk and uncertainty. In this situation, the judgement (and/or level of confidence) of the people over these probabilities becomes prominent. This way of thinking will become clearer after the "three different types of probability situation" (Knight 1921: 224) are introduced:

1   A priori probability. Absolutely homogeneous classification of instances completely identical except for really indeterminate factors. This judgment of probability is on the same logic plane as the propositions of mathematics....[8]

2   Statistical probability. Empirical evaluation of the frequency of association between predicates, not analyzable into varying combination of equally probable alternatives. It must be emphasized that any high degree of confidence that the proportions found in the past will hold in the future is still based on a priori judgment of indeterminateness.[9]

3   Estimates. The distinction here is that there is *no valid basis of any kind* for classifying instances.

(Ibid.: 224–225; original emphasis)

The third type is the closest to the concept of uncertainty – and the most difficult to analyse:

> this form of probability is involved in the greatest logical difficulties of all,
> and no very satisfactory discussion of it can be given, but its distinction
> from the other types must be emphasized and some of its complicated rela-
> tions indicated.
>
> (Ibid.: 225)

To explain his purpose, Knight took the example of a business decision. Every
business decision is unique and it is, therefore, difficult to precisely
calculate risk:

> The businessman "figures" more or less on the proposition, taking account
> as well as possible of the various factors [that are] more or less susceptible of
> measurement, but the final result is an "estimate" of the probable outcome
> of any proposed course of action. What is the "probability" of error (strictly,
> of any assigned degree of error) in the judgment?
>
> (Ibid.: 227)

Thus, the entrepreneur should estimate the accuracy of his first estimate, which
is the probability of her/his first prediction being fulfilled (ibid.; see also Langlois
and Cosgel 1993: 459). There is, therefore, a double operation of judgement:
the first to estimate the probability of the "thing" occurring and the second to
estimate the validity of the first judgement. Finally, the progression from pure
certainty (as in the first proposition) to full uncertainty is reinforced by the fact
that probabilities are not always "calculated". And, even when they are, people
may not always have access to them or be able to make good use of them.[10]

Returning to the first two propositions, Knight found the pure, mathemat-
ical, probability only in the first one. In the second type of probability, the level
of uncertainty was already higher: the risk of a house fire or car accident was
calculated based on past events, but there was no complete guarantee that the
same trend would continue in the future – most likely it would, but this conclusion already introduced a judgement. Another, more sophisticated, form of
judgement can be isolated from the way insurance premiums are calculated. If
probabilities and statistics were sufficient to determine these premiums accu-
rately, then, according to Knight, insurance companies would be unable to
profit, as they, holding the same set of statistics and full information, would
have to compete with each other and, thus, would propose the same contracts
that only cover their expenditures.[11] Thus, profits can only be explained by an
inherent uncertainty over the future: like businesspeople, the acumen of insurance companies and their agents play a major role in generating profits.

To summarize, after assessing the necessity of risk and uncertainty for human
life (a point often minimized by specialists[12]), Knight proposed a method to
lower uncertainty. This is done by affecting probabilities for the different states

of the world. When probabilities can be calculated, uncertainties are transformed into "things" (in Knight's language) that acquire a similar status as full certainty. But Knight showed that this process is incomplete and uncertainties remain at every level – from the construction of the states of the world to the assignment of probabilities. In this situation, people cannot base their decisions on probability alone, but have to rely on their judgements. The second section of this chapter will analyse more deeply the role of judgements in relation to risk and uncertainty.

An analytical framework of judgements

Knight did not fully analyse the formation of judgements, which remained somewhat beyond his focus. But he still provided the author with a starting point by linking judgements to "intuition", which becomes sharper with experience:

> The judgment or estimate as to the value of a man is a probability judgment of a complex nature, indeed. More or less based on experience and observation of the outcome of his predictions, it is doubtless principally after all simply an intuitive judgment or "unconscious induction," as one prefers.…[13]
>
> However, we cannot extend our inquiry to cover all the grounds on which men, even educated men, actually make decisions, or it will degenerate into a catalogue of superstitions.
>
> (Knight 1921: 229)

Interestingly, Knight's analyses echoed more recent discoveries in social psychology. For instance, Kahneman also noticed the role of experience in making accurate intuitive judgements, although he added that intuition can be misleading, even for experts:

> If the individual has relevant expertise, she will recognize the situation, and the intuitive solution that comes to her mind is likely to be correct. This is what happens when a chess master looks at a complex position: the few moves that immediately occur to him are all strong. When the question is difficult and a skilled solution is not available, intuition still has a shot: an answer may come to mind quickly – but it is not an answer to the original question.
>
> (Kahneman 2011: 12)

To support this last point, Kahneman took the example of a chief investment officer for a large financial firm who decided to invest tens of millions of dollars in Ford Motor Company stock. The decision was motivated not by the price level of the stocks, but by a recent visit to an automobile show that made a strong impression on him (ibid.).

The problem, then, has shifted. It is no longer about separating predictable risks from unpredictable uncertainties; it is also not about rejecting (or ignoring) probabilities on the grounds that they may be unreliable and biased – or, in extreme cases, when their calculations become useless because risks overwhelm us. It is to analyse the embeddedness of uncertainties and risks and, consequently, to see how judgements are embedded in the construction of risk.

Before developing this point, it should be noted that the key role of judgement in risk assessment, as well as for setting up standards and norms, is universally acknowledged (at least indirectly). This can even be verified in professional and technical guides that boldly underline the central role of "science in risk assessment". For example, the word, "judgement", appears 19 times in the 102-page FAO guide for national food safety authorities, while "uncertainty/ uncertainties" is mentioned 70 times (FAO 2009).

Thus, uncertainties remain, including in scientific evaluations, which lead to considerable divergences at both the scientific and political levels.[14] At the scientific level, the disagreements highlight a contradiction between the scientific process itself – in which controversies are essential – and the expertise, which does not tolerate these very same controversies. Notwithstanding scientific disputes, in practice, uncertainties are often incorporated into risk assessments and become invisible from the outside: with their concise shape, risks are supposed to be fully tackled, but this is, for a part, a fiction.

Indeed, uncertainties do not vanish by magic; they re-emerge at times – for example in the form of experts' diverging discourses in the media, which do much to confuse the public and policymakers alike.

At other times, scientific uncertainty and the plurality of judgements open the door to the politicization of science (Lin 2013; Augustin-Jean and Xie 2016; amongst others). The process assumes at least two different shapes. The first arises from the actions of scientists and/or experts who just hope to promote their views in the political sphere: "Hence technical experts are given pole position to define agendas and impose bounding premises a priori on risk discourses" (Beck 1992b: 4). This may be voluntary (e.g. when the experts aim to promote the goals of the organization they belong to – including private companies or the government) or involuntary in relation to scientists' unconscious biases. A second possibility for the politicization of science is just the other way around: governments and policymakers may affect the expertise in the ways they wish by selecting scientists who are closer to their views (see the next section).

Then if, in most cases, risk assessments incorporate de facto uncertainties and judgements, how is it possible to analyse (the formation of) these judgements? Such analysis should consider at least three aspects. First, in accordance with the cultural approach to risk (Douglas), judgements are culturally and socially determined and, thus, vary by time and place. This cultural influence can be felt at all levels, including the evaluation and acceptance of risk: even if it could be precisely assessed (in which case no uncertainty would remain), people may judge it differently, depending on their cultural background. A typical example is camembert cheese made with raw milk, which is considered risky in the United States (and its sale is illegal), but a premium food in France. Since any food ingestion involves risk (as "zero risk" does not exist), this calls for a more democratic control of experts who should not be left alone to decide the proper level of socially acceptable risk (Ilbert *et al.* 2014; Augustin-Jean and Xie 2016).

The second point is directly related: judgements are not only culturally determined, but also vary from individual to individual. They are subjective – in theory, there are as many judgements as people. In practice, however, judgements are ranked by a limited number of principles so that coordination of actions becomes possible.

Third, like probabilities, judgements are also judged (i.e. the people judge the accuracy of previous judgements). However, contrary to probability, the process is potentially infinite, as there can be judgements of judgements of judgements, *ad infinitum*, and a mechanism is necessary for stopping this chain of judgements and allowing for actions to occur.

The concept of "judgemental devices" proposed by Lucien Karpik (Karpik 2010) provides the tools to address these points. Judgemental devices are plural (they can be guides, labels, standards, experts' judgements, traditions, personal relations, etc.) and people use them differently, depending on their culture, knowledge, experiences, etc. These devices do not pretend to be objective and cannot solve the fundamental uncertainty; they are simply intermediaries between the object being judged and the subject and provide a certain degree of security to the people.

> There are ... pluralities of devices, which may be grouped according to different principles.... An easy way to distinguish them is to separate the personal devices (friends, family, alumni, etc.) from the impersonal ones (Karpik, 2010). An additional delimitation may be to differentiate the devices issued by the government as public goods (labels, regulation, standards, etc.), [from those] created by consumers themselves (specialized magazines, websites created by associations of consumers, etc.) or by the media ([articles written by] ... journalists, experts, professionals, etc.), and [from] those promoted by private companies (brands, trademarks, advertising, etc.).
> (Augustin-Jean 2014: 52)

In other words, a judgement of judgement is replaced by a judgement of a device and by a (relative) trust in the device, which is not objective. The chain of judgements stops when people can link the device to a higher principle of qualification (Thévenot 2001). For example, one may think it is "relatively" safe or healthy to eat certain foods because an expert says so (trust in science). Or an individual may do so because her grandmother told her (trust in tradition or family values). Other times trust is guaranteed by a standard...[15] One's judgement of another is replaced by a trust in an expert or a family member, or a standard, or a food guide, etc. which incorporates some elements of culture, the level of experience and expertise of certain individuals, and so on. In short, people do not assess directly the risk; they judge the reliability of the device.[16]

Thus, the chain of judgements is replaced by a unique question: how much trust should an individual grant a specific device? To answer this question requires an existing definition of trust. The following one, borrowed from Karpik, has three advantages: first, it includes the symbolic dimension of trust; second, it also shows that trust is beyond knowledge and, therefore, is particularly suited to the judgement of uncertainty; third, it insists on the fact that trust in something can eventually be removed:

> Trust is defined as a *relation of delegation embedded in the symbolic*. The reference to the symbolic system means: 1/ Trust cannot be based only on knowledge alone, because knowledge is to remain incomplete; only trust can fill the gap; 2/ a belief has the power to transform a representation into a reality; 3/ a belief varies from weak to strong; it is maximum when an actor sticks to it by a link of adhesion that removes her/his usage of free decision; it is minimum when it is replaced, without difficulty, by another belief; 4/ trust obeys to a symbolic logic; that explains why its effects are often characterized by excess and unexpected.
>
> (Karpik 2010: 174–175; original emphasis)

When an individual stops adhering to a device, like in the third proposition, he shifts his trust to another device. For example, when a food manufacturer is implicated in a food safety crisis, its customers may shift their loyalty to another brand. An alternative is to replace a specific food with another one – such as people shifting from beef to another meat during a BSE crisis.

Similarly, during the milk powder crisis in China (2008), when the adjunction of melamine to milk caused the death of six babies and sickened a total of 300,000 children, Chinese consumers lost trust in their own country's milk powder manufacturers (Delman and Yang 2012; Augustin-Jean 2015). The crisis eventually extended to the whole food system, including its systems of control. In this situation of generalized mistrust, both aforementioned solutions (replacement and loyalty shift) were impracticable. To restore trust – after all, people must eat, independently of the risk they face – the Chinese Government reacted promptly and issued the country's first food safety law (2009), as well as an array of measures (Snyder 2015, amongst others) to reassure the public.

If these measures are not implemented or if they are judged not credible enough, consumers would be left in disarray. The nuclear accident in Fukushima and the related (risk of) food contamination that followed was an extreme example of a generalized mistrust of the food system, including the judgement devices. The author will examine this case in the last part of this chapter using the theoretical background presented in the first two sections.

Risks, judgements and food contamination after the Fukushima nuclear disaster

The nuclear accident at the Fukushima Number 1 Nuclear Power Plant on 11 March 2011 led to a major food safety crisis, particularly in the area from Tokyo to the northern part of Honshu Island. The evolution of the crisis, as well as the way its risks were evaluated and perceived, showed the pertinence of Knight's theses and the importance of judgements for laypeople and experts alike.

On 19 March 2011, eight days after the disaster, a first case of contamination was detected in a dairy farm located about 30 kilometres from the plant. This was soon followed by reports of contaminated spinach grown in the nearby prefectures of Gunma, Tochigi and Ibaraki. The crisis peaked in June 2011 when the expression, "colossal blunder", was used by the media to qualify the distribution and sale of contaminated beef in 45 of Japan's 47 prefectures (*Daily Yomiuri* 2011).

In this context, the first pitfall for all parties – government, experts, consumers, etc. – was to decide what was contaminated and what was not, as no external sign indicated if a certain food was safe (contaminated food has no specific odour, taste or appearance). Because Japan did not have proper regulations for radionuclide-contaminated food prior to the Fukushima accident (Berends and Kobayashi 2012), this decision had to be made in under emergency conditions. Provisional regulations were issued a week after the accident, but only for some products, while a standard for seafood, so important in the Japanese diet, was not adopted until 5 April (Hamada *et al.* 2012; Augustin-Jean and Baumert 2014: 52). For basic foods, the benchmark, calculated in becquerels per kilogrammes (Bq/kg), was fixed at 500. A year later, in April 2012, this threshold was lowered to 100 Bq/kg (and 10 Bq/kg and 50 Bq/kg for water and milk, respectively, instead of 200 Bq/kg for both after the accident) – a change that was not without controversy (see below). In setting these norms:

> … the Japanese government relied upon the International Committee on Radiological Protection (ICRP) recommendations but their legitimacy is … highly contested. For instance, the food standard of 100 Bq/kg (for general foodstuffs) was derived from complex calculations that involve estimates of consumption volume of different categories of food, different sensitivities to exposure by age groups, and so on…. Some international organizations such as the European Commission of Radiological Risk criticised the ICRP's standards, arguing "that the ICRP risk coefficients are out of date…. Employing the ICRP risk model to predict the health effects of radiation leads to error which are at least ten fold" (González 2012: 247).
>
> (Kimura 2016: 40–41)

Scientific disagreements went beyond this point and some specialists such as Kodama Tatsuhiko, a medical doctor with expertise in radiation protection and a professor at the University of Tokyo, went as far as criticizing the pertinence of some indicators:

In his testimony to the House of Representatives' Labor Committee on July 27, 2011, for instance, he said, "To say 'X mSv,[17] in relation to internal radiation is meaningless. Iodine 131 accumulates in the thyroid, Thorotrast in the liver. Cesium accumulates in the urothelium and bladder" (Kodama, 2011: 19). From this perspective, each radionuclide … exerts differentiated and localized effects.

(Kimura 2016: 41)

On the other hand, experts close to the government brushed aside these scientific concerns and put on confident public faces, even though their explanations were unconvincing to many. In this respect, the expert cited by Sternsdorff-Cisterna was particularly caricatural:

This brought to mind the skepticism I heard about Dr. Yamashita, one of the leading government experts on radiation and a professor at Nagasaki Medical University. At the beginning of the crisis he said that people could be exposed up to 100 mSv/year without considerable health effects, and that people should smile to protect themselves from radiation.

(Sternsdorff-Cisterna 2013)

Thus, standards developed and/or guaranteed by experts comprise a great deal of uncertainty at all levels. First, uncertainties were incorporated into the construction of categories. This is not only evident in the way the "safe" and "unsafe" were defined, but also in the exact meaning of what was measured: the result of the test, whether it was in mSv/year or in Bq/kg, was not contested, but what the consequences could be were. The measurement gave realism to invisible contamination, but its interpretation was prone to uncertainty.

Second, if risk assessments are not as objective as they should be and include hidden uncertainties, then these uncertainties often resurface in the public sphere sooner or later (see the first section). As a result, the disagreements between government experts and other scientists were largely reported in the media and became sources of anxiety for Japanese consumers. They also strongly eroded the trust in government regulations: how could consumers objectively judge the safety of a food that contains 100 Bq/kg when the experts themselves disagree over this benchmark? Also, in accordance with Knight, how do they judge the probability of risk in this context and how can they interpret this new regulation when the government already assured them a year earlier that food with no more than 500 Bq/kg was safe? Differently stated, if a food was safe at 500 Bq/kg, then why did the government need to change the threshold? These questions and many similar ones were commonly asked by consumers and citizens and figured prominently in the media.

This contributed to a generalized climate of uncertainty over, and mistrust in, the food system, including for many judgement devices (see below). The mistrust, as seen earlier, came from at least three sources: (1) scientific uncertainty and the conflicting messages of experts in the media; (2) the benchmarks set up by the government; and (3) the systems of control (paradoxically, this type of mistrust was also triggered by the fact that some contaminated food was detected *before* it reached the market).

This lack of trust was well captured by data. A survey conducted by *Nikkei* at the beginning of 2012 indicated that "[m]ore than 70% of Japanese consumers grew more interested in food safety in the wake of last year's disaster at the Fukushima Daiichi nuclear power plant, and 70% remain highly concerned about contaminated food" (*Nikkei* 2012). Another study, issued in 2012 by the Japanese Government's Food Safety Commission, showed an even higher level of worry, since it pointed out that 87.6 per cent of women and 68.9 per cent of men expressed at least some concern over food safety (Kimura 2016: 34). The more pronounced lack of trust on the part of women, especially those who had young children, was confirmed by another survey:

> Kiyokazu Ujiie, assistant professor … at the University of Tsukuba, inter-viewed 5,614 married women about rice harvested in Fukushima, Miyagi and Ibaraki prefectures this year. Valid responses were received from 1,760.
>
> More than 50 percent of the respondents from the Tokyo metropolitan area and more than 60 percent in the Kansai region said they would not buy rice from the three prefectures, even if the cesium amount detected was lower than the government's provisional permissible standards.
>
> In fact, about 30 percent in the Tokyo area and more than 40 percent in Kansai said they would not buy rice from the three prefectures even if no cesium was detected.
>
> (Kimura *et al.* 2011)

Before commenting on this last bit of data, it should be pointed out that a final survey confirmed that the distrust extended beyond food safety and standards implementation to include government actions. According to Carola Hom-merich, a scholar from Hokkaido University, 75.6 per cent of the people she interviewed in the Kanto region would "rather not trust" governmental institu-tions, while only 14.6 per cent would (Hommerich 2012: 55).

Thus, in accordance with this widespread lack of trust, people are left on their own to evaluate risk (Beck 2006). Most previous judgement devices were not fully operational after 11 March 2011. While Karpik mentioned that a belief can eventually be removed by another belief, in this context of general mistrust, this type of replacement was difficult. One solution for the people was to develop their own judgements to gain a better sense of security – even though such judgements were not more objective than previous ones. This was most clearly emphasized by a young mother: "I feel a sense of crisis over food safety … and I can't trust the government. *I have to set my own standards* and make my own choices" (quoted in Aoki 2012; my emphasis).

In relation to this comment, the last part of this chapter will present how people have developed devices depending on their relationship to food, their immediate environments, and knowledge. While people have different connections to food and, thus, may set up a diversity of devices, in practice, their behaviours clustered around three courses of action.

A first group of people did not significantly change its food habits after the catastrophe. Due to this apparent passivity, this group, which is nonetheless the largest, is difficult to precisely identify and its motivations are not easy to grasp with certainty. However, three major reasons can still be pinpointed. First, some people adhered to the government's rationale, as the mistrust of its discourse and new standards, while widespread, was not universal (see above). Second, as the government condemned the spread of "harmful rumours", such as those stating that the official threshold was unsafe, social pressure was sufficiently strong in Japan to deter deviant behaviours. Thus, some people followed the government's regulations and advice, even when they did not fully trust them. As a result, many young mothers who showed concern over food safety were stigmatized as "radiation brain moms" – the title of Kimura's book (Kimura 2016).[18] Finally, a third reason for not changing previous habits was the "head-in-the-sand attitude": as individuals receive a mass of contradictory information that they may not fully understand or digest, they are in a state of great anxiety. To avoid any resulting mental confusion, they simply chose to tune out reality and pretend everything was just fine. In other words, they were not (and did not want to be) in the position to make any judgement and assess risk, which led them to inaction.

Apart from this apparent passivity, a second attitude was to purposely consume (in the two senses of buying and eating) food from contaminated areas. This behaviour has been actively encouraged by the government, which wants to minimize the negative economic impact of the disaster on these agricultural regions.[19] Several promotional campaigns were launched, starting with a photography session of the then-Chief Cabinet Secretary, Edano Yukio, eating strawberries from Fukushima just after the catastrophe (Harlan 2011). In the following months, campaigns became more institutionalized and included *Destination Tohoku*, which aimed to redevelop tourism in this prefecture, as well as the "eat to support" fairs that promoted food produced in the devastated areas (MAFF 2011; Augustin-Jean and Baumert 2014; Kimura 2016: 7). Slogans such as "Buy, Eat, and Encourage Fukushima" were launched in support of such campaigns (Baumert 2015). They were completed by governmental messages aiming to stop or curb the attempts of NPOs/NGOs (non-profit or non-governmental organizations) and distributors to test for possible nuclear contamination in food (see below).

Such campaigns were barely successful and interviews with scholars, as well as casual observations in Tokyo supermarkets, showed that Fukushima products had largely disappeared from their shelves.[20] However, they still appealed to some, most notably the elderly. This attitude by some Japanese senior citizens is not surprising, as they had already volunteered to "tackle the nuclear crisis at the Fukushima power station" (Buerk 2011). That did not mean they all agreed with the government's rationale or judged the level of risk negligible – far from it. But their time horizon and future were different than those for younger people, which influenced their judgement of risk: "I am 72 and, on average, I probably have 13 to 15 years left to live. Even if I were exposed to radiation, cancer could take 20 or 30 years or longer to develop. Therefore, [we] older ones have less chance of getting cancer" (quoted in Buerk 2011). In other words, while these elderly fully accepted the definition of risk that was introduced in the first section, albeit unconsciously, they judged the probability of developing cancer to be quite low due to their age. They also performed an indirect cost–benefit calculation and concluded that the limited risk for them would be compensated by higher benefits for the region and country – not to mention their own psychological and personal satisfaction to fulfil their civic duty, and help Japan (Augustin-Jean and Baumert 2014: 56).

The last attitude was for the average Japanese to conspicuously modify her/his own dietary habits. People who adopted this behaviour came from a diversity of backgrounds. Some were already concerned about food issues (e.g. they joined consumer cooperatives before the disaster, already bought organic food, etc.), while others became especially sensitive to food safety after the disaster (e.g. pregnant women and young mothers; see above). Overall, these people rejected the government's official take on the disaster and did not trust the new standards. But, unlike the first group, they collected and analysed the available information – at first individually and then collectively. Sternsdorff-Cisterna participated in one of these collective activities with the "Reading Club", which was formed in September 2011 by members of a Tokyo cooperative that aimed "to bring consumers and producers together in a virtuous cycle" (Sternsdorff-Cisterna 2015: 461). Its members gave short talks and shared readings on, and experiences with, food and radiation:

> Nakamura-san [a member of the club] said that it was so difficult to know the proper course of action. We reflected that asking laypeople to know an acceptable level of risk is a challenging proposition and that it was unfair to require us to shoulder such a burden…. Many times we raised questions such as the wisdom of eating at restaurants where they might be taking advantage of the cheaper prices for Fukushima products, but no one had a good answer for what we should do. We tried to the best of our abilities to interpret the available information and reassure each other that we were being conscientious about the moment, but the magnitude of the monumental task of managing risk after Fukushima always hovered in the background, never completely resolved.
>
> (Ibid.: 462)

In short, the members shared a general confusion over food safety and could not estimate risk, which was not unexpected due to scientific uncertainty (discussed above). For them, sharing experiences and readings was a way to ease their anxiety. The club operated privately so that trust could be built up between members. This was also the first step to reconstructing new judgement devices.

This self-reconstruction of judgement devices assumed three main forms, each of which was more complementary than exclusive of the other. The first was to adopt an "exclusion zone" and avoid buying food produced in certain areas. This zone would cover Fukushima Prefecture only or could include nearby prefectures such as Ibaraki, Tochigi, Gunma and Chiba.[21] This strategy could concern all foodstuffs or only some of them. For specific products known to contain higher levels of radiation (e.g. spinach, mushrooms or tea), the safety zone could be further enlarged: low levels of contamination were found in tea from Shizuoka, located 360 kilometres from Fukushima), which led some consumers to avoid buying tea from this region. At the extreme, these products could be entirely excluded from one's diet.

The second strategy was to rely on tradition: many traditional Japanese foods are supposed to promote good health and are used to prevent sickness. For example, people have been eating miso soup or seaweed to counter the effects of nuclear contamination.[22] It is difficult to know the extent of this practice, but it has been strong enough to influence businesses to promote it in their advertisements (more on this below).

The last strategy was to adopt lower benchmarks than the government's regulations.[23] This type of action corresponds to the matching of two principles of coordination (which can be rapidly defined as the aggregation of individual decisions). The first one can be termed "civic". It corresponds to the different actions undertaken by civil society movements, such as NGOs and NPOs, to test the presence of radionuclides in food, dispatch the results and explain them to their members and/or customers. These organizations, which Kimura termed "citizen radiation-measuring organizations" (CMRO), were of five different types. These included organizations created by previous antinuclear activists, people already engaged in consumers' rights or environmental causes, those who had no social movement experience prior to the accident, etc. (Kimura 2016: 111–116). These groups were politically engaged[24] in the sense that their tests not only operate in defiance of national regulations, but are also firmly opposed by the authorities. The government has constantly blasted the CMROs for sabotaging the country's reconstructive efforts. It also tried to discredit the CMROs for their lack of professionalism including, for example, testing food with scintillation detectors, which are not as reliable as germanium semiconductor detectors, as the latter are much more expensive and less accessible for most CMROs (Kimura 2016: 130).

Thus far, the government has been aggressively condemning any attempt to conduct independent tests or implement standards higher than its own (see below). However, it could not prevent their development. In fact, the action to have stricter benchmarks than the official ones was not only the apanage of the NGOs and NPOs, which follow a "civic principle of coordination", but it was also adopted by the industry and major retailers, which were quick to detect the shifting consumer sentiment. This corresponded to a "market's principle of coordination" and is remarkable because the large retailers were, at first, keen to follow the government's instructions and food from the vicinity of Fukushima figured prominently in their stores – before they practically disappeared due to a lack of demand. The Aeon/Jusco Group, one of Japan's major supermarket chains, was among the first to implement a private norm (*Daily Yomiuri* 12 April 2012), which was fixed at 50 Bq/kg, or 90 per cent lower than the provisional norm issued by the government in March 2011 (Augustin-Jean and Baumert 2014). In November 2011, Aeon/Jusco "announced that it would aim for 'tolerance zero' and publicize its own test results on its website" (Kimura 2016: 47). Even though Aeon did not test all of its products, it still tested a wider range of products than its competitors. That strongly helped it to maintain its brand image (ibid.: 47–48). Some independent restaurants followed the same policy and soon became "non-becquereled restaurants", after which they were imitated by a few national restaurant chains. But others did exactly the opposite, using their large-scale and central purchasing units to mix food from different geographical origins (including Fukushima) for their restaurants and, thus, dilute the effect of radiation.

The same economic exploitation also concerned the second type of device, which relied on tradition – at times, in a contestable way. Books that promoted traditional Japanese food culture were published with recipes to allegedly counter radiation. Titles included: *Don't Succumb to Radiation! Eighty-Eight Macrobiotic Recipes* (Okubo 2011) and *Detoxing Radiation: The Power of Japanese Food: Brown Rice, Miso and Seaweed Recipes* (Shufuno Tomo 2011; both titles – and others – cited in Kimura 2016: 48). Private companies, such as those that manufactured miso, also claimed their products were effective in mitigating radiation. These claims did not have much scientific validity, but, in the face of uncertainty, they were part of the business community's efforts to exploit the concerns of the public through the development of new and "more trustworthy standards".

As indicated above, the government negatively reacted to all these actions. It slammed what it called "harmful rumours" and a "becquerel war" and criticized companies and citizens who aimed to disrupt the norms enacted by the authorities:

> On April 23, a few days before the start of Japan's Golden Week holidays, phones at the farm ministry's Food Industry Affairs Bureau were ringing off the hook.
>
> Callers were furious at an advisory, issued by the ministry three days before, urging food companies, shops and restaurants to stay in line with new national maximums for radioactive cesium in food and drop their own more stringent standards.
>
> Ministry officials said they were concerned about an escalating "becquerel war" in which food industry players were competing with each other on radiation guarantees....
>
> But the official line cut across the efforts of private sector companies that said they were doing nothing more than trying to respond to the priorities of their consumers.
>
> (Furukawa 2012)

This attitude of the Japanese government can be explained by its efforts to balance the interests of consumers with the need to rebuild the affected areas and protect its economy. In fact, in the face of the costs of reconstruction and decontamination, the government chose to support local businesses to the detriment of Japanese citizens and consumers. But, to some extent, its efforts are a lost cause and the disappearance of food from Fukushima in Tokyo's supermarket shows it. In fact, it shows that judgements tend to aggregate and develop into "new" norms. These norms may not be based on science and are certainly subjective, but in the face of existing uncertainties, they provide a release for people. When they are also accepted and refined by the private sector, then they may not really become "public" norms, but they do gain credentials.

Conclusion

Frank Knight is generally remembered for his theory of risk and uncertainty. However, from his perspective, that did not mean there was a clear separation between the two. On the contrary, to Knight, the two concepts were tightly intertwined and a "pure" quantification of risk is rare: there is some uncertainty in most types of risk and the proportion of the unquantifiable has a tendency to increase when an event is rare or unique. To support his statement, Knight took the example of business decisions, which are, by definition, unique and make calculations of probabilities regarding the prospects of these decisions hazardous.

The Fukushima disaster offers an even more extreme example of the difficulty to estimate risks in the case of rare events. Nuclear disasters are rare and their consequences are still not fully understood. In this situation, the meaning of probability is closer to the third type identified by Knight than to his second one: judgements take prominence when uncertainties increase. As a result, traditional benchmarks and standards, which integrated these uncertainties, did not fulfil their roles and were contested by experts, leaving customers and citizens feeling insecure.

The seminal work of Knight did not fully address the issue of the formation of judgements, but he did mention the role of experience – to which knowledge could be added. Experience and knowledge are used by individuals to form an opinion on judgement devices. An example noted by Karpik concerned buying a CD that contains Beethoven's Fifth Symphony. A layman would probably ask the shop assistant to make his choice, while an experienced listener may base his/her decision on the name of the conductor. Neither device is objective, but both help people make a decision. They also displace judgements from the objects (in this case the recordings) to the devices. In this process, trust plays an important role.

After the Fukushima disaster, however, the existing devices could no longer be trusted. If Fukushima Prefecture was famous before 2011 for its high-quality agricultural products, the same could not be said after the nuclear meltdown. Again, since contaminated foods could not be distinguished from their non-contaminated counterparts, customers were left in a state of uncertainty, which, as seen above, was not eased by the new devices implemented in haste in 2011 and revised in 2012. The solution, criticized by the government, was to develop "new" standards that were certainly not more objective than those put out by the Japanese authorities, but provided a certain sense of relief to people.

In developing these standards, people often relied on their knowledge and experiences, which might have been linked to their proximity to food (if they belonged to a cooperative of customers, for example), their understanding of the risk of nuclear contamination, etc. The link could also be to tradition and relations of proximity (e.g. friends, family and neighbours). More fundamentally, some people have developed their own specific knowledge regarding food safety and nuclear contamination, due to uncertainties that might not have helped them gain a better idea of which foods are safe enough, but which did help them build a language sufficient to communicate with the local authorities and scientists. In some cases, while this communication did not lead to cooperation, it still pushed local governments to implement more stringent tests, particularly for school lunches. Similarly, consumer demand has prompted the private sector to meet it and implement more stringent norms than those of the government. In short, even though people may not have systematic scientific knowledge of nuclear disasters, they could still bend existing norms and modify market conditions through their actions. It is in this sense that judgements play a decisive role in uncertain situations.

All in all, the lessons of Knight are mostly forgotten today, but they are still useful, as they provide an analytical framework in which further research can easily fit. Knight's theory provides the missing link between the risk perception of Paul Slovic (2000), the risk society of Beck (uncertainties are everywhere and not measurable), and the cultural approach of Douglas (judgements are forged by culture and vary by society). Risks and uncertainties are and will remain everywhere. This is not necessarily a bad thing, but the question, then, is how one can deal with and limit them. Answers vary by time and place and depend on individual and collective judgements.

Notes

1 Alessandro Stanziani (2005) provided in-depth analyses of the economic pressure leading to counterfeiting and adulteration in nineteenth-century France.
2 See the Centre for Food Safety (n.d.), the government of the Hong Kong Special Administrative Region, www.cfs.gov.hk/english/multimedia/multimedia_pub/multimedia_pub_fsf_01_02.html (accessed 26 April 2017).
3 Even Ulrich Beck, despite having little appetite for probabilities (see Introduction), accepted this reliance on statistics:

> Consequences that at first affect only the individual become "risks", systematically caused, statistically describable and in that sense "predictable" types of events, which can therefore also be subjected to supraindividual and political rules of recognition, compensation and avoidance.
>
> (Beck 1992b: 99)

4 It should, however, be noted that risk, such as that accepted by an entrepreneur, may have a positive connotation. Similarly, Deborah Lupton, in her presentation of the history of the concept of risk, notes that until recently, risk could be either good or bad (Lupton 1999: 8).

5 As stated by Langlois and Cosgel, for Knight, "uncertainty arises out of our partial knowledge" (1993: 459). On the role of judgements in the construction of statistics, see also Desrosières (2002).

6 More precisely, in the wording of Kahneman:

> Framing effects: Different ways of presenting the same information often evoke different emotions. The statement that "the odds of survival one month after surgery are 90%" is more reassuring than the equivalent statement that "mortality within one month of surgery is 10%".
>
> (Kahneman 2011: 88)

7 Basically, Brussels stated that the measures implemented by the UK were efficient and the risk greatly reduced, while the French agency indicated that the risk was not completely under control and uncertainty remained.

8 In the words of Knight, "as an illustration of the first type of probability, we may take throwing a perfect die" (Knight 1921: 214–215).

9 Here, Knight referred mainly to insurance and the risk of fire. In short, the probability of a specific house catching fire is very different from that of throwing a six with a dice.

10 This is a point confirmed by recent findings in social psychology (Kahneman 2011) and behavioural economics (Thaler and Sunstein 2008). These works indicate that people have stronger reactions to salient phenomena (e.g. the description/visualization of a car accident that results in injury) than to "cold" statistical data (e.g. how many people have been injured each year by not fastening their seat belts).

11 The same applies to consumers, who may not have the same information as insurance companies, but can still compare packages and make informed choices. Of course, this argument is only theoretical, as Thaler and Sunstein have shown that it is impossible for a professional, never mind a layperson to select the best health insurance package (2008, chapter 10).

12 To be fair, Douglas and Wildavsky, among others, briefly discussed the issue when they stressed the impossibility of drawing a line between irreversible risks and other types of risk:

> If uncertainty prevents or inhibits risk taking, when would risk taking be justified? Hardly ever. For it is precisely these issues that divide us: we are entitled to a different view just because knowledge is limited, alternatives imperfectly understood, and the consequences disputed. The very uncertainty that is here presented as the basis for avoiding risk in another context would be the good reason for taking risk; otherwise we would be unable to learn how to do better. Risk is also opportunity. If whether to risk and what kind of risk to take are the questions, they cannot be answered by saying that if we don't know, we shouldn't take any at all.
>
> (Douglas and Wildavsky 1982: 22)

However, the point raised by Knight is more inclusive because for him, uncertainty is an integral part of the future. Risk, then, was constructed to limit, but not eliminate, this uncertainty.

13 He differentiated people who are able to make more accurate judgements compared to their peers. For Knight, business decisions, which are, by definition, unique, are the typical examples that require judgements: an entrepreneur is a risk-taker, which was a major difference from Schumpeter who defined a few years later that an entrepreneur was an innovator.

14 References to political influences are multiple in the document. See, for example:

> When risk management options are being evaluated, the risk analysis process sometimes becomes an overtly political one, with different interests within a society each seeking to persuade the government to choose the risk management options they prefer. This can be a useful phase.

(FAO 2009: 70)

15 The principle at work here is more difficult to analyse. On one hand, the standard can be seen as a scientific device. On the other hand, it can also be considered as an element of the market, leading to competition between companies or states for the use of specific standards (see Büthe and Mattli 2011; Augustin-Jean and Xie 2016).

16 The judgement on any of these devices can also vary according to circumstances, because other social factors are in play. For example, an individual may think it is not too healthy (or it is slightly risky) to eat certain foods. But s/he may still do it if it is offered by a family member, etc. – unless s/he judges the food really too risky. As the third section will show, social pressure may also be strong enough to push people to adopt practices they may judge unsafe.

17 A becquerel (Bq) measures the activity of the radioactive source, i.e. the number of atoms that, per unit of time, emit a radiation. The Sievert (Sv) is a measure of the health effect of low levels of ionizing radiation on the human body. Thus, even though some correspondences are possible (depending, in particular, on the types of nuclide concerned), the two units measure different things.

18 This pressure, being widespread, directly contradicted the general attitude of mistrust towards norms and food safety in general. Kimura, who analysed the phenomenon in depth, did not address this point. It could be that many people were worried, but did not want to appear as such in public.

19 One flagship product from Fukushima is peaches. These peaches fetched very high prices before the accident, but cost 20 per cent less than the national average thereafter (cited by Kimura 2016: 30).

20 Interviews were conducted with participants during the seminar *Risques Alimentaires, Perceptions Comparées* [Food Risks, Comparative Perspectives], the Maison Franco-Japonaise, 14 December 2014, and the international seminar, Historical and Cultural Studies of Food and Disasters in Japan, at the University of Nagoya, 22–23 February 2014. Casual observations in supermarkets were realized by the author making repeat visits to Tokyo from 2012 to 2016.

21 This is what the author of this chapter did just after the disaster, when he was working at the University of Tsukuba. This action, which was first unconscious, was at the root of this study on food safety in Japan.

22 The Merriam-Webster dictionary defines miso as "a high-protein fermented food paste consisting chiefly of soybeans, salt, and usually grain (such as barley or rice) and ranging in taste from very salty to very sweet". See www.merriam-webster.com/dictionary/miso, consulted on 1 June 2017.

23 Sternsdorff-Cisterna (2013) estimated these norms to be fixed at 10 per cent of the government's norms before the 2012 changes. Some individuals have even stricter standards and separate "becquereled" and "non-becquereled" food.

24 Arguing that participants in the CRMO usually claim that their actions apolitical, Kimura would disagree with this statement.

References

Aoki, M. (2012) "Mothers First to Shed Food-Safety Complacency", *Japan Times*, 4 January.

Augustin-Jean, L. (2014) "An Approach to Food Quality in China: An Agenda for Future Research", in L. Augustin-Jean and B. Alpermann (eds), *The Political Economy of Agro-Food Markets in China: The Social Construction of the Markets in an Era of Globalization*, Houndmills, Basingstoke: Palgrave Macmillan.

Augustin-Jean, L. (2015) "When Risks Turn to Uncertainties: Insights from the Food Market in China and Japan", *China Journal of Social Work*, 8(3): 247–267.

Augustin-Jean, L. and N. Baumert (2014) "Les réactions des consommateurs japonais suite à la contamination nucléaire de mars 2011 et leurs conséquences sur le rapport au territoire", *Géographie et Cultures*, 86: 49–64.

Augustin-Jean, L. and L. Xie (2016) "Rules and Standards between Global Public Goods and Elements of Competition: Case Studies from China's Agro-food Industry", in L. Augustin-Jean (guest ed.), "Food Risks, Food Safety and International Trade", Special Section, *Asian Journal of WTO & Int'l Health Law & Policy*, 11(2): 289–324.

Baumert, N. (2015) "Eating in Japan after March 2011: Geographical Consequences Concerning the Origin of Food", International Seminar, Food, Risks and Sustainability: An Asian Perspective, 6–7 July 2015, Hong Kong. www.polyu.edu.hk/apss/others/food/4.3.pdf [accessed 20 May 2017].

Beck, U. (1992a) *Risk Society: Towards a New Modernity*, London: Sage.

Beck, U. (1992b) "From Industrial Society to the Risk Society: Questions of Survival, Social Structure and Ecological Environment", *Theory, Culture & Society*, 9: 97–123.

Beck, U. (1999) *World Risk Society*, Cambridge: Polity.

Beck, U. (2006) "Living in the World Risk Society", *Economy and Society*, 35(3): 329–345.

Berends, G. and M. Kobayashi (2012) "Food after Fukushima: Japan's Regulatory Response to the Radioactive Contamination of its Food Chain", *Food and Drug Law Journal*, 67(1): 51–64.

Buerk, R. (2011) "Japan Pensioners Volunteer to Tackle Nuclear Crisis" [Online]. BBC, 31 May. www.bbc.co.uk/news/world-asia-pacific-13598607 [accessed 17 April 2017].

Büthe, T. and W. Mattli (2011) *The New Global Rulers: The Privatization of Regulation and the World Economy*, Princeton, NJ: Princeton University Press.

Centre for Food Safety, The Government of the Hong Kong Special Administrative Region (n.d.) "Hazard and Risk in Food Safety (Part I)". www.cfs.gov.hk/english/multimedia/multimedia_pub/multimedia_pub_fsf_01_02.html [accessed 17 April 2017].

Daily Yomiuri (2011) "'Colossal Blunder' on Radioactive Cattle Feed: Govt Officials Admit Responsibility for Foul-up That Let Tainted Beef Enter Nation's Food Supply", 18 July.

Daily Yomiuri (2012), "Gvt Asks Businesses Not to Set Cesium Limits", 12 April.

Delman, J. and M. H. Yang (2012) "A Value Chain Gone Awry: Implications of the 'Tainted Milk Scandal' in 2008 for Political and Social Organization in Rural China", in A. Bislev, S. Thogersen, and J. Unger (eds), *Organizing Rural China – Rural China Organizing*, Lanham, MD: Lexington Books.

Desrosières, A. (2002) *The Politics of Large Numbers: A History of Statistical Reasoning*, Cambridge, MA: Harvard University Press.

Douglas, M. and A. Wildavsky (1982) *Risk and Culture*, Berkeley, CA: University of California Press.

Elster, J. (1979) "Risk, Uncertainty and Nuclear Power", *Social Science Information*, 18(3): 371–400.

Flanquart, H. (2016) *Des Risques et des Hommes*, Paris: Presses Universitaires de France.

Food and Agricultural Organization (FAO) (2009) *Food Safety Risk Analysis: A Guide for National Food Safety Authorities*, FAO Food and Nutrition Paper 87, Rome: FAO/WHO.

Furukawa, M. (2012) "Farm Ministry Effort to Stop 'Becquerel War' Draws Fire", *Asahi Shinbum*, 7 May.

González, A. J. (2012) "The Recommendation of the ICRP Vis-à-vis the Fukushima Dai-Ichi NPP Accident Aftermath", *Journal of Radiology Protection*, 31(1): N1–7.

Hamada, N., H. Ogino and Y. Fujimichi (2012) "Safety Regulations of Food and Water Implemented in the First Year Following the Fukushima Nuclear Accident" *Journal of Radiation Research*, 53(5): 641–671.

Harlan, C. (2011) "Safety Regulations of Food and Water Implemented in the First Year Following the Fukushima Nuclear Accident", *Washington Post*, 24 April.

Hommerich, C. (2012) "Trust and Subjective Well-being after the Great East Japan Earthquake, Tsunami and Nuclear Meltdown: Preliminary Results", *International of Japanese Sociology*, 21(1): 46–64.

Ilbert, H., M. Petit and L. Augustin-Jean (2014) "Le respect des normes de sûreté sanitaire des aliments et des spécificités culturelles de l'alimentation: une double injonction contradictoire?" International Conference, Renouveler les Approches Institutionnalistes sur l'Agriculture et l'Alimentation: la "Grande Transformation" 20 ans après. https://esrcarto.supagro.inra.fr/seminaire2014/index.php/articles/session-3/26-ilbert-helene-augustin-jean-louis-petit-michel [accessed 17 April 2017].

Kahneman, D. (2011) *Thinking, Fast and Slow*, London: Penguin.

Karpik, L. (2010) *Valuing the Unique: The Economics of Singularities*, Princeton, NJ: Princeton University Press.

Kimura, H. A. (2016) *Radiation Brain Moms and Citizen Scientists: The Gender Politics of Food Contamination*, Durham, NC and London: Duke University Press.

Kimura, H., K. Nannichi, N. Sawa and M. Kobayashi (2011) "Distrust of Government Standards Fuels Avoidance of Tohoku Food", *Asahi Shinbun*, 17 September.

Knight, F. H. (1921) *Risks, Uncertainty and Profit*, New York: Reprints of Economic Classic, Augustus M. Kelley, Bookseller (1964). http://mises.org/sites/default/files/Risk%2C%20Uncertainty%2C%20and%20Profit_4.pdf [accessed 11 June 2018].

Kodama, T. (2011) *Naibuhibakuno Shinjitsu* [The Truth about Internal Radiation], Tokyo: Gentosha.

Langlois, R. N. and M. M. Cosgel (1993) "Frank Knight on Risk, Uncertainty, and the Firm: A New Interpretation", *Economic Inquiry*, 31(3): 456–465.

Lin, C. F. (2013) "Scientification of Politics or Politicization of Science: Reassessing the Limits of International Food Safety Lawmaking", *Columbia Science and Technology Law Review*, 15: 1–40.

Lupton, D. (1999) *Risks*, London: Routledge.

Marsal, P. (2000) "La vache, l'expert et le politique. Le Courrier de l'environnement", 39. www7.inra.fr/lecourrier//wp-content/uploads/2013/03/C39Marsal_Vache-folle.pdf [accessed 31 May 2017].

Ministry of Agriculture, Forestry and Fisheries (MAFF) (2011) *Annual Report. Special Feature: "Great East Japan Earthquake"*, Tokyo, Japan. www.maff.go.jp/e/annual_report/2010/pdf/e_feature.pdf [accessed 5 June 2017].

Nikkei (2012) "Fukushima Disaster Raised Awareness of Food Safety: Polls", *Nikkei Report*, 7 March.

Simon, H. A. (1997) *Administrative Behavior: A Study of Decision-Making Processes in Administrative Organizations* (4th edn), New York: Free Press.

Slovic, P., ed. (2000) *The Perception of Risks*, London: Earthscan.

Snyder, F. (2015) *Food Safety Law in China: Making Transnational Law*, Leiden and Boston: Brill Nijhoff.

Stanziani, A. (2005) *Histoire de la qualité alimentaire, XIXe–XXe siècle*, Paris: Seuil.

Sternsdorff-Cisterna, N. (2013) "Safe and Trustworthy? Food Safety after Fukushima". Paper presented at the STS Forum on the East Japan Disaster, University of California, Berkeley, 11–14 May. https://fukushimaforum.wordpress.com/workshops/sts-forum-on-the-2011-fukushima-eastjapan-disaster/manuscripts/session-4a-when-disasters-end-part-i/safe-and-trustworthy-foodsafety-after-fukushima/ [accessed 27 April 2017].

Sternsdorff-Cisterna, N. (2015) "Food after Fukushima: Risk and Scientific Citizenship in Japan", *American Anthropologist*, 117(3): 455–467.

Thaler, R. and C. R. Sunstein (2008) *Nudge: Improving Decisions about Health, Wealth, and Happiness*, New Haven, CT: Yale University Press.

Thévenot, L. (2001) "Organized Complexity: Conventions of Coordination and the Composition of Economic Arrangements", *European Journal of Social Theory*, 4(4): 405–425.

Wikipedia (n.d.) "List of Food Contamination Incidents". https://en.wikipedia.org/wiki/List_of_food_contamination_incidents#2001_to_present, last [accessed 8 June 2017].

Wynne, B. (1996). "May the Sheep Safely Graze? A Reflexive View of the Expert–Lay Knowledge Divide", in S. Lash, B. Szerszynski and B. Wynne (eds), *Risk, Environment and Modernity: Towards a New Ecology*, London: Sage.

5 Essential elements for interactive risk communication in food-related emergencies

A model and experiments on the health effects of radioactive substances

Yoko Niiyama

Introduction

Risk communication is considered an essential part of the framework of risk analysis for food safety (FAO/WHO 2006, 2016; CAC (Codex Alimentarius Commission) 2007). Risk communication has been defined by Codex as:

> The interactive exchange of information and opinions throughout the risk analysis process concerning risk, risk-related factors and risk perceptions, among risk assessors, risk managers, consumers, industry, the academic community and other interested parties, including the explanation of risk assessment findings and the basis of risk management decisions.
>
> (FAO/WHO 2006; CAC 2007)

However, structured elements and procedures, such as "risk management" and "risk assessment", have not yet been specified.

Risk communication is assumed to take place in a variety of contexts, including between risk assessors and risk managers on the subject of risk assessment policies and assessment outcomes, as well as between experts and citizens regarding the outcomes of risk assessment and the selection and implementation of risk management measures.

While each of these contexts has its own challenges, we here discuss the issue of communication between experts and citizens. With many difficulties and few successes, an effective interactive communication model is yet to be found. As parts of its background, we point it out that there is a significant gap between psychological and subjective public risk evaluation and science-based risk assessment, and public knowledge is limited by a restricted information environment.

In the first half of this chapter, we will discuss the purpose of risk communication in the food safety field, the implications of interactivity, the cases and methods of implementation and the risk perception of citizens. In the latter half of the chapter, the interactive risk communication model (i.e. the interactive information summarizing and horizontal discussion model) and its essential elements are presented and the verification result of its effects in the following emergency is shown.

We present the case of food-related health effects of radioactive substances derived from the Fukushima Daiichi Nuclear Power Plant disaster due to the earthquake on the Pacific coast of Tohoku (11 March 2011). In order to respond to citizens' strong anxiety about it, we urgently created the interactive risk communication model and applied it.[1] This chapter is based on the articles arising from the results of this enforcement.

Purposes and methods of risk communication between experts and citizens

Implications of interactivity for the purposes of risk communication

The goal of risk communication, developed in the United States, has changed from (i) information disclosure (mid-1970s–mid-1980s), to (ii) persuasion (mid-1980s–mid-1990s), to (iii) mutual understanding (since the mid-1990s) (NRC 1989; FAO/WHO 1998; Harada 2007).

Along with these changes, the concept of the information provided and the direction of transmission have changed significantly. In concept (ii), risk communication aimed to obtain people's understanding by explaining information from experts on risks such as probability of loss. This is characterized as one-way transmission, in which experts select appropriate information and present it to people. However, from many experiences such as informed consent in the medical field, it has become known that achieving unity on risk information is difficult. As a result, it has come to be thought that it will be sufficient if mutual understanding might be made, and the aim has become to interactively transmit not only information on risk itself but also on all relevant information and opinions as much as possible.

As a background to this change, it has been noted that it is neither the experts nor the parties themselves who make risk decisions and it is based on the agreement of stakeholders. It also reflects on the fact that the characterization of risk perception has been clarified by the development of cognitive science.

Risk analysis for food safety can be regarded as a framework for risk reduction based on the agreement of stakeholders. Therefore, risk communication is required at each stage of risk analysis (see Table 5.1; FAO/WHO 2006, 2016). Communication among all stakeholders is required for some steps of preliminary risk management, including explanation of constraints, assumptions and uncertainty, and minority opinions. Close communication between risk managers and risk assessors is necessary for developing risk profiles and commission risk assessment. For identification and selection of risk management options, government risk managers need to communicate effectively to industries and consumers.

Risk communication is fundamentally a two-way process. It involves sharing information. That risk managers provide the public with clear and timely

Table 5.1 Communication point and participants

Communication point in risk management process	Participants in risk communication
1 Preliminary Risk Management Activities	
(1) Identifying food safety issue	All parties
(2) Developing risk profile	Risk managers and risk assessors or other scientists
(3) Establishing goals of RM	Risk managers, risk assessors and external stakeholders
(4) Establishing risk assessment policy	Risk assessors, risk managers, and stakeholders
(5) Commissioning risk assessment if necessary	Risk assessors and risk managers
(6) During the conduct of a risk assessment	Risk assessors and risk managers, and encouraging more participation by external stakeholders
(7) When the risk assessment is completed	Risk assessors, risk managers, interested parties and the public
(8) Ranking risks if necessary	Risk managers and relevant stakeholder groups
2 Identification and Selection of Risk Management Options	Government risk managers, industry and consumer
3 Implementation of Risk Management Decision	Government risk manager and those implementing risk management measures (industry and consumer)
4 Monitoring and Review	Government risk manager and those implementing risk management measures (industry and consumer)

Source: made by the author based on FAO/WHO (2006).

information is one of the critical functions of risk communication as an "outgoing" process. However, as "incoming" communication, decision makers can obtain vital information and opinions through soliciting feedback from affected stakeholders and can provide input to the basis for decision-making (FAO/WHO 2006).

We have faced challenges at each stage and it is a particularly difficult issue to ensure effective risk communication between experts and citizens. We are still seeking an effective model worldwide.

Purposes of risk communication and the implementation environment

Risk communication has been carried out with a number of objectives. We can describe four typical purposes:[2] (1) sharing and exchanging risk-related information, (2) societal consensus-building, (3) contributing to individual choices and (4) acquiring the ability to examine risk-related information (Table 5.2). These types of risk communication are conducted in the following cases: (1) when performing preventive responses to anticipated situations and (2) when responding to an emergency situation that has occurred. Also, differences in environments regarding seriousness, trust and perception have been found. Corresponding to these situations, the state of information exchange assumed is also different, as is shown in Table 5.2.

Emergency communication (e.g. at the time of occurrence of the following events: the former BSE, highly pathogenic avian influenza and the release of radioactive materials due to nuclear power plant accidents) is more difficult than other preventive types of communication in terms of time margin and response to serious situations. Nonetheless, it takes a certain amount of time to take control of the situation and summarize the necessary scientific information. It is during this time that various sources of information are released from the media and the initial impression is determined. Effective risk communication cannot be started unless we understand the status of citizens' risk perceptions and the kind of information the citizen is seeking, but this process takes time. Also, we cannot predict the kind of time scale on which the situation will change.

In these emergency situations, the environment of communication will depend on the level of trust in the administration, the experts and the media and the gap between risk assessment by experts and citizens' risk perceptions. If trust is lost and citizens' level of perceived risk is higher than the risk as assessed by experts, or even in the case of an emergency that fails in the initial communication, citizens are less likely to accept expert information.

When one responds to the situation of information exchange, it is necessary to consider the content of scientific information to be provided and how to provide it. In particular, in cases where the situation is serious and deep scientific knowledge is needed and in the case of a low trust level among citizens and high-risk perception, experts need to provide systematic scientific information and citizens need to find a place for elaborate information processing.

Interactivity, range and speed in risk communication methods: the Japanese example

In order to think concretely, we can consider the types of risk communication from two perspectives. This is to say the range and speed of communication and the style of communication which is one direction or interactive. Figure 5.1 shows the types of risk communication implemented in Japan. The Roman text

Table 5.2 Between government officials/experts and citizens, purposes, circumstances and environments of risk communication

		Probable steps in risk analysis (Table 5.1)
1 What is the purpose?		
(1) Sharing and exchanging scientific knowledge on hazards and risks		1–1), 6), 7), 8)
(2) Building a social consensus regarding risk management goals and setting standards/regulations		Especially 2
(3) Contributing to individual choice regarding food behaviour and home food handling		Especially 2, 3
(4) Acquiring ability to examine government/media information and scientific information regarding the specific event faced		Above basis
2 What kind of circumstances should be implemented?		Status of information exchange
(1) When doing preventive response to anticipated situation		There is a time margin
(2) When responding to an emergency situation that has occurred		There is no time margin, it is often a serious situation
3 Environment of communication		Status of information exchange
(1) Degree of seriousness and the necessary scientific knowledge	a When it is high	Systematic knowledge and sophisticated information examination process required
	b When it is low	Information examination is not so difficult
(2) Status of trust in administration, experts and media	a When it is high	Information is easy to accept
	b When it is low	Elaborate information examination process required, due to doubt
(3) Status of public risk perception	a When it is high	Since low risk information is difficult to accept, elaborate information examination process required
	b When it is low	High risk information is easy to accept

Source: made by the author based on Niiyama *et al.* (2015a).

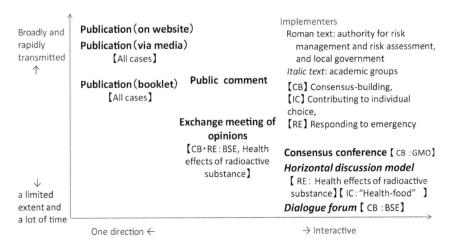

Figure 5.1 The types of risk communication and experience in Japan.

Source: made by author based on Niiyama *et al.* (2015a).

represents items conducted by risk management and risk assessment authorities and local governments, while the italic text represents items conducted on the part of academics.

The authorities, in one direction but broadly and rapidly, produce publications on websites and via media to transmit information for all purposes. Also, on the other hand, they interactively conduct many "exchange meetings of opinions" and public comments to solicit opinions regarding regulatory measures and to respond to emergencies.

More interactive initiatives have been experimentally implemented in authoritative and academic settings. Consensus conferences and dialogue forums are conducted with the aim of consensus-building in public policy. The horizontal discussion model that we propose has been conducted with regard to responding to emergencies (progress of citizens' elaborate information examination) as well as to individual choices.

The "opinion exchange meeting" is a method peculiar to Japan and heavily used in risk communication conducted by governments and local authorities. The general example is a style in which participants are recruited on a scale of 100–200 people, experts and administrative staff speak, questions are received from participants in the venue and the speakers respond. The original purpose, as inferred from the name, is an exchange of opinions on risk assessment and risk management measures (1–7 and 2 in Table 5.1). However, in reality, the emphasis is often placed on information penetration. So, this gives citizens the impression of unilateral information provision from the administration and the executing agency has come to recognize that participant understanding levels are poor (FSCJ 2006, 2008).

The consensus conference was conducted for GM crops (Kobayashi 2004), nanotechnology application to foods (Tachikawa and Mikami 2013), etc. by the Ministry of Agriculture and by academics. The objective was, rather than risk communication, to examine the direction of advanced technology with citizen participation and to obtain citizen engagement in social treatment and ethical consideration. The "Dialogue forum" (Iizawa 2010) is an example of applying this method to risk communication on the academic side. It was implemented in the Hokkaido area for the purpose of exchange of opinions of stakeholders on BSE measures, etc. Applicability will be further explored in the future.[3]

In addition, the search for interactive risk communication between experts and citizens is prominent in the field of nuclear power and the insufficiency of existing methods has been pointed out. There, over the establishment of nuclear facilities, continuous communications for a certain period between the facility engineer and local residents, such as through the "Dialogue forum", have been experimented with. Also, with regard to the method, it has been pointed out as a constraint that the outcome depends on the skill of the facilitator (Yagi *et al.* 2007; Tsuchiya *et al.* 2009).

In these cases, the scope of stakeholders is limited to the specific facility and the residents in the surrounding area. On the other hand, in the case of food-derived risk, stakeholders are widespread. Although regulators comprise the specific government agency, there are a large number of food business operators implementing regulatory measures, foods with contamination potential and the number of citizens exposed to the risk is unspecified. Due to these conditions, it seems that risk communication in the food field has fundamental difficulties in ensuring interactivity.

Status of risk perception of citizens and risk assessment of experts in the food field

There is a significant gap between experts and the public regarding risk assessment approaches, particularly for concepts of risk and risk estimation procedures. Food-related risk is defined as a function of the probability of an adverse health effect and the severity of that effect and is estimated based on scientific data and processes by experts. Public risk assessment, in contrast, is conducted in an intuitive fashion. Slovic (1999) indicated that the public has a broad conception of risk, qualitative and complex, that incorporates considerations, such as uncertainty, dread, catastrophic potential, controllability, equity, risk to future generations and so forth, into the risk equation. Rohrmann and Renn (2000) present a conceptual model in which personal and social factors influence risk perception in addition to risk characteristics.

> The public is not irrational. Their judgments about risk are influenced by emotion and affect in a way that is both simple and sophisticated. The same holds true for scientists. Public views are also influenced by worldviews, ideologies and values; so are scientists' views, particularly when they are

working at the limits of their expertise. The limitations of risk science, the importance and difficulty of maintaining trust and the complex, sociopolitical nature of risk point to the need for a new approach – one that focuses upon introducing more public participation into both risk assessment and risk decision making in order to make the decision process more democratic, improve the relevance and quality of technical analysis and increase the legitimacy and public acceptance of the resulting decisions.

(Slovic 1999: 689)

The considerable point in citizens' perception about food-related risk is that the probability of adverse effects is difficult to perceive (Niiyama *et al.* 2011a). In the structure of risk perception, the following latent factors have been found: mass media coverage, trust for regulatory measures, affective association (evoked images), knowledge and perceived characteristics of risk (severity of health effects, accumulation in the body/delay of influence, and difficulty of control). In particular, it has been clarified that the evoked serious image strongly influences the perceived risk characteristics. As the result, the severity is strongly perceived and such the causal sequence leads to the perceived magnitude of the risk (Niiyama *et al.* 2011b).

Regarding the health effects of radioactive substances released by accidents at Fukushima Daiichi nuclear power plant, it has been found that the influence of evoked images is more significant and the influence of knowledge is smaller (Kito *et al.* 2014). According to supplemental hearing in our survey discussed later, participant citizens explain reasons for not considering the probability of occurrence of health damage as follows: Despite being provided with a definition of risk, we will start thinking from a situation in which health effects have occurred. They said that they noticed that they unconsciously avoided considering the probability of occurrence and the lowering of the probability of occurrence by regulatory measures.

This phenomenon seems to correspond to the following points. When people assess risk, they replace tasks to be assessed, if doing so is difficult, with easy-to-estimate elements and do so based on accessible events and clues. There, we can find a tendency to obtain clues by associations such as images accumulated in memory through past experiences. This eliminates the load of information processing, leading to faster processing and action (Stanovich and West 2000; Slovic *et al.* 2004; Kahneman 2012). This is a universal approach to risk for human beings and it is by no means lacking in thought. However, it is also true that there may be a large deviation from realistic risk, which may cause people to become more anxious.

We obtained the following data. After the Fukushima disaster, the public assessed the health risk of radioactive substances by associations with images. These images are serious and have been obtained in the past from graphics of the atomic bombings in Hiroshima and Nagasaki and news of the Chernobyl accident (Niiyama *et al.* 2015b). This process leads the public to make assessments of serious deterministic effects, such as deformity, genetic effects or death.

It is well known that these effects are not observed under low-dose exposure like this time. We also found that systematic scientific information has not been provided and the public has not been able to recognize the difference in the effects of high- and low-level exposure.

The interactive information summarizing and horizontal discussion model: what communication would be effective?[4]

As we have already discussed, today we know that public persuasion by experts is regarded as difficult. We focus on mutual understanding and interaction. Moreover, after a failure of initial risk communication, any act of persuasion invites public protest and suspicion.

We have developed a model for responding to emergency, following the Fukushima Daiichi Nuclear Power Plant disaster. People were lacking systematic scientific information, were strongly injured by information from the media and accompanied by strong anxiety; they were placed in a condition under which they operated in their daily lives with a strong level of stress. As shown in Table 5.2 above, the information needs of people were extremely high, but communication has been extremely difficult. Consequently, we have judged that the only effective communication is to closely respond to people's knowledge level, questions, anxiety, concerns and information-processing processes. We aim to enhance people's ability to examine media information for the purpose of communication.

The model we prepared includes the following three elements. First, public participants present questions and concerns. Second, a team of experts systematically summarize scientific information responding to the public questions. Third, a team of experts and/or communicators provides a stage for public discussion in their own style to allow elaborate information processing on the scientific information.

Our model is carried out in three stages, as Figure 5.2 describes. The first stage is built upon focus group communications (FGC) conducted by a team of experts (TE). During this stage, the TE prepares basic scientific information. The second stage aims for training of communicators. In the third stage, widespread communications are conducted by communicators, who are local government officials, corporations and other operators, using the basic scientific information prepared for the first stage.

In the FCG, our model consists of four steps including two-round communication, as Figure 5.2 shows. First, the TE prepares the first round of scientific information with its explanatory text. In the second step, which is the first-round discussion, the experts explain the scientific information to participating citizens, and participants then advance group discussion on the information in small groups of 5–6 people and organize the points of understanding and questions. The moderator chooses from participants and experts do not intervene at all (so we call this "horizontal discussion"). In the third step, the TE extracts questions from the group discussions and prepares the second round of scientific

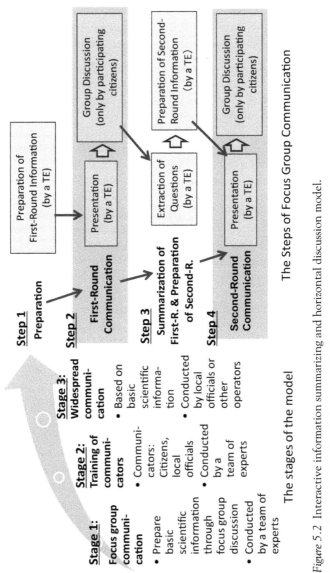

Figure 5.2 Interactive information summarizing and horizontal discussion model.

Source: made by author based on Niiyama *et al.* (2015a).

information with its explanatory text to respond to these questions. In the fourth step, that is the second round of the discussion, the TE explains this information and participants then advance a second round of group discussion. The TE organizes the whole body of scientific information based on the results.

The following widespread communications in the second stage start from the second step. If additional scientific information is required depending on the questions raised, the communicator requests cooperation from the TE at the third step. Since the scientific information prepared in the first step has an explanatory text, the communicators can easily explain it to participant citizens and this can be widely practised.

This model consists of four essential factors as follows.

First, the model aims to create a foundation for citizens to examine and judge the information presented by the government and the media. It is not aimed at persuasion (non-persuasive).

Second, the scientific information is prepared via communication. Two types of information – the information that experts wish to convey and the information that the public feel essential to answer their questions – will be integrated during the four-step communication process in the FGC (interactivity).

Third, no facilitators or experts participate in the group discussion.[5] The discussion is conducted only by citizens, according to their own style. We call this "horizontal discussion". Tasks for the discussion are to share new findings, questions and matters that require additional information. Acceptance of scientific information is left to the citizens. Experts do not respond on the spot to citizens' doubts. The response to the question is made through the provision of the second round of scientific information. This format allows participants to examine the information closely until they are satisfied in their own way and can then re-evaluate their viewpoints (horizontal discussion).

Fourth, communication is repeated twice. Using this style, we integrate scientific information with interactivity and secure interactivity of communication. Participating citizens can accumulate their own understanding by taking time and receiving scientific information to respond to their questions (interactivity).

Verification of focus group communication: how was it implemented and how did participants accept it?[6]

Overview of focus group communication implementation

FGC was conducted in Tokyo and Kyoto from June to August 2011. Participants included both males and females aged from 30 to 49 years old with children, living in Kanto (three groups of seven females, two groups of six men) and in Kansai (three groups of six women), totalling 51 people (Figure 5.3). However, as the typhoon changed the schedule in Kansai, the number of participants in the second round declined to 44 in total. Kanto was selected as a population confining area a relatively short distance away from the accident facility and Kansai as a relatively long distance area.

Venue	Subjects (aged from 30 to 49 who have school children)	Date	The team of experts:
Tokyo	Women (living in Kanto area) 3 groups × 7 women	June 2nd and July 22nd, 2011	• Radiology (National Institute of Radiological Sciences)
Kyoto	Women (living in Kansai area) 3 groups × 6 women	June 4th and August 3rd, 2011	• Mechanical Engineering (Kansai Univ.) • Risk Communication (Kyoto Univ. and Consumer Affairs Agency)
Tokyo	Men (living in Kanto area) 2 groups × 6 men	July 2nd and August 6th, 2011	

Total 8 groups 51 Participants

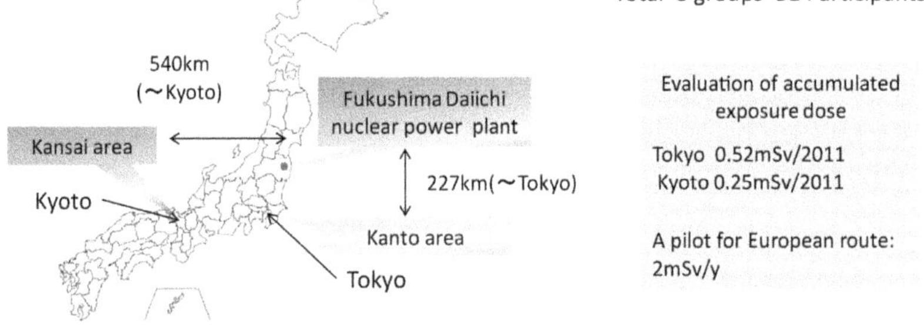

540km
(~Kyoto)
Fukushima Daiichi
nuclear power plant
Kansai area
Kyoto
227km(~Tokyo)
Kanto area
Tokyo

Evaluation of accumulated exposure dose

Tokyo 0.52mSv/2011
Kyoto 0.25mSv/2011

A pilot for European route:
2mSv/y

Figure 5.3 Implementation of the focus group communication.

Source: made by author based on Niiyama *et al.* (2015a) and "Scientific Information in the Second-Round Communication".

In order to know the state of radiation exposure in the area, the estimated total exposure dose combined with internal exposure from food, water, air and external exposure to body surface in 2011 is shown in Figure 5.3. It was evaluated as 0.52 mSv in Tokyo and 0.25 mSv in Kyoto. For comparison, Figure 5.3 shows the dose of natural radiation that pilots taking the European route will be additionally exposed to in one year (it is 2 mSv/y). These figures were included in the scientific information presented to the participants.

Participant recruitment was conducted by Nihon Research Center Co., Ltd, excluding those involved in radioactive materials and nuclear power plants.

A team of experts consisted of the examiners (including the author) in the areas of risk communication from Kyoto University, cooperative researchers in the area of radiobiology from the National Institute of Radiological Sciences (Dr Makoto Akashi) and mechanical engineering from Kansai University (Dr Mamoru Ozawa) and Consumer Affairs Agency personnel.

Questions of participating citizens and providing scientific information to respond to them

Table 5.3 shows the contents of scientific information prepared for the first round of communication, which includes the following topics: "The accident at the Fukushima Daiichi plant", "Effects of radioactive substances on the human

Table 5.3 Scientific information in the first-round communication

1 The accident at Fukushima Daiichi nuclear power plant	• <u>Functions of nuclear reactor</u> • The background of hydrogen explosion
2 Effects of radioactive substances on the human body	*1) Radiation in everyday life* <ul><li><u>Radiation received from the natural world</u></li><li>Radiation exposure from medical exams and procedures</li></ul>*2) Variety and disposition of radiation* *3) Effects of radiation on the human body* <ul><li>Deterministic effect and stochastic effect of radiation</li><li><u>Threshold for deterministic effect/acute disorder</u></li><li><u>Radiation-induced DNA damage and DNA repair</u></li><li>Stochastic effect and increase of cancer death rate</li></ul>
3 Effects of radioactive substances in food on the human body and the regulatory standards	• The rationale of regulation standards • Physical half-life, biological half-life and radiation dose estimate

Source: made by author based on Niiyama *et al.* (2015a).

Note
The underlines show new knowledge for participants.

body" and "Effects of via food on the human body and regulatory standards" with 34 pages of slides.

We spent 20 minutes presenting these contents to the participants and then asked them to discuss the given information for about 30 minutes. The topics discussed by the participants were largely identical in all groups.

The participants reported that this was the first time they had received coherent, comprehensive information on the items, functions of the nuclear reactor, radiation received from the natural world, the threshold for deterministic effects, radiation-induced DNA damage and DNA repair.

Many questions, however, were raised during the discussion. Figure 5.4 shows those questions.

With regard to effects on health, the participants first asked what kind of data was used to evaluate the relationship between radiation dose and the occurrence of disease and whether the amount of data observed was sufficient, especially in relation to genetic effects.

The second question was: "Is there really no possibility of delayed effects, although it was explained that these were not found?"

The third question was: "Was there really no increase in accumulated radioactive substances in the body in continuous exposure, although the physical

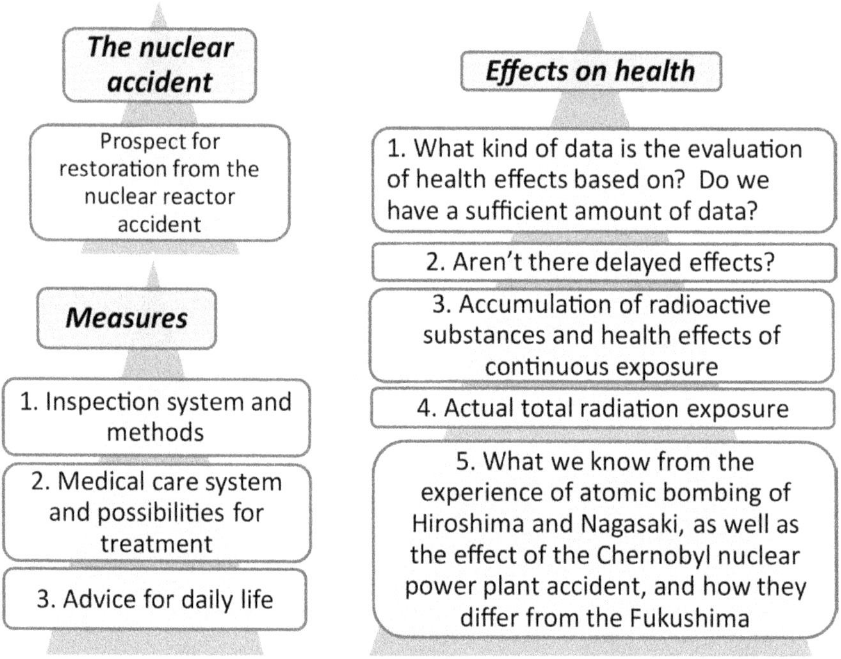

Figure 5.4 Participants' questions in the first-round group discussion.
Source: made by author based on Niiyama *et al.* (2015a).

half-life of radioactive material and its physiological half-life due to external discharge have been explained?"

Fourth, they strongly wanted to know the actual total exposure according to each situation, including not only those through foods but also direct exposure.

Lastly, the participants asked what could be learnt from the experience of past atomic bombings in Hiroshima and Nagasaki and the effect of the Chernobyl accident and how these events differed from the Fukushima accident. The participants requested detailed data on these questions.

They also asked about the inspection system and requested information about the medical care system and aspects of daily life. Furthermore, they asked about prospects for restoration from the nuclear reactor accident.

From this, our team of experts got the impression that they could hardly discriminate between deterministic and stochastic effects.

In order to respond to the above questions, the team of experts prepared further scientific information with 52 slides over a month, and provided in the second round of communication (Table 5.4).

We presented the information to the participants for 30 minutes and asked them to discuss it for approximately 60 minutes.

Table 5.4 Scientific information in the second-round communication

1 Radiation epidemiology data	• Chernobyl Nuclear Power Plant accident survivors, Mayak Nuclear Plant workers • Survivors of atomic bombings of Hiroshima and Nagasaki
2 Effects of radioactive substances (RS) on the human body	*1) Manifestation of the impact – especially stochastic and genetic effects* (1) Radiation effects on human body (2) Repair of DNA damage caused by radiation (3) Probabilistic effects of radiation (4) Increase in cases of radiation cancer (5) Increase in the mortality rates of cancer by 100 mSv radiation exposure (6) Effect on, and threshold dose for, the foetus (7) Genetic effects of radiation (effects not found in past epidemiological studies) *2) Total exposure dosage and cumulative dosage from RS* (1) Natural background radiation per year, radiation humans are exposed to, main absorption route of RS into crops, half-life of radiation entering the body, decay of RS by the effective half-life, calculation of the amount of radiation, survey of environmental radioactivity level (2) Estimation method (e.g. total radiation dose per year)
3 Past Cases	*1) Health effects of the atomic bombs on Hiroshima and Nagasaki* (1) Relationship between distance from the hypocentre and radiation doses (2) Estimated number of deaths and injuries, early and delayed effects *2) Damage caused by the Chernobyl Nuclear Power Plant accident* (1) Comparison with the Chernobyl Nuclear Power Plant accident (2) Actual damage reported after Chernobyl
4 Inspection System and Decontamination Method	(1) Views on inspection system (2) Measurement and analysis methods (3) Inspection agencies and items subject to inspection (4) Plan and implementation of inspecting radioactive substances in food (5) Mechanism of caesium removal (6) Method for removing radioactive substances in food

Source: made by author based on Niiyama *et al.* (2015a).

Acceptance of participants, changes in knowledge and risk perception

After the second-round discussion, as a result of asking the participants what they could understand via a questionnaire survey of free description, the majority stated the following opinions: "The information responding to the questions at first-round discussion promoted my understanding" or "The systematic detailed date, numerical values and graphs helped deepen my understanding". We make no mistake in thinking that this opinion shows that this model is acceptable to them.

As mentioned in the explanation of this model, there is no intention to improve knowledge and risk perception, but it is meaningful to confirm what kind of change has occurred in the participants. This will be considered based on the results of the questionnaire survey carried out before the first round of discussion and after the second round of discussion.

Public knowledge of risk is limited because of the information environment. On the health risks of radioactive substances, under conditions of high anxiety and distrust in the government, the public has gathered information available to them as individuals. Accordingly, they have formed strong beliefs about the events based on this information and demonstrate a lack of knowledge about information they could not obtain.

Before the first-round discussion, major items of low levels of the participant knowledge were as follows: natural radiation exposure, mechanisms of health effects and regulatory measures and inspections. Aspects of the health effect mechanisms not known were as follows: the threshold for deterministic effects, DNA repair at the time of low dose exposure, cancer development triggered by faulty DNA repair and the physical and biological half-life of radioactive substances. As shown in Figure 5.5, these missing items of knowledge were acquired after the second round of discussion.

The participant estimations of risk dimensions for health effects of radioactive substances via foods released after the Fukushima Daiichi accident of 2011 are shown in Figure 5.6. Before the first-round discussion, high response rates were found for "fatal and leading to death",[7] "the negative health effects occur at later time", "leading to illnesses", "stored in the body", "difficult to identify" and "cannot trust government regulatory measures". After the second-round discussion, as Figure 5.6 indicates, the ratings on the severity of health effects declined by approximately one point. This suggests that the change corresponded to the shift in knowledge level. The figure also shows a shift in participants' trust in government regulatory measures from negative to neutral.

These changes resulted in a one-point decline from 7.4 in the mean rating of the magnitude of perceived risks. We believe this is a significant change. However, it is an important fact that the ratings remained unchanged or increased for some participants (Figure 5.7). This finding shows the significance of accepting the diversity of public information processing. Even if people participate in the same discussion by using the same scientific information, that people may handle that information differently ought to be considered.

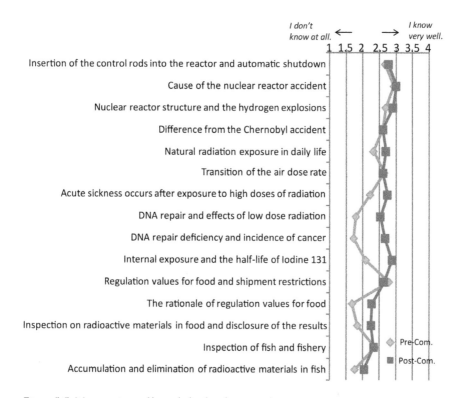

Figure 5.5 Mean ratings of knowledge level: pre- and post-communication.

Source: made by author based on Niiyama *et al.* (2015a). Questionnaire surveys of subjects who attended both sessions (10 males and 21 females in Kanto; 13 females in Kansai).

Scrutinizing scientific information of participants in the horizontal discussion

These changes are the result of the horizontal discussion by the participants themselves: that is, careful examination of scientific information in the two rounds of the group discussion. This finding was verified through the process of group discussion.

For a characteristic example of participant judgements on scientific information according to the free description survey following the first round of discussion, participants who stated that "the current human intake due to the accident does not have much impact on the human body" were roughly one-quarter. Since this communication model did not aim at persuasion, any evaluation concerning the safety of the current state was not mentioned in the provided scientific information at all. Therefore, the participant statements reflected only their own judgements based on the information (Niiyama 2012; Niiyama *et al.* 2015a).

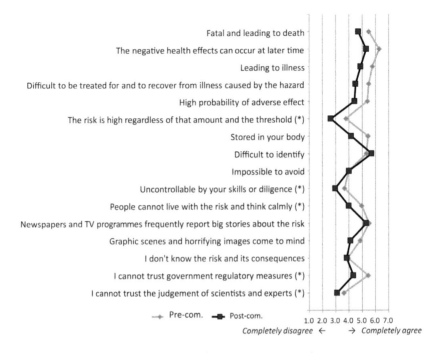

Figure 5.6 Mean ratings of risk/hazard characteristics: pre- and post-communication.

Source: made by author based on Niiyama *et al.* (2015a). Questionnaire surveys of subjects who attended both sessions (10 males and 21 females in Kanto; 13 females in Kansai).

Note
The items marked with asterisks are converted into to a negative notion question.

However, this decision was not made smoothly. In the discussion, when the participants examined scientific information, they took up each of its important parts one by one and checked it while returning back and forth many times in light of the wondered facts about received information from the media and of the questions they had posed themselves over their lives. The opinion was not uniform at that time (Niiyama 2012). Following such process, reviewing scientific information from various aspects progressed.

In the actual discussion, it was repeatedly examined as "slightly relieved" → "doubtful" → "full of unknown things" → "I think it is correct but still uneasy" as follows (Niiyama 2012). The sentence following the # symbol shows a summarizing protocol data of a part of the first-round discussion of one focus group in chronological order. The text in [ ] is by the author.

#1   [A little relieved] Looking at the explanation of regulation standards, it seems that we will not eat the reference amount in reality.

#2   [Doubtful] How large will be the amount from eating and from exposure to the body altogether?

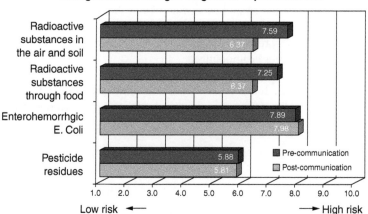

Change in mean rating of magnitude of perceived risk

Radioactive substances in the air and soil: 7.59 (Pre-communication), 6.37 (Post-communication)

Radioactive substances through food: 7.25 (Pre-communication), 6.37 (Post-communication)

Enterohemorrhgic E. Coli: 7.89 (Pre-communication), 7.98 (Post-communication)

Pesticide residues: 5.88 (Pre-communication), 5.81 (Post-communication)

Low risk ← → High risk

Number of participants whose perceived risk scores have risen/decreased

	Number of participants					
	have decreased		no change	have risen		total
	<−3	−1, −2	0	+1, +2	+3<	
Radioactive substances through food	9	15	7	8	4	43
Radioactive substances in the air and soil	12	15	8	5	3	43

Figure 5.7 Magnitude of perceived risks: pre- and post-communication.

Source: made by author based on Niiyama *et al.* (2015a). Questionnaire surveys of subjects who attended both sessions (10 males and 21 females in Kanto; 13 females in Kansai).

#3 [Doubtful] It is better to not take contaminated food. Consideration of various things in our daily lives is necessary (cannot let children play outside, must use the shower when going home and have to be cautious about bathing, water, food and so on). How long do we have to keep doing these things?

#4 [Question] It is full of things we do not understand even when checking this information (reasons for the difference between infants and young children with effective dose factors and no information about fish and shellfish, fish paste/solidified paste made with minced fish, seaweed, and clam dug or swimming in the sea).

#5 [Criticism] When we look at the government and TEPCO's correspondence, we do not really know that what they are saying is true.

#6 [Relieved] We think this information is correct, but still we feel uneasy.

#7 [Doubtful] As most experts are right, we are relieved, but another expert denies it. So, even this information does not seem to be okay.

#8 [Doubtful] With reference to inspections, which part is examined in which way? Facing the report of inspection results, we feel safe with

　　　regard to the inspected parts, on the other hand we have come to feel
　　　uneasy about the uninspected parts.

＃9　[Doubtful] What should we buy and what should we make for meals?
　　　Going shopping is not fun. I am frustrated by having to act in accord-
　　　ance with only reported information. It may be that the truth is found
　　　later. It may not be announced.

For the influence on the human body, the participants acquired certain judgements based on scientific information, but on the other hand, also noticed some
new content to think about as follows.

＃11　[A little relieved] (Looking at the information showing the exposed
　　　dose and the period until onset of typical diseases, deterministic influ-
　　　ence when exposed to a large dose) If we can get such numbers prop-
　　　erly, we can feel a little bit relieved.

＃13　[Relieved] When the exposure is 100 mSv or less per year, no physical
　　　dysfunction of the body occurs. When the food contamination of
　　　radioactive substances is below the reference value, accumulation will
　　　be limited to under 5 mSv per year. Not much influence has been
　　　found from food. There is no need to be over-sensitive. But, if facing
　　　something that is not trusted, everything becomes frightening.

＃14　[Question] How much is the external exposure dose?

＃15　[Question] To what extent is the survey of vegetable contamination
　　　done? How well does the government recognize and report on the
　　　extent of pollution?

＃16　[Turning back] Hearing a rumour of worker exposure, I cannot trust
　　　the figure: There is no effect if it is less than 100 mSv.

＃17　[Question] For radioactive substances, which function with a half-life,
　　　becoming zero is not possible. When radiation exposure continues
　　　even at low doses, accumulation in the body surely increases? It is
　　　better not to eat.

＃18　[Relieved and doubtful] Taking this information, there seems to be
　　　little effect on health. However, not all fields can be examined. The
　　　fact that mistakenly shipped shipments were withdrawn is there. I do
　　　not know how to believe it.

＃19　[Question] What was the radiation dose of the Hiroshima and Naga-
　　　saki atomic bomb and its impact? We want information that can be
　　　studied compared to this accident.

＃20　[Strong doubt] Media are competing for audience ratings, which just
　　　had the effect of arousing public anxiety. We want a route to obtain
　　　exact reliable information from experts. We want to know, so we are
　　　seeing various kinds of news. However, the more we see it, the less
　　　trustworthy it is and the more we feel we do not understand.

＃21　[Question] In the case of onset, what kind of treatment is available?
　　　A bit of anxiety disappears.

The process of reviewing and evaluating information iteratively in the light of these various elements as seen in the group discussion is considered to be the thinking method itself through which people obtain recognition through information. Scientists also carefully examine risk from various viewpoints when conducting risk assessment. The process of information evaluation through such a scrutineering process is considered to be an indispensable element in order for people to acquire the knowledge based on scientific information and to ease anxiety as much as possible.

Conclusion

We confirmed that all stakeholders, including citizens, are decision makers in the risk management process and ensured that we emphasized interactive risk communication. We also confirmed the characteristics of the human risk perception process.

Based on this, from the search for the interactive risk communication model and the result of its implementation, we found that the following elements are required for emergency risk communication. First, providing scientific information that responds to citizens' questions and sufficiently detailed data and information that allows citizens to closely examine and judge the situation by themselves. Second, providing a stage for discussion that enables people to scrutinize scientific information independently in their own style. Despite the fact that scientific knowledge is necessary, systematic and sufficient scientific information was not provided before the accident, so if it is more strongly dependent on affective association, the model is effective.[8] It can also be applied to cases for individual choice and agreement formation.

We accept the following four items of basic scientific information, summarized from Tables 5.4 and 5.5 regarding the health effects of radioactive substances and believe that they can be applied to various emergency situations: first, the root cause of disaster and prospects for resolution; second, the basic and detailed data and information for estimates of health effect, especially physiological mechanisms; third, the actual conditions of contamination and exposure as per the distance and sensitivity of each person; fourth, response measures and implementation against these problems, including enabled measures by individuals.

We can expect that various communication methods will be developed according to their purposes and situations. We need more experience and further research to better develop them.

Notes

1 This study was conducted with Grant-in-Aid for Scientific Research (S) "Risk Perception and Risk Communication, and the Establishment of Food and Agricultural Ethics/Profession" (Representative: Yoko Niiyama) and as delegated research of Consumer Affairs Agency, Japan. A part of this study was published in the following articles: Niiyama 2012, 2013; Niiyama *et al.* 2013, 2015a.

2 Lundgren and McMakin (1994) assumed three types of communication, consensus, crisis and care, on the other hand, NRC (1989) and Kikkawa (1999) in Japan assumed the situation of social controversy and personal choice.

3 The improved consensus conference in Denmark is notorious as a way to summarize the evaluation of and suggestions for science and technology by citizen participation. In the implementation in Japan, participating citizens discuss together under the progress of the facilitator and at a later date, they carry out the question-and-answer session about it with experts (Kobayashi 2004; Tachikawa and Mikami 2013), so that experts' and citizens' direct dialogue is emphasized. Also, a discussion between citizens, experts and stakeholders (Iizawa 2010) was attempted and facilitators' involvement is also different, so its operation has a wide range. The discussion is continued several times, but since it is done only by the group convoked, broad communication is not secured.

4 This section is based on Niiyama (2012, 2013) and Niiyama *et al.* (2013, 2015a).

5 Since the role of the facilitator is to coordinate the discussion smoothly, it is incompatible with the style of coming back and forth while affirming or denying and fully discussing the scientific information provided. Also, as the facilitator advances discussions while organizing topics, for the participants, it is hard to cope with talking about topics with detailed lines of sight and examining information from various angles. The better the skill, the more the coordination function will be demonstrated in discussion. Furthermore, regarding the skills of the person of the investigation company, in order for the facilitator to function as a neutral coordinator, it is said that he/she needs a lot of training; securing the facilitator is difficult now and it is a barrier for widening communication.

6 This section is based on Niiyama (2012, 2013) and Niiyama *et al.* (2013, 2015a).

7 For acute death due to radiation, it is said that 50 per cent of people died with a marrow dose of 2.9–3.3 Gy (= 2,900–3,300 mSv). For acute disorders, cataracts, there are threshold values of exposure dose (below which there are no symptoms). For cataracts it is 1.5 Gy (1.5 Sv). Deformity (effect on the foetus) is a threshold dose of 0.1 Gy (100 mSv), 0.12–0.2 Gy (120–200 mSv) when exposed in the body during organogenesis and organ completion. Based on the information on the special distribution applicant (for pregnant women) at the time, 90 per cent or more of pregnant women in Hiroshima and Nagasaki city were confirmed and investigated. Genetic influences have not been found in epidemiological surveys targeting children of atomic bomb survivors (median exposure doses of the parents are about 140 mSv). The above are based on the Radiation Effects Research Institute (2008), for genetics in addition to Nakamura (2006).

8 Even with this model and implementation experiments, it was difficult for participants to understand probabilistic events of risk as follows, so we need to explore improvements. For one, a random health effect, such as cancer development, has multiple potential triggers and a time lag between exposure and response. Another one, reducing the probability of contamination by regulatory measures, such as inspection, achieves an adequate level but does not reduce it to zero.

References

CAC (Codex Alimentarius Commission) (2007) *Working Principles for Risk Analysis for Food Safety for Application by Governments*, Rome: CAC, www.fao.org/3/a-a1550t.pdf [accessed 20 June 2018].

FAO/WHO (1998) "The Application of Risk Communication to Food Standards and Safety Matters". FAO Food and Nutrition Paper 70, Rome: FAO, www.fao.org/docrep/005/x1271e/X1271E00.HTM [accessed 12 June 2018].

FAO/WHO (2006) *Food Safety Risk Analysis: A Guide for National Food Safety Authorities*, Rome: FAO/WHO, www.fao.org/docrep/012/a0822e/a0822e00.htm [accessed 20 June 2018].

FAO/WHO (2016) *Risk Communication Applied to Food Safety: Handbook*, www.fao.org/3/a-i5863e.pdf [accessed 12 June 2018].

FSCJ (Food Safety Commission, Japan 食品安全委員会) (2006) *To Improve Risk Communication Related to Food Safety* 食の安全に関するリスクコミュニケーションの改善に向けて, www.fsc.go.jp/osirase/pc2_ri_arikata_270527.data/riskomiarikata.pdf [accessed 20 June 2018].

FSCJ (Food Safety Commission, Japan 食品安全委員会) (2008) *Guideline on Implementation and Evaluation of Opinion Exchange Meeting* 意見交換会の実施と評価に関するガイドライン, www.fsc.go.jp/senmon/risk/riskcom_guideline.pdf [accessed 20 June 2018].

Harada Hidemi 原田英美 (2007) "A Study on Risk Communication Concept and Problem" リスクコミュニケーションの考え方と課題に関する一考察フードシステム研究, *Journal of Food System Research*, 13 (3).

Iizawa, R. 飯澤理一郎 (2010) *Social Technology Research and Development Project 2010 Report: A Study for Modeling on Interactive Risk Communication by Cooperation of Actors* 社会技術研究開発事業平成 22 年度研究開発報告書：アクターの協働による双方向的リスクコミュニケーションのモデル化研究. https://ristex.jst.go.jp/result/science/interaction/pdf/H22_iizawa_houkokusho.pdf [accessed 20 June 2018].

Kahneman, D. (2012) *Thinking, Fast and Slow*, London: Penguin Books.

Kikkawa, T. 吉川肇子 (1999) *Risk and Communication: Aiming for Mutual Understanding and Better Decision-Making* リスク・コミュニケーション 相互理解とよりよい意思決定をめざして, Tokyo: Fukumura-Syuppan.

Kito, Y., Niiyama, Y. and Kudo, H. (2014) "Structural Models of Japanese Public Perception: Regarding the Risk of Radioactive Substances in Food", SRA 2014 Annual Meeting, 8–11 December, Denver, USA.

Kobayashi, D. 小林傳司 (2004) *Who Is Thinking about Science and Technology: An Experiment Called Consensus Meeting* 誰が科学技術について考えているのか―コンセンサス会議という実験, Nagoya: Nagoya-daigaku-syuppankai.

Lundgren, R. E. and McMakin, A. H. (1994) *Risk Communication: A Handbook for Communicating Environmental, Safety and Health Risks*, Piscataway, NJ: IEEA Press.

Nakamura, N. (2006) "Genetic Effects on Radiation in Atomic-Bomb Survivors and Their Children: Past, Present and Future", *Journal of Radiation Research*, 47 (Suppl): 67–73.

Niiyama, Y. 新山陽子 (2012) "The Public Psychology and an Interactive Risk Communication on Effects of Radiation Contamination of Food on Health: Scrutinizing Information Necessary for Acquisition of Knowledge" 放射性物質の健康影響に対する市民の心理と双方向で密なリスクコミュニケーション―知識の獲得に必要な精緻な情報吟味プロセス―, *Journal of Rural Problems*農林業問題研究, 48 (3): 346–354.

Niiyama, Y. (2013) "Applying an Interactive Model to Risk Communication: Effects of Radiation-Contaminated Food on Health", in *Japan-Canada Food Systems Resilience Symposium Conference Proceedings*, Toronto, 16–17 May 2012, Keynote Speech, pp. 36–48.

Niiyama, Y. 新山陽子, Hosono, H. 細野ひろみ, Kawamura, R. 河村律子, Kiyohara, A. 清原昭子, Kudo, H. 工藤春代, Kito, Y. 鬼頭弥生 and Tanaka, K. 田中敬子 (2011a) "Re-investigating the Factors Affecting Public Perception of Food-Related Risk: A Cross-national Studies by Laddering Method" 食品由来リスクの認知要因の再検

討－ラダリング法による国際研究－, *Journal of Rural Economics* 農業経済研究, 82 (4): 230–242.

Niiyama, Y. 新山陽子, Kito, Y. 鬼頭弥生, Hosono, H. 細野ひろみ, Kawamura, R. 河村 律子, Kudo, H. 工藤春代 and Kiyohara, A. 清原昭子 (2011b) "The Structural Models of Public Risk Perception of Typical Food-Related Hazards: An Analysis of the Structural Complexity of Incorporated Factors by SEM" 食品由来のハザード別にみ たリスク知覚構造モデル－SEMによる諸要因の複雑な連結状態の解析－, *Japanese Journal of Risk Analysis* 日本リスク研究学会誌, 21 (4): 295–306.

Niiyama, Y., Kito, Y. and Kudo, H. (2013) "An Experimental Interactive Risk Communication on the Health Effects of Radioactive Substances in Food", in S. Ikeda and Y. Maeda (eds), *Emerging Issues Learned from the 3.11 Disaster as Multiple Events of Earthquake, Tsunami and Fukushima Nuclear Accident*, Tokyo: The Committee of the Great East Japan Disaster, Society for Risk Analysis – Japan, pp. 54–58.

Niiyama, Y. 新山陽子, Kito, Y. 鬼頭弥生, Kudo, H. 工藤春代 and Matuo, K. 松尾敬子 (2015a) "An Interactive Risk Communication Model Based on Horizontal Discussion by Citizens and Examination of it through Focus Group Communication: Elaborate Information Processing on Health Effects by Radioactive Substances in Food" 市民の 水平的議論を基礎にした双方向リスクコ　ミュニケーションモデルとフォーカ スグループによる検証－食品を介した放射性物質の健康影　響に関する精緻な 情報吟味－, *Journal of Food System Research* フードシステム研究, 21 (4): 267–286.

Niiyama, Y., Kito, Y. and Kudo, H (2015b) "'Evoking Image' Factor for Public Risk Perception of Radioactive Substances in Food", World Congress on Risk 2015, 19–23 July, Singapore.

NRC: National Research Council (1989) *Improving Risk Communication*, Washington DC: National Academy Press.

Radiation Effects Research Institute (2008) *Handbook 2008*, Hiroshima, Japan.

Rohrmann, B, and Renn, O. (2000) "Risk Perception Research: An Introduction", in O. Renn and B. Rohrmann (eds), *Cross-Cultural Risk Perception: A Survey of Empirical Studies*, Dordrecht: Kluwer Academic Publishers, pp. 11–53.

Slovic, P. (1999) "Trust, Emotion, Sex, Politics, and Science: Surveying the Risk-Assessment Battlefield", *Risk Analysis*, 19 (4): 689–701.

Slovic, P., Finucane, M. L., Peters, E. and MacGregor, D. G. (2004) "Risk as Analysis and Risk as Feelings: Some Thoughts about Affect, Reason, Risk and Rationality", *Risk Analysis*, 24 (2): 311–322.

Stanovich, K. E. and West, R. F. (2000) "Individual Differences in Reasoning: Implications for the Rationality Debate?" *Behav Brain Sci*, 23 (5): 645–665.

Tachikawa, M. 立川雅司 and Mikami, N. 三上直之 (2013) *Sprout Science Technology and Citizens: Questions from Food Nanotechnology* 萌芽的科学技術と市民-フードナ ノテクからの問い, Tokyo: Nihon-keizai-hyoron-sya.

Tsuchiya, T. 土屋智子, Taniguchi, T. 谷口武俊, Kosugi, M. 小杉素子, Onodera, S. 小 野寺節雄, Takemura, K. 竹村和久, Tatewaki, O. 帯刀治, Nakamura, H. 中村博文, Yonezawa, R. 米沢理加 and Morioka, T. 盛岡通 (2009) "The Differing Points of View between Citizens and Experts on Risk Management of Nuclear Facilities: An Analysis of the Risk Communication Activity in Tokai, Japan" 市民と専門家の原子 力安全に対する視点の違い－東海村におけるリスクコミュニケーション活動の 実践から－, *Syakaigijutsu-ronbunsyu* 社会技術研究論文集, 6: 16–25.

Yagi, E., Takahashi, M. and Kitamura, M. (2007) "Clarification of Nuclear Risk Recognition Scheme through Dialogue Forum", *Transactions of the Atomic Energy Society of Japan*, 6 (2): 126–140.

6 The private–public complementary relationship for managing catastrophic risk in egg production and marketing in Japan

Michitoshi Yamaguchi

Introduction

In early 2004, the first epidemic of avian influenza in 79 years struck Japan. In that incident, one egg producer[1] hid the case from the authorities, which caused the spread of additional infection. Subsequently, all eggs and chickens within a 30-kilometre radius of the infected farms remained unshipped for at least one month. Even though a reliable monetary estimate is not available, this caused considerable economic loss. The culpable producer was prosecuted and eventually left his business.

In court, he said, "My company would go bankrupt if I disclosed the disease." This seems a somewhat odd comment because highly pathogenic avian influenza (HPAI) is a highly contagious and fatal disease for poultry, so it is hard to believe that an outbreak could be hidden, let alone the disposal of millions of dead hens. It cannot be hidden and he should have known that. Nevertheless, he gambled against great odds to save his business.

Why would his business go bankrupt under truthful disclosure of the disease? The possible reasons he perceived behind his misbehaviour can be identified as follows: a disproportionate quarantine scheme, harsh competition in the egg industry and insufficient compensation. First, the HPAI virus strain H5N1 became well known after a 1997 outbreak in Hong Kong. It could become the primary source of the next pandemic human influenza, which made quarantine policies at that time disproportionately stringent.

Second, supermarkets, the major egg retailers in Japan, consider eggs to be must-have items on their shelves to attract consumers. On the other hand, egg storage has become increasingly difficult because of the demand for fresher eggs. A brief cessation of egg shipments could incite supermarkets to change their egg suppliers or at least have second thoughts about continuing to do business with them. Anticipating a strict eradication process on one hand, and a switch in egg transaction on the other, might induce egg producers to hesitate about notifying the authorities immediately regarding the disease. However, and lastly, even if the consequential loss of business under compliance were significant, sufficient compensation for complying with strict eradication processes might encourage notification by producers, which could be justified from a public health perspective. In fact, though there were indemnity payments for culled animals, it was perceived as insufficient to continue to be in business.

Actually, as shown in the theoretical part of this chapter, sufficient public compensation cannot be justified from a theoretical perspective either. Immediate disease notification is still, of course, key for animal health, particularly in the case of a contagious animal disease such as the avian influenza. In the recent highly industrialized livestock production system, hygiene control is essential for business viability. Then disease transmitters should be kept away from livestock premises as far as possible. Even an inspector of the authority cannot enter the henhouse frequently because of the risk of disease transmission. So a "command and control" approach to contagious animal disease control is becoming increasingly difficult. That is, mandatory notification of the disease depends more or less on the voluntary action from the owner of the private information about the health of his animal. Under the impossibility of sufficient public compensation, a complementary loss reduction plan for infected sites is highly demanded. In the descriptive part of this chapter, a case study of such a practice in Japan is introduced.

Overview of the egg food system in Japan

In Japan, the number of laying hens per farm has grown rapidly. One reason is that animal welfare is not so popular in Japan, and battery cages are still dominant in Japanese egg laying facilities. In 2003, just before the avian influenza outbreak, 137.3 million laying chickens were kept by 4,340 farms, which works out at 31,600 hens per farm[2] (MAFF 2004). This average figure does not necessarily reflect the true nature of the industry, because 80–90 per cent of egg producers maintained more than 200,000 hens, corresponding to one large 10-tonne cargo truck a day. Shipments of this size qualified such producers to be regular trade partners of large wholesalers (Norinchukin Research Institute 2001).

The scale of egg production now is larger than ever before, and some wholesale processes such as grading and packing are often integrated into egg producing. One reason for this integration is that the production scale becomes large enough to meet the optimal scale of packing facilities; the other reason is to keep the egg fresh for as long as possible, which is demanded by Japanese consumers, who consider that eggs can be eaten raw. Wholesalers remain major trading partners of egg producers, and supermarkets are important customers for them. Supermarkets apply their own hygiene standards to suppliers, and therefore, they purchase eggs continuously from the same qualified producers through certain wholesalers. Table eggs are roughly classified into two categories: generic and specialized. Some of the nutrients such as vitamins are added to chicken feed to produce specialized eggs, which are branded thus. However, generic eggs can also be branded, and they tend to be traded continuously with same dyad relationships of egg producer and supermarket, rather than spot market.

Ten eggs per carton is the most popular egg package size in Japanese supermarkets, and even though eggs are treated as a fresh product, they tend to be bought over the weekend rather than on a daily basis. On the supply side, a single hen can lay at most one egg in one day. To supply fresh eggs on weekends, supermarkets discount egg prices one weekday each week (called "bargain day"), which clears the egg surplus before the weekend. Under pressure for freshness, policies such as the day-0-egg policy are followed, whereby eggs are delivered to a supermarket's shelf the day they are laid, eggs are usually overproduced to meet peak demand in supermarkets for the freshest eggs.

The animal health and trade situation in Japan

Animal health has a major impact on human infectious diseases. Many emerging diseases can be traced back to zoonosis, and the abuse of antimicrobial drugs in treating livestock is thought to be the major source of antimicrobial resistance. However, for listed diseases by Office International des Epizooties (OIE), including avian influenza, it is important to maintain the disease-free status not just because of animal health and public health, but because of economic concerns, too. Japan is not a major livestock-exporting country; however, a high-value product such as Wagyu (Japanese beef) needs a foreign market because of the ageing and shrinking domestic market. Japan having a disease-free status is important for exports of Japanese products. Moreover, because Japan is a major importer of livestock and livestock products, animal health concerns can be a legal trade barrier, protecting domestic producers under the Sanitary and Phytosanitary (SPS) agreement of the World Trade Organization (WTO).

For any country to be certified as disease-free for an avian influenza, vaccination is not allowed before outbreak. The possible options for keeping poultry farms virus-free are limited to activities such as hand washing, wearing disposable clothes, cleaning and disinfecting equipment and shutting out possible reservoirs such as wild birds or small ruminants from poultry houses. Even though emergency vaccinations are prepared, strict stamping out and quarantine policies are the first options that are adopted in the event of an outbreak. These actions are indispensable in keeping the virus out of farms. But for farmers, they are less cost-effective than vaccination.[3]

Theoretical analysis of public compensation for contagious animal diseases

Public compensation for a stamping-out policy in the case of animal disease outbreaks can be thought of as a means to encourage immediate notification. Conversely, this system could backfire if farmers know in advance that sufficient compensation is forthcoming when diseases occur. In economics, this problem is called a moral hazard. Kuchler and Hamm identified that in the US, notifying regarding animal disease by a farmer was indemnity-elastic (Kuchler and Hamm 2000). This suggests that farmers' efforts to prevent animal diseases are also indemnity-elastic but in the opposite direction. This does not necessarily mean that sufficient compensation encourages farmers to risk their livestock. However, we cannot expect the same level of effort without compensation. Therefore, the design of public compensation for culled animals should be balanced between encouraging early notification and discouraging a moral hazard.

A seminal paper in this field (Gramig *et al.* 2009) employs contract theory regarding this problem. The disease status of livestock is private information for a farmer, and for truthful disclosure, the adverse selection model in contract theory applies to the "hidden knowledge" side of the problem. Then, the moral hazard model in contract theory applies to the "hidden action" side of the problem, i.e. encouraging disease prevention. However, Gramig's model ignores limited liability constraints and assumes that no limit exists for fines imposed on farmers who hide the onset of diseases. In reality, though, fines that exceed farmers' payment ability do not provide additional incentives for disclosure. Therefore, we have developed a simple static model of indemnity design with limited liability constraints.

The model description[4]

Farmers choose the level of biosecurity *ex ante*, and they choose whether to report a disease to the authorities after the outbreak of the disease. In concrete terms, disease probability p has two levels, where p is defined as a function of farmers' efforts regarding keeping the virus out of their farm, namely, b_l and b_h (assuming $b_l < b_h$ and $p(b_l) > p(b_h)$). Once a disease breaks out at probability $p(.)$, farmers choose either to report it or not. If they report the disease, they incur loss L from culling their livestock and other disinfecting efforts while obtaining an indemnity payment t from the government. Conversely, if they hide the disease and if it is detected by the authorities at probability q, then they are fined f in addition to L. If not detected, the loss l is defined to be smaller than L ($l < L$), which reflects a possibly softer treatment than that in a public eradication policy. The game tree is depicted in Figure 6.1.

In the latter half of the model, the problem for the government is to choose optimal t and f, which induce truthful disclosure. The game tree is depicted in Figure 6.2. Omitting a mixed strategy for simplicity and assuming that truthful disclosure is always socially desirable, a fine f is never imposed; hence, "optimal" means minimizing the sum of t and farmers' subjective cost for the risk. Key model variables are summarized in Table 6.1.

Analysis of the model

A farmer's Bernoulli utility function is denoted by u with the assumption that $u' > 0$. Then, the farmer's expected utility under truthful disclosure U^R is represented as follows:

$$U^R = (1-p)\, u(0) + pu\, (t-L).$$

Effort on biosecurity by poultry farmer

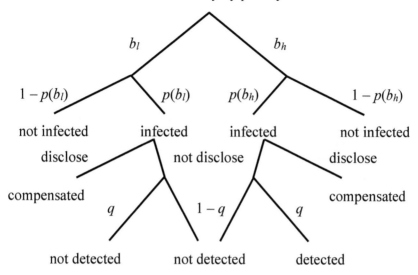

Figure 6.1 A game tree of the whole model.

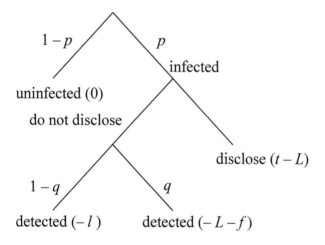

Figure 6.2 A game tree for an adverse selection part of the model (farmers' payoffs).

Similarly, a farmer's expected utility if hiding the case U^{NR} is as follows:

$$U^{NR} = (1-p)\, u(0) + p\, [qu\, (-L-f) + (1-q)\, u(-l)].$$

Hence, the incentive compatibility condition $U^R > U^{NR}$ is as follows:

$$u\, (t-L) > qu\, (-L-f) + (1-q)\, u(-l).$$

Table 6.1 Model variables

Variable	Description
p	Probability of disease onset
b_l	Lower biosecurity effort by farmer
b_h	Higher biosecurity effort by farmer
L	Economic loss for farmer under strict eradication process when disease outbreaks
l	Economic loss for farmer under "soft" eradication process when disease outbreaks
t	Indemnity payment from government to farmer for culled livestock
q	Probability for authority to detect deceive by farmer
f	Fines imposed on deceive

Let us assume that the above equation holds true in equality and not in inequality; taking the total derivative, we get the following:

$$df/dt = -u'(t-L)/qu'(-L-f) < 0.$$

This represents the slope of the frontier if the incentive compatibility condition holds true. In the $f-t$ plane, the intercept on the f axis of the frontier can be derived as $(1-q)(L-l)/q$. If f can be set above this value, truthful disclosure can be achieved without any compensation (see Figure 6.3). It takes a larger value in any or all of the following cases: when it is difficult for authorities to detect the disease (small q), the loss under a strict eradication process is high (large L) and when the loss under looser treatment is low (small l). Even if q were to be high,

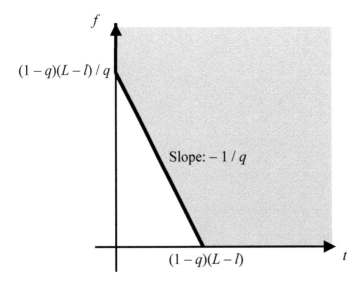

Figure 6.3 The $f-t$ plane satisfying incentive compatibility (shaded region).

because of high pathogenicity in the case of HPAI, a farmer's perceived q is not necessarily high, in which case this value grows. In these cases, it is not plausible that f can be set without an upper bound. Therefore, we define f_u as the upper bound for the fine that can be paid by a farmer (Figure 6.4). By definition, $f_u < (1-q)$ $(L-l)/q$. Then, the optimal f is f_u, and the optimal t is as follows:

$$t = -qf_u + (1-q)\,(L-l).$$

If farmers are risk averse ($u'' < 0$) as assumed in most cases, t on the frontier is not necessarily optimal because of farmers' subjective cost from the risk. Rather, it can be understood as a lower bound for a feasible t.[5]

The former part of the model, i.e. the moral hazard regarding *ex ante* choice of an effort, is depicted as follows. Two effort levels are chosen by a farmer as described above, and their costs are denoted by $c(.)$. We assume that the cost of more effort is higher, namely, $c(b_h) > c(b_l)$. We also assume that a farmer's utility function regarding these costs is additive and separable. The authorities cannot directly observe a farmer's effort; hence, b is a farmer's private information. In the following, incentive compatibility for truth disclosure is assumed to hold true.

A farmer chooses b_h rather than b_l in the following case under the conditions of truthful disclosure:

$$(1-p(b_h))\,u(0) + p(b_h)\,u(t-L) - c(b_h) > (1-p(b_l))\,u(0) + p(b_l)\,u(t-L) - c(b_l).$$

It can be rearranged as follows:

$$u(0) - u(t-L) > [c(b_h) - c(b_l)]/[p(b_l) - p(b_h)] > 0.$$

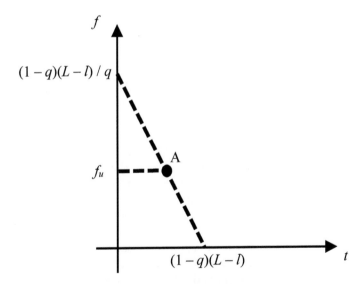

Figure 6.4 Optimal f and t with a liability constraint (point A).

The left-hand side of the first inequality is the utility difference between compensation and the status quo. The right-hand side can be interpreted as the inverse of the effort's cost-effective ratio for reducing the probability of disease. Therefore, this condition means that the higher this cost-effective ratio, the lower the right-hand side of the first inequality of the above condition, so it can be permitted that the difference of the utility between compensated and status quo is small. This means that the indemnity payment required to induce b_h can be large. Conversely, if the cost-effectiveness of an effort is low, then the indemnity payment should be small to induce high effort. According to Japanese quarantine guidelines, for Japan to remain disease-free, vaccination for avian influenza cannot be allowed. This means that only very limited measures are available to keep the virus out of the farm, such as the disinfection of hands and shoes when entering poultry houses. Whether this holds true or not, these measures are often perceived by farmers to be less cost-effective. It turns out that the upper bound for indemnity payments t in this case is so small that this upper bound might even be lower than the lower bound we have just derived in the latter part of the model, i.e. the adverse selection. In this case, no optimal t can exist for any value function. Put differently, we cannot compensate the farmer for truthful disclosure without slackening the effort, or we risk truthful disclosure.

Theoretical analysis above shows that the public compensation for culled animal alone cannot induce farmers' optimal decision from the public health point of view. This conclusion still holds true if the loss of business and its compensation are included in the model.[6]

Descriptive analysis of private safeguards in egg marketing[7]

As stated previously, supermarkets are important customers for egg producers, even though they may not be the direct trade partner. Eggs are popular bargain items that attract Japanese consumers. An egg shortage in stores means that they (supermarkets) lose the opportunity to sell other grocery items to consumers who visit them for the bargain eggs, so it should be avoided. When poultry diseases such as an avian influenza occur, egg shipments are banned for a certain period, which may cause supermarkets to switch their egg suppliers through wholesalers. Egg producers' losses from losing customers are so large that they cannot be compensated for by the indemnity payments analysed above.

Avoiding such consequential loss of business is essential not only for private business continuity, but for a high level of animal and public health with adequate compliance in the case of disease outbreak. For that purpose, some business continuity plan other than public indemnity payment is indispensable. The requirements for such plan include, as stated in the previous section, keep the input of farmers' effort at a high level. It turned out that a private alliance of egg producers for marketing purposes served as the possible business continuity plan during the avian influenza outbreak. The alliance is called the "egg safety net", whereby members ship substitute eggs during the quarantine period.

Two such cases are described below and summarized in Table 6.2.

Table 6.2 Summary of the "egg safety nets"

	Case A	Case B
Organizer	Feed company X	Wholesale company Y
Procedure of substitution	Prescribed in detail	Not thoroughly specified
Team merchandising	No	Yes
Meeting regularly	No	Yes
Egg type	Generic	Quality egg

Case A

The feed company X is the organizer of this egg safety net. In Japan, poultry feed is supplied to egg producers through roughly three routes: farmers' cooperatives; subsidiary feed companies of a general trading company called "Sogo Shosha"; and an independent feed company. X is the only independent feed company in Japan. During the development period of a modern poultry business, feed companies in any route described above wholesale their customers' eggs to secure payment for their feed. Today, feed companies take part in marketing a specialized egg by designing a specialized feed. This feed company X is not integrated into the egg production process, which is outsourced to egg-laying farms and packing stations.

After the first Japanese avian influenza case (in 79 years) in 2004, an egg-laying farm in a quarantine area consulted the feed company X regarding egg shipments. The feed company X arranged a safety net in April 2004 with seven large egg producers to cover all Japanese egg substitutions. The substitution capacity was 150 tonnes per week, which was about 5 per cent of their production. Beneath this nationwide safety net, four regional safety nets were formed, and a system of regulating egg quality standards by region was established. The original seven egg producers chaired each regional net, and there were 50 member farms.[8] Note that this safety net only provisioned generic eggs and not specialized "quality eggs".

The substitute shipping procedure was set as follows. First, a member farm asks the net for egg substitution. Subsequently, the feed company X, serving as the secretary of the net, collects information on other member farms' availability and informs the quarantined farm, which chooses the egg supplier and asks for shipment. While common cases and packs are prepared by each member farm in advance, backup eggs carry the supplier's label. Substituted egg prices are set to the supplier's wholesale price in their region of operation, and payment between farms is in cash. When the quarantine is lifted, egg substitution ends and normal trading resumes as soon as possible.

Member farms are required to explain the "safety net" to their trading partners, supermarkets in particular, and to get consent for substitution in advance. In addition to assuring the quality of eggs used as substitutions, they should get agreement that the supply of eggs to their own customer, i.e. some supermarkets, may be reduced slightly in case they supply the egg substitution to another member farm. The organizer of a safety net only commits to matching and information gathering. Shipping is the responsibility of member farms. This lack of enforcement may be the reason that egg substitution did not work until the 2010 avian influenza outbreak, even though this safety net represented a pioneering alliance after the 2004 outbreak.

To join a safety net, consensus of the existing member farms is required. This provides mutual recognition of hygiene levels and quality control in members' egg production systems, which is a key requirement to avoid the moral hazard problem in case of public compensation.

Case B

This egg safety net was in fact originally formed for marketing specialized "quality eggs" and not for emergency substitution. The organizer of this net was the western Japanese branch of the largest cooperative egg wholesaler Y.

The alliance was first organized in November 2003. Egg prices were very low at the time, and this alliance was formed to market surplus eggs. Member farms agreed to produce eggs under common hygiene standards and unified their feed designs to differentiate their eggs from low-priced generic ones. Because different supermarkets had slightly different quality control criteria, member farms had to establish a common standard that was satisfactory to all their customers. Originally, the major advantage of this alliance as a group was that it could absorb the daily fluctuation in the demand for eggs.

With the first avian influenza outbreak in 2004, one member farm of this alliance was quarantined. That farm was the main supplier of the private branded eggs for some large supermarket Z; those eggs were fully wholesaled by Y, the organizer of this alliance. Since supermarket Z was confident regarding these suppliers' quality standards, the egg trade was not interrupted; interruption could occur only if the process standard of the product was violated. The supermarket Z accepted another branded egg from other member farms within the alliance and resumed purchasing from the quarantined farm after the quarantine was lifted.

From this case, member farms realized that the function of the safety net of this alliance was effective. During negotiations over an item revision or new transaction, the organizer obtained consents from supermarkets for emergency egg substitution from member farms. At the end of 2006, a safety net agreement, incorporating common hygiene standards at farms and packing centres, was negotiated among 11 large farms, amounting to ten million layer chickens in the western part of Japan.

For this safety net, the substitution procedure was not specified in detail in the shared document. The organizer of this net was a wholesale price setter for several regions who knew the egg production schedule of every member farm. This information allowed the organizer to negotiate better with the member farms and supermarkets so that emergency substitution of eggs could be done without a detailed, prescribed procedure. It should be noted that the function of the safety net is to market branded eggs from multiple farms that meet the needs and the requirements of supermarkets. Without the nets, an egg producer's advantageous position alone probably would not be enough to successfully accomplish substitution and the resumption of the egg trade. This safety net is for branded eggs, which are sold in the competitive market for egg producers. To foster trust among branded egg producers, a summit meeting of top executives of egg farms is held three times a year.

Concluding remarks

In 2004, small epidemics of an avian influenza occurred in Japan for the first time in 79 years. One egg producer hid the incident, which eventually led to the infection spreading. Insufficient compensation, which was perceived as jeopardizing the continuation of the producer's egg production business, was one reason why the producer did not reveal the presence of the disease. Eggs are treated as fresh food and are often sold at discounted prices in Japanese supermarkets to attract consumers. Industrialized egg producers usually integrate wholesaling and sell some of their products to supermarkets through wholesalers. Eggs are usually overproduced to meet the demand for "bargain days". When an avian influenza outbreak occurs, egg producers whose livestock is affected by an avian influenza should cull their laying hens in the same location. In addition to this, other producers within the quarantined area also stop shipping eggs to customers. Supermarkets have to purchase eggs from another egg producer to avoid losing consumers, and this overproduction of eggs enables them to do so. Consequently, an egg producer in the quarantined area loses his customers. A public compensation to the infected farm for animal diseases does not cover consequent losses such as losing customers. An insufficient compensation plan can be justified by a simple, static game-theoretical model that combines the concepts of adverse selection and moral hazards. The model also implies that the lower cost-effectiveness of preventive measures against animal disease reduces compensation as is the case with an avian influenza. Given this situation, cooperative egg marketing agreements among large, industrialized egg producers were formed to supply each other's customers in the event of an avian influenza outbreak. This private agreement was successful in the case of "quality eggs".

Quarantine plans during an avian influenza outbreak have been revised to proportionate the risks and losses, shorten the time for egg quarantine and narrow down its area.[9] Egg producers can buy insurance, in addition to the indemnity payment from government, to prepare for losses caused by an influenza outbreak. Moreover, policy options such as cross-compliance might be used to prevent misbehaviour.[10] However, even with the options mentioned above, private–public complementary loss management seems to be important to ensure the compliance with disease eradication programmes.

Notes

1 In this chapter, "egg producer" means "farmer (of raising laying hen)" who integrates some wholesale facilities such as a grading and packing centre.
2 In 2016, these figures reached 173.3 million laying hens and 2,440 farms, or 71,000 hens per farm (MAFF 2016).
3 In Japan, vaccination is a major preventive treatment for many infectious poultry diseases, including Newcastle disease, Marek's disease and infectious bursal disease (IBD).
4 Thorough derivation of the model can be found in the author's book (Yamaguchi 2015: chapter 3). An extended model is developed there, including moral hazards about consequential loss of business after adverse selection of disclosures.
5 In this case, it can be shown that the frontier of incentive compatibility moves to the origin and that its slope becomes less steep. Hence, this lower bound for t lies below $-qf_u + (1-q)(L-l)$.
6 See the reference in note 4.
7 This section is based on interviews with the persons of feed company X, egg wholesaler Y, egg producers in the second case, and supermarket Z. They were the persons in charge of each decision described in this section. The interviews were held in the latter half of 2006 and early 2007.
8 Twelve for Hokkaido and the Northern Tohoku region, nine for the Kanto region, 19 for the Central and Kinki regions and ten for the Western and Kyushu regions.
9 One reason for this revision is that avian influenza is not a matter of food safety in Japan because there is no live bird market and consumers do not come into close contact with infected birds. Quarantine is entirely for preventing the spread of disease.
10 Ten articles of hygiene standards for animal husbandry are required to join the mutual assistance fund. However, these standards were not known by livestock farmers and thus were not complied with in the 2010 foot-and-mouth disease outbreak in Japan.

References

Gramig, B. M., R. D. Horan and C. A. Wolf (2009) "Livestock Disease Indemnity Design When Moral Hazard Is Followed by Adverse Selection", *American Journal of Agricultural Economics*, 91: 627–641.

Kuchler, F. and S. Hamm (2000) "Animal Disease Incidence and Indemnity Eradication Programs", *Agricultural Economics*, 22: 299–308.

Ministry of Agriculture, Forestry and Fishery 農林水産省 (MAFF) (2004) *Statistics of Livestock Industry* 畜産統計, www.e-stat.go.jp/SG1/estat/List.do?lid=000001060043 [accessed 1 April 2017].

Ministry of Agriculture, Forestry and Fishery 農林水産省 (MAFF) (2016) Statistics of Livestock Industry 畜産統計, www.e-stat.go.jp/SG1/estat/List.do?lid=000001160843 [accessed 1 April 2017].

Norinchukin Research Institute 農林中金総合研究所 (2001) *Futures Trading of Domestic Agricultural Products* 国内農産物の先物取引—リスク管理手法としての可能性, Tokyo: Ienohikari Kyokai.

Yamaguchi, M. 山口道利 (2015) *The Economic Analysis of Contagious Animal Disease* 家畜感染症の経済分析, Kyoto: Showado.

7 The rise of a risk-based approach to implementing food safety law in China

Yongkang An

Introduction

In recent years, a risk-based approach to implementing food safety law has drawn increasing attention from government regulators in China. As defined by the former China Food and Drug Administration (CFDA), it is an approach through which food authorities categorize food businesses based on their risk levels. The level of risk is determined by the type of food, the nature and size of the business, and internal food safety management. It is also an approach for optimizing the allocation of regulatory resources through adopting a varied level of oversight based on the level of risk.[1] This approach purports to address the tension between the massive size of the food industry being regulated and the scarce regulatory resources possessed by government food authorities.

This approach has arisen from the policy context that food safety risk causes wide concerns and that risk regulation becomes a key concept in government efforts for addressing these concerns. In the 农产品质量安全法 (Law on Quality and Safety of Agricultural Products 2006), the concepts of risk regulation and risk assessment regarding food safety were introduced for the first time in national legislation. This was followed by the first comprehensive 食品安全法 (Food Safety Law 2009 [FSL]). It requires the government to base the development of food safety standards on risk assessment. In cases of the detection of certain foods posing a high risk to public health, competent food authorities should take measures such as ordering the cessation of its supply and alerting the public.

However, a systematic incorporation of risk-based approaches to implementing food safety law did not happen until 2015. In early 2015, an amendment to the FSL was approved by the national legislative body. It requires competent authorities to determine the measures and frequencies of regulatory intervention according to the risk level of food businesses. Shortly afterwards, the CFDA further clarified this approach. It issued detailed guidelines for the application of this approach in an official document in late 2016, as mentioned in note 1.

Surrounding the topics of food safety risk and risk regulation in China, there has been broad discussion in various dimensions. For instance, researchers have analysed risk assessment (Shen Kui 2011; Qi Jiangang 2012) and risk communication (Wang Guisong 2011; Wang Dianhua *et al.* 2012) and their application in China. In light of the roles of different actors such as government, experts and the public, some researchers have advocated a model of co-governance (Qi Jiangang 2011). From the perspective of consumers, risk perception has been an important topic (Fan Chunmei *et al.* 2012).

Risk-based approaches to monitoring and enforcing the law, however, have been largely neglected. Researchers have noted that the arrangement exempting certain large food corporations from regulatory inspections was rather problematic,[2] because it failed to notice the character of food safety risk and the risk of this measure (Shen Kui 2009). From a legal perspective, Qi argued that the risk-based approach would help with improving the rationality and proportionality of administrative activities. It would also help with relieving the tension between the highly demanding administrative processes and the scarce resources (Qi Jiangang 2013). There is no systematic analysis from the perspective of regulation. Nor is there any close examination of the current practice in China. This chapter will bridge these gaps to some extent. It will examine what the "risk-based" approach has been and what strengths and weaknesses there are in the process of implementing food safety law.

This chapter is arranged as follows. The second section will focus on the relevant theoretical construction by examining the existing research on risk-based regulation conducted in different jurisdictions. The third section will turn to the current rising fashion of a risk-based approach to implementing food safety law in China. In the fourth section, I will examine the findings in the previous sections and highlight some critical issues that are associated with the current practice in China. This will be achieved by observation from a comparative perspective, more specifically, with the framework adopted by the Food Standards Agency (FSA) in the UK. This is because in the UK, there has been considerable experience of applying risk-based approaches to regulation. This chapter will conclude by highlighting the significance of this analysis in both theoretical and empirical dimensions.

Understanding risk-based approaches to regulatory implementation

The terms "risk" and "risk regulation" have been keywords in processes of public administration in the last two or three decades (Fisher 2010). It is not difficult to understand that risks concerning areas such as environment, food safety and finance have raised serious concerns around the world. Having recognized that these risks cannot be reduced to zero because "going the last mile" can be disproportionately costly to achieve, can create other risks or distract attention from other problems (Breyer 1993; Rothstein *et al.* 2013), governments in many jurisdictions have followed certain kinds of risk-based approach. The risk-based approach purports to achieve proportionate and targeted regulation by assessing the nature and magnitude of the risks being addressed (Bounds 2010).

Risks and motives

There are two different yet closely related sets of risk in discussions of risk-based regulation. One refers to the risk to the wider community. It concerns public health, the environment, food safety and so on. In this sense, policymakers deploy risk-based approaches to solve issues such as what to regulate and to what extent should it be regulated. So, these risks are mainly addressed at the stage of policymaking or standard-setting. There has been long experience of this type of risk-based regulatory practice across many countries such as the US, the UK, Australia and Canada (Rothstein *et al.* 2006, 2013).

The second set of risks points to those that threaten the effectiveness, efficiency and legitimacy of regulators, or the so-called "business risks" (Rothstein *et al.* 2006). It is the risk that regulators may not be able to achieve objectives such as promoting compliance by the regulatees, because of, for example, the scarcity of resources. To reduce these risks, regulators may choose to pay more attention to a certain group of regulatees and reduce their control over another group based on the assessment of the level of "business risks". The risk-based approaches to regulatory implementation, to a large degree, have been designed to address these risks (Black 2005, 2010). It is also these approaches that this chapter focuses on.

Following the second sense, risk-based frameworks can generate a number of benefits that encourage regulators to put the risk-based approach into practice. First, perhaps also the most straightforward reason is that a risk-based approach enables regulators to deploy their scarce resources to those regulatees that pose the greatest risk to the achievement of their objectives. Second, supervisors at higher levels are able to improve their management controls over field officers by developing general risk-based frameworks that the latter have to comply with. Third, by responding to different regulatees with a varied level of control, regulators have a defence of charges of over- or under-regulation. Last but not least, regulators are also able to gain another source of legitimacy by introducing a similar strategy, particularly when many jurisdictions have adopted risk-based approaches (Black 2010; Rothstein *et al.* 2006).

Elements and application of risk-based approaches to regulatory implementation

The starting point of a risk-based approach is risks instead of rules (Black 2010). A typical framework in practice usually contains a list of risk indicators, assignment of weight or scores to each indicator, determination of risk levels, and a varied level of regulatory implementation based on the level of risk. Risk-assessment is at the core of this process. It is often far more complex than simply quantifying objective indicators with numbers such as the limits of emission. As researchers have argued, regulators should also keep in mind the regulated bodies' behaviour, attitudes, and culture and the environment of the regulatory regime amongst other factors (Black and Baldwin 2010).

Risk-based approaches can be and have been applied across all of the three essential components of regulatory regimes. As defined from the cybernetic perspective, any effective regulatory process must contain capacity for setting standards, targets and goals (standard-setting); for gathering information to verify compliance (monitoring); and for enforcing rules to modify behaviours (enforcement) (Hood *et al.* 2001; Black 2002). In processes of standard-setting, a risk-based framework allows policy-makers to determine how and to what extent to intervene, for example, by setting limits for residue of certain pesticides in food (Rothstein and Downer 2012). When regulators conduct inspections or audits, or take enforcement decisions, they can allocate scarce resources wisely to optimize the achievement of their objectives. For instance, they can target the bulk of resources on certain groups of high risk businesses (Rothstein *et al.* 2013). This chapter examines the latter two processes, because the implementation of food safety law in China is far more complex as it involves three and, in many places, four tiers of government. A proper risk-based framework would help with improving the coordination between competent authorities at different levels and of different jurisdictions.

Challenges to risk-based approaches to regulatory implementation

Compared with many private regulatory regimes, risk-based approaches to conducting inspections are a strength of government regulators. As one research report assessing private assurance schemes in the UK noted, over 80 per cent of them maintained a fixed interval to monitor their regulated food businesses (Wright *et al.* 2013). However, it does not imply that the risk-based approach is free from problems. The most obvious one is that risk-based regulation is a zero-sum game (Black 2010). That is to say, while regulators' attention is drawn to regulatees with high risks, they will pull back resources from lower risks. However, the bulk of regulatees in practice belong to the latter group. It would be dangerous if regulators fail to keep lower risks under review, partly because risks are dynamic and low risk may increase (Black and Baldwin 2012). Also because of the large group of low risks, ignorance of them risks reducing public confidence in the regulators. Regulators need to carefully design their framework to attend to these lower risks properly.

Second, risk-based approaches shall not be understood as a free-standing mode of control. They are deployed in processes of regulation and will inevitably be in harness with other strategies and instruments. For example, Black and Baldwin suggested that regulators should keep in mind different logics of regulatory tools and the performance of the current tools amongst other elements as well as their changes over time (2010). This is particularly important and also challenging in cases in which regulatory strategies and instruments have been developed on an individual basis over time.

The risk-based approach to implementing food safety law in China

The growing fashion of the risk-based approach

As mentioned earlier, food safety risk and risk regulation have only occurred to Chinese regulators in the last decade. The Central Government created the National Committee for Food Safety Risk Assessment in 2009 and renamed it as the National Centre for Food Safety Risk Assessment in 2011. It is a scientific body offering technical support mainly for standard-setting and for alerting the public to food safety risk. In processes of implementing food safety law, the application of a risk-based approach came relatively late. The 食品安全法实施条例 (Implementing Regulations of the FSL) requires food authorities to tighten their control over food businesses that pose high risk, especially those may cause food safety accidents (Article 48). But it does not contain a complete risk-based approach. It does not address how to deal with low risk and the criteria for assessment are not clear.

The first relatively clear application of the risk-based approach was perhaps the food safety rating scheme which was developed by the then Ministry of Health (MoH) in regulating restaurants and caterers in 2010. In its 餐饮服务食品安全监督管理办法 (Administrative Measures on Food Safety in Catering Service 2010), the MoH required competent food authorities to categorize restaurants and caterers based on their food safety status and to adjust measures and level of regulatory control accordingly. The then State Food and Drug Administration (SFDA, the central competent authority for regulating food safety in catering sector) clarified that the criteria for assessment include licensing status, premises and facilities, food additives and internal food safety control arrangements.[3]

Before the CFDA issued its document in 2016, it had launched a pilot scheme regarding the application of the risk-based approach to food producing and processing businesses in 2014. The CFDA applied it to some local areas such as Fujian.[4] In 2016, the CFDA extended this approach to the whole food supply chain in 食品生产经营风险分级管理办法 (试行) (Measures for Risk-Based Regulation of Food Businesses [Provisional], CFDA 2016 document). It is also the CFDA 2016 document that addresses the risk-based approach to regulatory inspection in a systematic manner.

Risks and motives

According to the FSL and the CFDA 2016 document, the risks being addressed are those that impede the achievement of regulatory objectives, i.e. food safety and public health. The duty of food authorities is to control and reduce those risks. Following the risk-based approach, food authorities prioritize the control of higher risk businesses over the control of lower risk ones. The logic is to concentrate the bulk of regulatory resources on dealing with the main risks.

The main driving factor behind this growing fashion has been the sharp contrast between the large number of food businesses and the limited capacity of government regulatory authorities. As one CFDA officer explained during a focused training session about the application of this approach, by late 2016, there were over 11 million licenced food businesses regulated by quarter of a million officers. To deploy the scarce resources more effectively and efficiently, competent authorities should target regulatees that pose higher risk. By tightening the control over higher risk businesses, food authorities also expect them to improve their internal food safety management and procedural control, with a purpose of easing the burden on the government.[5]

The development of the risk-based approach is also encouraged by the observation that it is a "common international practice". Food authorities in countries such as the USA, the UK and Germany have adopted such an approach. It has proved to be a successful design.[6] By following the widely recognized approach, government regulators would gain more legitimacy. It is particularly important in an era when food safety incidents recur constantly.

The scoring system and application of results

According to the CFDA, the criteria for assessing the level of risk consist of three elements. Two of them constitute the two-part scoring system based on which competent authorities determine an initial risk level. The third element contains extra conditions that will directly increase or decrease the initial risk level. Table 7.1 briefly shows the two-part scoring system. It should be noted that this table does not cover all of the indicators as listed by the CFDA. But it captures the main features. For example, it shows that these indicators are actually a detailed breakdown and quantification of legal requirements. It also demonstrates that in determining the level of risk, competent authorities do not only consider the current status of compliance (food, premises, facilities, etc.), but also the internal food safety control arrangements. However, the assessment mainly relies upon the documented or formal evidence (such as whether there is a person in charge of food safety), rather than the substantive application (such as the knowledge of the responsible person). These features will be further discussed in the next section.

The third element contains negative or positive conditions. Negative conditions are those that the occurrence of which will directly increase the initial level of risk. Examples include deliberate food safety regulatory offences that incur administrative penalties; failure to meet food safety standards in national or provincial processes of monitoring sampling and testing; food safety accidents; failure to recall unsafe food or cease its supply; failure to cooperate with food officers to conduct inspections; and so on. Positive conditions are those that can directly decrease the initial level of risk. For instance, food businesses without extra negative conditions in the past three years, or that have obtained GMP or HACCP certificate or Government Quality Award (at or above the prefectural level) will meet this requirement.

Table 7.1 The two-part scoring system

Parts and weight	Indicators
Part I: 40 A fixed score is applied to each type of food or business	Food producers & processers: type of food & ingredients; complexity of formula; conditions for storage; targeted consumers; etc.
	Food distributors: size of premises; amount of prepacked/ other food; number of consumers.
	Catering service providers: type of business (restaurants, central kitchen, canteen, etc.) and size of restaurants/size of consumer groups; type and amount of food being supplied.
Part II: 60 Each indictor weighs 0.5 or 1 point	1 Qualification: licensing status and permitted content (e.g. type of food) (FSL Arts. 35, 39) 2 Conditions of premises/facilities: proper premises/facilities and cleanliness (FSL Art. 33(1)(2)) 3 Conditions of foodstuff: whether expired or abnormal (FSL Art. 34(6)); labelling (FSL Arts. 34(11),67); etc. 4 Food safety control department and person: whether there is any (FSL Art. 33(3)); etc. 5 Management of food handling staff: whether the person has a health certificate (FSL Art. 45); etc. 6 Procedural control of food safety: proper storage or not (FSL Arts. 33(6), 54, 56, etc.); etc.
	* 7–11 concerns special businesses, such as Internet platform providers for online food transaction; businesses providing food storage or transportation service; etc. (FSL Arts. 61, 62, 77–83, etc.)

Note
This table was drawn according to 食品生产经营风险分级管理办法 (试行) (Measures for Risk-Based Regulation of Food Businesses [Provisional] 2016).

The level of risk is finalized after the third element is considered. If none of these negative or positive conditions exists, the initial level of risk is the final decision. The CFDA requires the competent food authorities to take a varied frequency of inspection. Table 7.2 shows the level of risk and its corresponding minimum frequency of inspection per year.

Table 7.2 Risk levels and inspection frequency

	Level of risk	Scope of score	Frequency of inspection per year
High risk	D	Score >60	At least 3 ~ 4 times
↑	C	45< score ≤60	At least 2 ~ 3 times
	B	30< score ≤45	At least 1 ~ 2 times
Low risk	A	Score ≤30	At least 1 time

Note
This table was drawn according to 食品生产经营风险分级管理办法 (试行) (Measures for Risk-Based Regulation of Food Businesses [Provisional] 2016).

It should be noted that the system developed by the CFDA only provides guidance. Food authorities at the provincial level may make adjustment and tailor it to their local needs. Up until the beginning of November 2017, there were 25 out of 31 authorities that had issued specific documents to apply the risk-based approach to monitoring inspection. In all of the other six provinces, according to news reports and government reports, there has been relevant practice. Amongst the 25 authorities, 21 have applied this approach to monitor food production; 11 to food distribution, and 11 to the catering sector. None of them applied this approach to small food workshops, food vendors or and small catering service providers (the "three smalls"), which has been delegated by the CFDA to food authorities at the provincial level.

According to the current documents, local food authorities have copied the risk-based approach as explained by the CFDA to a large extent. The main difference lies in some specific indicators that influence the calculation of risk levels. Since the end of 2016, local food authorities have started putting this approach into practice. However, thinking critically, there are some issues that may cause the practice to deviate from the objective of the risk-based approach. The following section will examine these issues.

Critical issues in practice

As researchers have observed, risk-based regulation applies in many countries but varies from one jurisdiction to another (Krieger 2013). It would be helpful to examine the current practice in China from a comparative perspective, especially by looking at some jurisdiction with rich experience. The UK has stood out regarding the application of a risk-based approach. At the central level, the previous Regulators' Compliance Code 2007 and now the Regulators' Code 2014 have both made it clear that all relevant regulators should follow a risk-based, proportionate and targeted approach to regulatory inspection and enforcement. Up until now, this requirement has applied to the vast majority of regulators, including food safety regulators. Indeed, in processes of food safety regulation, a risk-based framework for taking regulatory interventions was designed even earlier, as reflected in the Food Law Code of Practice 1995. It is further refined by the FSA under the EU legislative framework.[7]

The objective of the FSA is to direct more intensive regulation at those food businesses that present the greatest risk to public health. The risk-based approach applies to taking interventions and also to taking enforcement measures. Interventions include official controls (such as inspections, audits and sampling) and other measures such as education, advice and information gathering. Competent authorities are instructed to determine the intervention frequency on the basis of risk levels. To low-risk businesses, authorities may apply alternative enforcement strategies that involve no less than one intervention every three years. Enforcement measures include informal ones (educating, giving advice, etc.) and formal ones (Hygiene Improvement Notice, Hygiene Prohibition Notice, etc.). Food officers operate a graduated and educative approach, starting from informal action and only move to more formal action where the informal action does not achieve the desired effect.[8]

The highlights of the UK approach lie in the indicators for assessing the level of risk and the application of the results of assessment. They show some significant contrasts with the CFDA framework. Table 7.3 briefly compares the CFDA scoring system and the FSA scoring system in England. It should be noted that in the other three regions (Wales, Scotland and Northern Ireland) of the UK, a similar framework exists, though in separate Codes of Practice. This section will discuss these contrasts and critical issues surrounding the CFDA framework.

Risk-based or rule-based assessment

As noted in the previous section, indicators under the CFDA framework are details of legal requirements. The "risk assessment" is simply a quantitative approach to counting the number of legal requirements that are complied with or breached by a regulatee. It is perhaps more like a "rule-based" rather than a "risk-based" approach to conducting inspections. In contrast, under the FSA framework, there is more direct consideration of risk. For instance, it distinguishes "non-compliance but not significant in terms of risk" from "major non-compliance". In the Chinese case, thinking about the detailed indicators, high score is not necessarily associated with high risk. For example, in the case of Tianjin, failure to display 食品安全承诺 (Food Safety Declaration) weighs two points, whereas failure to maintain personal hygiene of employees and clean lavatories weigh one point respectively. It is hard to say that simple display of one declaration is more important than personal hygiene to food safety. Additionally, the "rule-based" style risks causing creative compliance. Both regulators and regulatees may follow the rules but evade the spirit of the law (McBarnet and Whelan 1991; Braithwaite and Braithwaite 1995; Black 2008).

A relevant issue is that the CFDA framework pays more attention to the documented or formal food safety control arrangements. For example, it considers whether there is a dedicated person managing food safety; or whether there is a documented risk control procedure. In contrast, the FSA framework also evaluates the substantive dimension of internal food safety control. For instance, food officers would assess the knowledge of responsible persons, and the attitude of the present management towards food safety. Comparatively speaking, the FSA framework is more likely to achieve somewhat precise risk assessment. But, unquestionably, it is also more challenging for food officers to put it into practice.

Coverage of the risk-based approach

A horizontal observation of the existing documents reveals at least three gaps in the coverage of the risk-based approach in China. These gaps concern businesses of small size, different stages of food supply chains and the process for

Table 7.3 A brief comparison between the CFDA scoring system and the FSA scoring system

	China CFDA	UK FSA
Indicators	**Part I**: type of food; nature of business (separate criteria for producers/processors, distributors and catering service providers). **Part II**: current status of compliance; internal food safety control arrangements (documentation). **Part III**: extra conditions that will directly increase or decrease the risk level.	**Part I**: Potential hazard (type of food & method of handling; specific method of processing; consumers at risk, e.g. local/nationwide, vulnerable groups). **Part II**: Level of current compliance (hygiene: handling practices/temperature control/procedures, etc.; structure: cleanliness, layout, lightning, ventilation, facilities, etc.). **Part III**: Confidence in management/control procedures (documented procedures and subjective factors, such as attitude of the present management toward food safety and risk control; relevant knowledge possessed by the managing person, etc.; reassurance provided by checks undertaken on food safety management system via an independent third party as part of an assurance scheme that addresses application legislation).
Way of calculating	Specific scores to specific factor. E.g. the fact that the food being inspected has expired will incur 1 point; the fact that the labelling is not clear or incomplete will incur 1 point; no Chinese labelling on imported food will incur 1 point; no food safety managing person will incur 0.5 point; food handling persons without health certificates will incur 0.5 point; etc.	For **Part I**, fixed scores for specific indicator. E.g. manufacturers or distributors whose food is distributed nationally receive 15 points under "consumers at risk". For **Part II**, scores are based on the level of compliance. E.g. high standard of compliance, good compliance, non-compliance but not significant in terms of risk, some major non-compliance and so on. Consideration is given to compliance with industry codes of recommended practice and good practice in trade while determining high standards of compliance. For **Part III**, scores are based on the level of satisfaction. E.g. excellent track record of correcting non-compliance, knowledgeable and competent business operators or managers, good or poor appreciation of food safety risk control, etc.

Note
This table was drawn according to 食品生产经营风险分级管理办法（试行）(Measures for Risk-Based Regulation of Food Businesses [Provisional] 2016) and the Food Law Code of Practice (England) (March 2017).

enforcing food safety law. First, the FSL has delegated the regulation of the "three smalls" to governments at the provincial level. Accordingly, the CFDA 2016 document has directed food authorities at the provincial level to develop and apply a risk-based approach to control the "three smalls". However, up until the beginning of November 2017, none of those authorities had taken this step yet. In addition, the current scoring system does not distinguish businesses of medium size from large ones. Regulatory burdens are bound to be heavier for smaller businesses than bigger ones.

Second, as noted in the previous section, the risk-based approach has been developed for food production, distribution and catering service separately. However, there are still about one-third of all provinces which have not applied it to food production, and about two-thirds not to food distribution and catering service respectively. The distinction between different stages of food supply chains may be explained from two perspectives. Historically, there was a segmented regulatory regime, with different authorities regulating different stages of the food supply chain. In the legislative dimension, the FSL has laid down detailed requirements for different stages separately.

The third gap concerns the application of the risk-based approach to processes of enforcement. The current framework only covers processes of monitoring in China. But in the UK, food authorities also follow this approach to take enforcement measures. The FSA has introduced the "enforcement pyramid" which was originally drawn by Ayres and Braithwaite (1992) into practice. Food officers prioritize informal action over formal ones. Only where an informal action does not achieve the desired effect, may officers move up to a formal action. This is consistent with the claim that the best approach to securing compliance is often a combination of "carrots" and "sticks" (Braithwaite 1997).

Track records in risk assessment

The third critical issue concerns track records of food businesses. Under the CFDA framework, track records documenting administrative penalties are additional conditions for decreasing or increasing the initial risk level. In contrast, in the FSA system, it is the track records documenting the willingness of "the regulatees" to act on previous advice and enforcement, and the history of compliance that are considered in determining the risk level. The problem with the CFDA framework is that penalties in the past do not necessarily imply high risk in the future. This is because non-compliance arises for multiple reasons. It is often the case in China that people have failed to comply with the law because of lack of capacity or knowledge. Following previous penalties, they may change their behaviour in accordance with the law. More importantly, regulatees comply with regulatory requirements mostly because of the value of addressing a given problem (May 2004, 2005; Tyler 2006). It is the subjective commitment that weighs more. Hence, focusing on penalties in the past is not a wise step.

Contribution of private assurance schemes

Last but not least, it concerns the involvement of third parties. Under the CFDA framework, the contribution of private assurance schemes has no influence on risk levels. But the FSA system reflects the significance of checks undertaken by independent third parties as part of assurance schemes that address applicable legislation. However, it should not be forgotten that this is based on a well-established system of private regulation. While this is the case in the UK (Flynn *et al.* 1999; Marsden *et al.* 2000), it is far from being true in China. For a long time there has not been a friendly environment for the development of private food safety regulation (Liu 2010). Recently, some food businesses have obtained or sought to obtain certificates based on certain private schemes. For example, Junlebao Dairy Co., Ltd has successfully obtained certificates issued by SGS (China) based on the BRC Global Standards for Food Safety and the IFS standards in 2014 (君乐宝乳业 Junlebao Dairy Co. Ltd 2014). Yet, this practice has not been widely recognized amongst food businesses and also regulators.

Conclusion

This chapter has examined the rise of a risk-based approach to implementing food safety law in China. We may count this approach as another "imported" term but with Chinese characteristics. Or more fundamentally, we may call it a "rule-based" approach, as explained in the last section. It is questionable whether this approach starts from risk or from rules. As this chapter has explained, Chinese regulators have learnt the experience from other countries. They expect to optimize the allocation of regulatory resources and achieve regulatory goals more effectively by following this approach. However, the design of this approach in China shows unique features.

By comparing with the approach maintained by the FSA in the UK, this chapter explains that the Chinese approach faces a number of challenges to meet regulators' expectations. From the perspective of risk assessment, it is doubtful whether the detailed indicators of risk and the formal assessment will produce reasonable results. The consideration of track records documenting penalties in the past risks misleading local food officers, too. As to the application of this approach, the limited coverage has left a significant group of food businesses beyond the reach of the risk-based approach. Consequently, Chinese food safety regulators encounter more challenges than what have been noted by the existing research. This is partly a consequence of the detailed legislative style in China. But food authorities could have made efforts to reduce this kind of influence to some extent.

Regarding risk assessment, possible improvement may come from four aspects. First, the CFDA and food authorities at the provincial level may determine the risk level based on regulatees' level of compliance, such as full compliance, compliance, minor non-compliance and so on, rather than simply counting the number of legal requirements being breached. Second, food authorities may pay more attention to the substantive factors apart from formal documentation. Third, track records of penalties should not weigh too much in determining risk levels. Food authorities may consider this together with the other indicators. However, it should not directly lead to the increase or decrease of risk levels. Fourth, also in the long run, food authorities may consider the contribution of private assurance schemes. Indeed, these schemes have played an important role in controlling food businesses and, hence, easing the regulatory burden on government regulators in some industrialized countries. While this might be difficult to achieve in China in the near future, it is a beneficial development in the long run.

Regarding the application of the risk-based approach, there is a great potential to expand in China. Although researchers have warned of low-risk groups, the more urgent need in China is to apply a risk-based approach to the whole food supply chain. It does not only include businesses of bigger sizes, but also smaller sizes and those "three smalls"; and does not only apply to food production, but also to distribution and the catering sector. In fact, the CFDA has designed this approach with full coverage. However, it always takes time for local authorities to make adjustment or to put it into practice. Thinking positively, this challenge may be solved in time. Another critical issue concerns the application of a risk-based approach to regulatory enforcement. To meet this challenge, both the legislature and the government authorities will need to make changes. The legislature needs to give more leeway to food authorities by changing the prescriptive legislative style. Food authorities need to communicate more with food businesses by adopting an educative and compliance-oriented strategy for enforcing the law.

The risk-based approach to legal implementation has grown in popularity in recent years. If well designed and applied, regulators will benefit from it greatly. But as with many regulatory instruments, there are always challenges in practice. Issues concerning the coordination between different regulatory instruments are not examined in this chapter. As the CFDA explained, earlier schemes such as the food safety rating scheme and food safety credit records have been incorporated into the risk-based approach.[9] To what extent this is true, or how this can be achieved, still needs time to tell. In short, there may be no best instrument or strategy, but regulatory tools can get better and better by being tested and improved in practice.

Notes

1 In late 2016, the CFDA issued 食品生产经营风险分级管理办法（试行）（食药监食监一〔2016〕115号）(Measures for Risk-based Regulation of Food Businesses (Provisional)) and defined the term in Article 2.

2 This was a measure which was designed to reduce the regulatory burden both on regulators and regulatees by exempting large corporations with good record of compliance from regulatory inspections for three years, and this term was renewable. It was created by the State Council in 1999 and applied by the department of quality supervision in

2001. Following the outbreak of the melamine-contaminated baby formula incident in 2008, which was partly blamed on this arrangement, the State Council immediately abolished this measure.

3 See 关于实施餐饮服务食品安全监督量化分级管理工作的指导意见 (国食药监食 [2012]5号) (SFDA Guidance for Implementing Food Safety Rating Scheme in the Catering Service Sector 2012).

4 See 食品生产企业风险分级监管指导意见 (试点稿) (CFDA Guidance for Risk-Based Regulation of Food Producers and Processors (Pilot Version)).

5 www.sda.gov.cn/WS01/CL1786/164246.html, accessed 2 November 2017.

6 Ibid.

7 After the plague of food safety scares in the last two decades of the twentieth century, risk analysis became a key concept in processes of food safety regulation under the EU legislative framework. This has been clarified in the Regulation (EC) No. 178/2002 of 28 January 2002 laying down the general principles and requirements of food law, establishing the European Food Safety Authority and laying down procedures in matters of food safety [2002] OJ L31/1. In taking official controls, the EU regulation requires competent authorities to base on risk levels, taking into consideration:

> (a) identified risks associated with [food or food businesses, the use of food or any process, material, substance, activity or operation that may influence food safety];
> (b) food business operators' past record as regards compliance with food law …;
> (c) the reliability of any own checks that have already been carried out; and
> (d) any information that might indicate non-compliance.

See Regulation (EC) No. 882/2004 of 29 April 2004 of the European Parliament and of the Council on official controls performed to ensure the verification of compliance with feed and food law, animal health and animal welfare rules [2004] OJ L165/1, art. 3.

8 For more details, see Food Law Code of Practice (England) (March 2017) and Food Law Practice Guidance (England) (October 2015).

9 www.sda.gov.cn/WS01/CL1786/164246.html, accessed 2 November 2017.

References

Ayres, I. and J. Braithwaite (1992) *Responsive Regulation: Transcending the Deregulation Debate*, Oxford: Oxford University Press.

Black, J. (2002) "Critical Reflections on Regulation", *Australian Journal of Legal Philosophy*, 27: 1–35.

Black, J. (2005) "The Emergence of Risk-Based Regulation and the New Public Risk Management in the United Kingdom", *Public Law*, 512–548.

Black, J. (2008) "Forms and Paradoxes of Principles-Based Regulation", *Capital Markets Law Journal*, 3: 425–457.

Black, J. (2010) "Risk-Based Regulation: Choices, Practices and Lessons Being Learnt", in OECD (ed.), *Risk and Regulatory Policy: Improving the Governance of Risk*, Paris: OECD Publishing.

Black, J. and R. Baldwin (2010) "Really Responsive Risk-Based Regulation", *Law & Policy*, 32: 181–213.

Black, J. and R. Baldwin (2012) "When Risk-Based Regulation Aims Low: Approaches and Challenges", *Regulation & Governance*, 6: 2–22.

Bounds, G. (2010) "Challenges to Designing Regulatory Policy Frameworks to Manage Risks", in OECD (ed.), *Risk and Regulatory Policy: Improving the Governance of Risk*, Paris: OECD Publishing.

Braithwaite, J. (1997) "On Speaking Softly and Carrying Big Sticks: Neglected Dimensions of a Republication Separation of Powers", *University of Toronto Law Journal*, 47: 305–361.

Braithwaite, J. and V. Braithwaite (1995) "The Politics of Legalism: Rules Versus Standards in Nursing Home Regulation", *Social & Legal Studies*, 4: 307.

Breyer, S. G. (1993) *Breaking the Vicious Circle: Toward Effective Risk Regulation*, Cambridge, MA: Harvard University Press.

Fan Chunmei 范春梅, Jia Jianmin 贾建民 and Li Huaqiang 李华强 (2012) "Public Risk Perception and Responses in Food Safety Incidents" 食品安全事件中的公众风险感知及应对行为研究, *Management Review* 管理评论, 163–168 + 176.

Fisher, E. (2010) "Risk Regulatory Concepts and the Law", in OECD (ed.), *Risk and Regulatory Policy: Improving the Governance of Risk*, Paris: OECD Publishing.

Flynn, A., T. Marsden and M. Harrison (1999) "The Regulation of Food in Britain in the 1990s", *Policy & Politics*, 27: 435–446.

Hood, C., H. Rothstein and R. Baldwin (2001) *The Government of Risk: Understanding Risk Regulation Regimes*, Oxford: Oxford University Press.

Junlebao Dairy Co. Ltd 君乐宝乳业 (2014) Junlebao Milk Powder Is Certified against BRC Global Standards, a Pass for Exporting to the EU 君乐宝奶粉率先获得BRC认证 取得出口欧盟通行证, www.junlebaoruye.com/News.aspx [accessed 10 November 2014].

Krieger, K. (2013) "The Limits and Variety of Risk-Based Governance: The Case of Flood Management in Germany and England", *Regulation & Governance*, 7: 236–257.

Liu, P. (2010) "Tracing and Periodizing China's Food Safety Regulation: A Study on China's Food Safety Regime Change", *Regulation & Governance*, 4: 244–260.

Marsden, T., A. Flynn and M. Harrison (2000) *Consuming Interests: The Social Provision of Foods*, London: UCL Press.

May, P. J. (2004) "Compliance Motivations: Affirmative and Negative Bases", *Law and Society Review*, 38: 41–68.

May, P. J. (2005) "Regulation and Compliance Motivations: Examining Different Approaches", *Public Administration Review*, 65: 31–44.

McBarnet, D. and C. Whelan (1991) "The Elusive Spirit of the Law: Formalism and the Struggle for Legal Control", *The Modern Law Review*, 54: 848–873.

Rothstein, H. and J. Downer (2012) "'Renewing Defra': Exploring the Emergence of Risk-Based Policymaking in UK Central Government", *Public Administration*, 90: 781–799.

Rothstein, H., P. Irving, T. Walden and R. Yearsley (2006) "The Risks of Risk-Based Regulation: Insights from the Environmental Policy Domain", *Environment International*, 32: 1056–1065.

Rothstein, H., O. Borraz and M. Huber (2013) "Risk and the Limits of Governance: Exploring Varied Patterns of Risk-Based Governance across Europe", *Regulation & Governance*, 7: 215–235.

Qi Jiangang 戚建刚 (2011) "The Transformation of Food Safety Risk Regulation in China" 我国食品安全风险规制模式之转型, *Chinese Journal of Law* 法学研究, 33–49.

Qi Jiangang 戚建刚 (2012) "The Multifacets of Food Hazards and Risk Assessment" 食品危害多重属性与风险评估制度的重构, *Contemporary Law Review* 当代法学, 49–56.

Qi Jiangang 戚建刚 (2013) "Administrative Inspections of Food Safety based on Risk Assessment" 论基于风险评估的食品安全风险行政调查, *The Jurist* 法学家, 55–69.

Shen Kui 沈岿 (2009) "Rethinking the Measure of Exemption from Inspections in Food Regulation: From the Perspective of Risk Governance" 食品免检制之反思：以风险治理为视角, *Studies in Law and Business* 法商研究, 3–10.

Shen Kui 沈岿 (2011) "Administrative Law in Risk Assessment: The Case of Food Safety Regulation" 风险评估的行政法治问题：以食品安全监管领域为例, *Zhejiang Academic Journal* 浙江学刊, 16–27.

Tyler, T. R. (2006) *Why People Obey the Law*, Princeton, NJ: Princeton University Press.

Wang Dianhua 王殿华, Su Yiqing 苏毅清, Zhong Kai 钟凯 and Zhao Yaling 赵雅玲 (2012) "Risk Communication: New Approach to Prevention of Food Safety Risk" 风险交流：食品安全风险防范新途径, *China Emergency Management* 中国应急管理, 42–47.

Wang Guisong 王贵松 (2011) "The Boundary and Responsibility in Food Safety Risk Communication" 食品安全风险公告的界限与责任, *Journal of the East China University of Political Science and Law* 华东政法大学学报, 28–38.

Wright, M., G. Palmer, A. Shahriyer, R. Williams and R. Smith (2013) "Assessment and Comparison of Third Party Assurance Schemes in the Food Sector: Towards A Common Framework", *Final Report for the Food Standards Agency CR2435 R2 V8*.

8 A study on peasant behaviour and peasant niche in contemporary China's agri-food supply system

Evidence from Henan province

Jinghan Ke and Shuji Hisano

Introduction

Industrialized agricultural production in the conventional agri-food supply[1] system is characterized by a continual increase in the use of artificial growth factors such as chemical fertilizers, pesticides, industrial feed and new hybrid seeds (van der Ploeg 2010). It is expected to contribute to the eradication of hunger by improving the yield worldwide, and in the meantime it supposedly benefits different groups of stakeholders within the agri-food value chain: domestic suppliers of production input factors, scattered small retailers, large-scale supermarket chains, and transnational dealers and food corporations (Burch and Lawrence 2009; Hisano 2014). In the contemporary consumption-driven era (Wunder 2012), it seems achievable to meet consumers' diversified demand. Urban consumers can access abundant varieties of agricultural produce and processed food such as off-season vegetables and fruits. However, industrialized agricultural production also has resulted in tremendous negative consequences. On the one hand, it has brought about negative impacts on the eco-system through direct environmental pollution and increasing disconnection of farming from nature (Kloppenburg *et al.* 1996). On the other hand, it has led to serious problems in food safety and public health through food contamination (Maye and Kirwan 2010).

This circumstance is particularly evident in China (Liu and Diamond 2005; Thiers 2005; Gong *et al.* 2012). China is one of the largest agricultural producers in the world. Over the past few decades, it has been promoting the "industrialization and modernization of agriculture" (Ye 2015). One measure is to expand external inputs and new sophisticated technologies (van der Ploeg and Ye 2016). Commercial mass production and widespread use of chemical inputs have destroyed the stability and balance of entire ecosystems (Wang 2005), and have resulted in direct chemical impacts and indirect impacts on aquatic, terrestrial and soil organisms through changes in food resources and natural predators (Liu and Diamond 2005). Since the 2000s, a series of widespread panics has been sparked by agri-food safety scandals at home and abroad, such as frozen dumplings with pesticide residues exported to Japan in 2008 and the "scallion poisoning" and "cowpea poisoning" in 2010. According to estimates from the

Chinese Ministry of Health and Ministry of Agriculture, there are over 200,000 pesticide-poisoning accidents each year (Peng 2001).

There is evidence to show that Chinese peasants are likely to overuse or mix chemical pesticides, unaware of their negative impacts, and continue in this excessive use even after introducing new technologies, such as pest-resistant Bt cotton (Liu and Huang 2013; Yang *et al.* 2014). It is said that farmers usually divide their land and differentiate produce for their own consumption from those for the market (van der Ploeg and Ye 2016), as also pointed out by the ex-Mayor of Beijing, Wang Qishan, during his speech in the 11th National People's Congress in 2011.[2] However, our field surveys conducted in Henan province in the past four years (as explained later) have revealed a different but more distressing phenomenon occurring on the ground across rural China. Among the 155 peasant households interviewed, nearly 80 per cent applied chemical inputs in an arbitrary way without considering the negative impact. Approximately 70 per cent were conscious of the fact that they could not guarantee the safety of their produce, but they also consume what they sell without caring about their own health. Why does this phenomenon take place? How have they formed this kind of behaviour? How do peasants make decisions in terms of pesticide use? This chapter aims to explore these questions.

Many studies have discussed the issue of pesticide use in China as well as in other countries such as the USA, European countries and South Africa (e.g. Lichtenberg and Zimmerman 1999; Phipps and Park 2002; Hofs *et al.* 2006). Still, there is a lack of attention given to the chemical use behaviour of small-scale scattered peasants. Most Chinese scholars tend to investigate farmers involved in large-scale production projects such as "pollution-free[3] agri-food production bases" or demonstration zones (Zhou and Jin 2009; Jiang *et al.* 2012). However, the farmers in those projects are equipped with better technical training, supervision and sales channel than small-scale peasants. Although some scholars have analysed what factors may influence peasants' pesticide use (Wei and Lu 2004; Zhang and Lu 2007; Xu *et al.* 2008; Liu and Huang 2013; Yang *et al.* 2014), they largely fail to look at structural elements within the agri-food supply system. They mainly focus on cognitive elements (awareness of safety, risk and the environment; sense of moral responsibility; expected profit; and satisfaction degree of information dissemination), household profile (age, education, cultivation area, production years, family size, agricultural income and technical skills). Even when they take into account the external political environment such as the involvement of farmers' cooperatives, supporting policies and administrative regulation, they treat peasant households as a single production unit with the hypothetical condition that all of the factors are independent and parallel, and do not look into peasant behaviour in the supply system operated by different actors. They therefore lose sight of the interactions between the intrinsic elements and the exogenous ones. In particular, they neglect power relations with other influential actors in the current agri-food system, in which the political and economic elites aim to eliminate smallholders in the capitalist industrialization of agriculture (Schneider 2015).

In this chapter, we do not intend to figure out all-embracing elements regarding peasant behaviour. Rather, we would discuss the structural element of the current agri-food supply system. Structure is not external to peasants, it is more internal than external as instantiated in production activities. As Giddens (1986) asserted, within the structure of systems, power presumes regularized relations of autonomy and dependence between actors in contexts of social interactions. We argue that the supply mechanism determines peasants' narrow room for autonomy and heavy dependence on other actors in the current agri-food supply system, and this strongly affects peasant behaviour of synthetic chemical usage. Here, we propose the concept of a "peasant niche"[4] to describe peasants' situation in the agri-food supply system. If we take an ecosystem as a metaphor for the agri-food supply system, it also includes the biotic (agricultural material suppliers, peasants, big-scale farmers, wholesalers, retailers and consumers) and abiotic factors (the socio-economic and political environment) in this system. In this vein, a peasant niche represents the role and position in a specific environment of the agri-food system. Considering the complexity of the Chinese agri-food supply system, we categorize it into three models: the wholesale market-centred model, the leading enterprise-centred model and the farming-supermarket docking model. This categorization draws from the existing literature (e.g. Ling and Zhu 2006; Chen and Ren 2012) as well as our observation of the supply mechanism in our field surveys. By so doing, we explicitly interpret the relationship between peasants and other actors, and highlight peasants' subordinate status and very narrow room for autonomy in the agri-food system.

In the rest of the chapter, we will first discuss how peasant behaviour and Chinese peasants have been theoretically portrayed. Second, we will outline the landscape of the contemporary agri-food supply system in China, beginning with the socio-economic context. This is to underline how the conventional agri-food supply system has been shaped and developed till now. Third, three models will be introduced to manifest the conventional agri-food supply mechanism. Fourth, situated in each model, the peasant niche will be analysed with the evidence from Henan province. To support our evidence, we will explain how the data of our fieldworks were collected. Lastly, we will discuss how we should understand Chinese peasant behaviour in agri-food safety issue, and conclude with the future work of this study.

Peasant behaviour and Chinese peasants

China's agricultural growth is a peasant-managed process, in which millions of peasant households decide what to produce, how and for what reasons (van der Ploeg and Ye 2016). Nowadays, the majority of agri-food is still produced by peasants.[5] About 70 per cent of the cultivated land is managed by peasants and not by large-scale farmers,[6] and 45.2 per cent of registered rural residents are involved in farming (National Bureau of Statistics of the People's Republic of China 2015). Under this situation, supporting small-scale peasantry farming seems a logical objective for China's agriculture (Schneider 2015). As van der Ploeg (2013) argues, any discussion today on sustainability has to debate the role of peasantries; the peasant and small-scale farming are supposed to be important issues related to agriculture and rural development.

There have been significant debates on the peasant over the past decades. Among others, Chayanov points out in *The Theory of Peasant Economy* (1966) that the purpose of peasant production is to meet the subsistence needs of family consumption, not to pursue profit maximization. This is the fundamental premise of peasants' economic activities, explaining that peasants pursue a balance between household consumption and agricultural labour inputs, rather than a balance between profit and cost. Given a lack of land, capital and external employment opportunities, peasants keep high labour intensity in order to increase yield as much as possible; however, this comes with low returns, which is called "self-exploitation" (Chayanov 1966). Scott (1976) focuses on the perspective of "subsistence ethic" to identify peasant behaviour. He claims that the peasant family is a subsistence-oriented unit; it is a unit of both consumption and production; when choosing the means of production, timing and technique, the peasant family unit will decide upon its minimal human needs in a reliable and stable way, and this makes it different from a capitalist enterprise. Roumasset (1971) argues that peasants follow the "safety-first" principle to avoid risks when they decide on seeds and farming techniques, because they want to minimize the probability of having a disaster, rather than maximizing their average return. These scholars identify peasant behaviour with an emphasis on subsistence ethic, rather than profit.

In contrast, another school believes that peasants pursue profit maximization as rationally as capital entrepreneurs. Schultz (1964) considers the peasant as "Economic Man" exactly as any capital entrepreneur, and the way to transform the traditional agriculture is to provide the peasant with modern factors of production at affordable prices and to leave the small farm structure intact without intervening. Drawing from Schultz, Popkin (1979) takes the peasant farm as a capitalist farm, whereby peasants act to maximize profits by rationalizing their production and balancing their short-term and long-term interests. He argues that we should respect peasants' ability to solve problems in resource allocation and conflicts. These scholars believe that peasant behaviour is characterized by maximizing profit.

As for Chinese peasants, there have been some key studies in the past decades. Philip Huang (1985) argues that peasant behaviour could not be easily concluded as irrational or not from the single point of profit maximization. He applies the concept of "marginal utility" to comprehend peasant behaviour because utility allows for subjective preferences related to a particular circumstance. Van der Ploeg and Ye (2016) consider that Chinese peasants are identified and specified as a social actor by their relations with work, land and household. They highly evaluate current Chinese peasants, arguing that Chinese peasants are enlarging their autonomy and the amount of created value (van der Ploeg *et al.* 2014). Day (2008, 2013) analyses how the figure of the peasant fits into history. He argues that the peasant represents a broad range of political concerns in Chinese political discussions, and the marginalization of the Chinese peasantry is part of a global trend. Schneider (2015) identifies Chinese peasants as a social category used by political and economic elites to represent the ills of China's agri-food system. She explains that how the peasant is constructed in *nongmin* (农民, i.e. farmer or peasant) discourses has a political significance.

The above-mentioned theories and studies have given specific elaboration on peasant behaviour from different points of view. Unfortunately, none of them looks deeply into Chinese peasants' specific behaviour in terms of pesticide use. Although small-scale farming is characterized by peasants' practices of permanent, sustainable agriculture in China's long history (Netting 1993), peasants often make a significant and long-standing impact on the local ecosystem and environment through pesticide use (Zhang and Lu 2007). Pesticide overuse by Chinese peasants seems like an irrational choice from both an economic and a moral perspective. On one hand, pesticides and other chemicals contaminate soil, air and water, damaging non-target organisms and resulting in the reduction of the marginal productivity of farmland (Wasim *et al.* 2009). At the same time, the consumption of contaminated agri-food products may lead to food poisoning, which damages the peasants' health and weakens their labour force and productivity as well. On the other hand, the contaminations affect public health and deteriorate consumers' trust in their produce, which in turn affects their sales. Most of the peasants act as entrepreneurs to maximize their interests, but they also exploit their own labour force and time to continue their improper production behaviour, and disregard the health of the public and themselves. However, the behaviour they choose is derived from the socio-economic conditions. Therefore, the key question is not if Chinese peasants are rational or if they have a different form of rationality, but rather how peasants make decisions when facing the constraints from a specific niche. As van der Ploeg and Ye (2016) claim, the existing literature related to Chinese agriculture and peasants is missing detailed studies that pay attention to the grassroots realities and dynamics of farming. In order to give a complete portrayal of the contemporary Chinese peasants and the reality of their farming, the issue of pesticide overuse needs to be investigated and interpreted in association with the external conditions.

Economic reforms and the conventional agri-food supply system

The conventional agri-food supply system in China has been formed and evolved in the context of several economic reforms in the past decades. Drawing from Yang (2001), Wu (2008) and Ma and Chen (2009), we divide the past decades into the following five reform periods.

During the first reform period between 1978 and 1984, the so-called "household contract responsibility system" was established to endow peasants with the right of land use. In that way, the agricultural productivity was no longer bound by the collective economy, and peasants were enabled to produce varied crops based on the comparative advantage and market demands. Partial deregulation of agricultural markets and prices provided peasants with economic freedom and opportunities to increase their income. This was the starting point of the formation of the contemporary agri-food supply system.

The second reform period is from 1984 to 1991, when the planned economy was gradually shrinking but was still dominant in China. To put it differently, the market economy slowly expanded but was at the edge of the planned economy in this period. The key focus of the reform included the introduction of a price adjustment mechanism, the implementation of the enterprise contract management responsibility system, the delegation of fiscal rights to local governments and the promotion of township enterprises. After the household contract responsibility system permeated to broader rural areas, the production yield and the peasants' income as well as their purchasing power largely increased. In the meantime, surplus labour appeared in the countryside. Previous enterprises led by "people's communes" developed to be township enterprises, which covered a wide range of business sectors, including processing, catering, transportation and housing industries. The development of township enterprises, which later on grew to be leading enterprises,[7] further stimulated the agri-food production and processing, and expanded the market for multitudes of smallholders. Thanks to the cancellation of state monopoly policy for purchase and marketing, agri-food markets became more dynamic and active. Agricultural wholesale markets were increasingly founded during this period to facilitate the efficient distribution and price formation of agri-food products.

The third reform period is from 1992 to 1997. Based on the political principle of "open-door to the outside world" proposed by Deng Xiaoping (Ji 1984), the main measures included broader privatization of the enterprises involved in the international trade, improving special economic zones to attract foreign investments, and increasing export. On the agriculture side, township enterprises achieved fast growth and started to show their interest in new products, innovative technologies and cooperation with research institutions or state-owned enterprises to improve product quality and management. They started to produce agricultural inputs such as fertilizers, pesticides and farm implements in abundance, and took charge of processing, transporting, marketing and selling for peasants. Meanwhile, the wholesale markets stepped into an era of being multilevel. They formed a structure centring on big cities but with small ones spreading over towns and villages.

The fourth reform period is from 1997 to 2006. The purpose was to deepen the reform of state-owned enterprises and start a diversified ownership system. However, in the face of the Asian financial crisis, China's exports diminished, while the reform of state-owned enterprises resulted in an increasingly serious unemployment problem. During 1997 to 2006, the increase of rural residents' income was 6.2 per cent, which was only two-thirds of the increase of the urban residents' income.[8] This period witnessed the dramatically growing income gap between the urban and the rural residents. Along with the more extensive privatization and the establishment of market economy, the conventional agrifood supply system in China has been formed as diverse and multidimensional as Figure 8.1 shows. It is a network that includes producers in the upstream stage, processors and wholesalers at the intermediate stage, retailers in the downstream stage and consumers at the terminal stage. It covers distinct actors, such as peasants, big-scale farmers, farmers' cooperatives, middlemen, state-owned enterprises, local leading enterprises, supermarkets, individual restaurants and transnational corporations. The intermediate part usually consists of individual middlemen, wholesalers in local wholesale markets and wholesalers in distant wholesale markets of other cities or provinces. Hence, China's supply chains are so lengthy that agri-food products reach the hands of consumers with a final price that is much higher than the producer price after passing through the hands of several intermediate actors (e.g. Zhang 2016).

Since 2006, a new era has started. The construction of the "socialist new countryside" has been considered an important historical target of the central government. In the government documents, increasing farmers' income, improving agricultural productivity, developing modern agriculture and strengthening agricultural infrastructure were strongly emphasized (Central Document No. 1, 2006). Particularly in recent years, the so-called "new types of agricultural management entities" have been energetically promoted with the aim of optimizing the agricultural structure. These new entities include specialized households (专业大户), family farms (家庭农场), farmers' professional cooperatives (农民专业合作社, hereafter "farmers' cooperatives" for short), and leading enterprise of agricultural industrialization[9] (农业产业化龙头企业, hereafter "leading enterprises" for short) (see Table 8.1). Since 2015, 20 per cent of general agricultural subsidies granted by the central government has been allocated to support the above-mentioned four types of entities. In 2016, the number

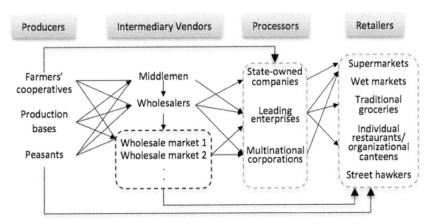

Figure 8.1 The conventional vegetable supply system in China.

Source: authors' elaboration.

Table 8.1 Four "new types of new agricultural management entity"

Type	Definition	Qualifying standard	Amount
Specialized household (*Zhuanye dahu* in Chinese)	Focus on one kind of agricultural product in a certain production scale at professional level	No unified standard. Each provincial government has its own standard (e.g. over 500 *mu* cultivation area).	No statistics
Family farm (*Jiating nongchang*)	Updated version of specialized household. The family members are main labour force, engaged in large-scale, intensified and commercialized agricultural production, and the agricultural income is the main income source.	No unified standard. Each provincial government has its own standard (e.g. commercial crop: over 30 *mu*, field crop: over 50 *mu* cultivation area).	0.877 million (0.414 million certified) (2016)
Farmers' professional cooperative (*Nongmin zhuanye hezuoshe*)	Voluntarily cooperative, mutually beneficial and autonomous economic organization whose members are producing similar crops or providing related service based on the household contract.	More than five members consist of individuals or organizations, among whom farmers account for at least 80 per cent; new applicants should abstain consent and meet the requirements of each cooperative (e.g. membership fee).	1.794 million (2016)
Leading enterprises of agricultural industrialization (*Nongye chanyehua longtou qiye*)	Enterprises certified by the government, engaged in agricultural products processing in a certain scale, distribution and marketing, and help farmers access the market.	Registered with the Department of Industry and Commerce and certified as different levels: National, provincial and city.	0.386 million (2016)

Source: authors' elaboration. Information is collected from website of Ministry of Agriculture.

Note
Specialized household and family farm are sometimes seen as one type.

of certified new entities[10] rose to 2.8 million.[11] As a whole, the production area of all new entities in total accounts for 30 per cent of the national production area.[12] The remaining area is in the charge of peasants who are out of the scope of the new policies. China has 220 million rural households and the average production area per rural household is merely 9 *mu* (0.6 hectares).[13] The main body of agri-food production is still those peasants. This also indicates the above-mentioned large-scale new entities would be coexisting with peasant smallholders for a long time and they could not replace the role of peasants in agri-food supply in China, as claimed by Han (2014), the Vice President of Development Research Center of The State Council.[14]

Three mainstream models of China's agri-food supply system

In the agri-food supply system, scattered smallholders at the upstream are organized and cooperate with the processing and distribution nodes of intermediaries to efficiently and safely provide high value-added agri-food products. The agri-food supply chains have been increasingly internationalized along with the globalization of the food market (Burch and Lawrence 2009). In China, some scholars claim that the agri-food supply system in the domestic market is a dualistic structure dominated by wholesale markets and supermarket chains (e.g. Yang 2007). The primary conventional agri-food supply approach is the wholesale market-centred chain. Of the total vegetable product, 80 per cent is through the "peasants + wholesalers" chain (Chen and Ren 2012). Ling and Zhu (2006) believe that supermarkets play a core role in providing fresh agri-food products and ensuring safety and quality to meet consumers' demand. Based on these previous studies as well as the current situation according to our field observation, the remainder of this section will categorize the domestic agri-food supply system into the following three mainstream models. What needs noting is that in this chapter we only focus on the most ordinary peasant households surviving in the domestic conventional supply system, so we will not take into consideration the specialized households that work for the big transnational corporations such as McDonald's and KFC, and those households involved in special supply for assigned canteens of government, factories, schools and other organizations when analysing the supply chains.

The wholesale market-centred model

The wholesale market-centred model is the dominant pattern in the agri-food supply in contemporary China. It offers a platform for wholesalers and agri-food enterprises to interact and collaborate with each other for selling similar or complementary products. In 2013, there were 1,708 wholesale markets and the transaction volume reached over ten billion yuan, increasing by 54 per cent from 2000. The overall volume of transactions was 22,621 billion yuan[15] (Ministry of Agriculture 2015). In this model, producers autonomously select and produce crops according to their own estimation of market demand. Then, the products reach consumers through several steps of distribution among intermediate operators. The producers here include peasants, enterprises that have large-scale production bases, and farmers' cooperatives. The peasants who are not a member of farmers' cooperatives or have no contract with enterprises have two ways to sell their products: one is to wait at home for middlemen to come and collect their products; the other is to bring and sell their products at nearby wholesale markets by themselves (see Figure 8.2). Wholesale markets are situated in the centre of this supply model as an integrated service platform, where plenty of migratory wholesale dealers from local towns or other provinces and other agri-food-related organizations gather and complete transactions. Some of the products are sold in local markets and some others are distributed to outside markets. The retailing sector consists of supermarkets, chain grocery stores, agri-food wet markets and catering organizations such as individual restaurants and some organizational canteens. Wholesale markets are equipped with modern facilities for fresh keeping, packaging, transporting, storage and electronic payment in order to handle a large number and volume of daily transactions. There are three types of wholesale markets depending on spatial distance. The first type is local wholesale markets in producing areas, comprising the producing and processing clusters, to gain access to cheap and abundant products. These wholesale markets are functioning as a stage of presenting products and serving various actors of the processing cluster. The second is wholesale markets in consuming areas, which are close to the terminal of the supply chain in the consumption market. These wholesale markets are located in medium- to large-scale cities with advanced retail businesses and large consumption demands. The third one is secondary wholesale markets, usually located between the former two types of wholesale markets, so as to easily collect and transfer products and act as distribution centres. These three types of wholesale markets respectively account for 63 per cent, 27 per cent and 10 per cent of the total number of agri-food wholesale markets in China (Chen and Ren 2012). Taking Beijing as an example, most of the agri-food products provided to Beijing's consumers go through wholesale markets. Approximately 90 per cent of vegetables consumed in Beijing are distributed through wholesale markets. The Xinfadi

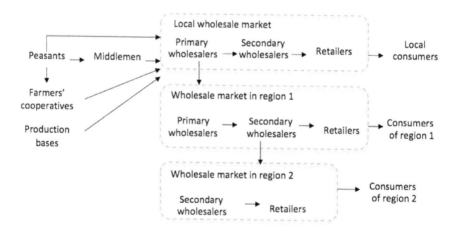

Figure 8.2 The wholesale market-centred model.
Source: authors' elaboration.

Wholesale Market is the biggest one, accounting for 80 per cent of the agri-food supply for the whole city. It supplies vegetables sourced from 26 regions to most of supermarkets, secondary wholesale markets and wet markets in Beijing and other regions all over the country. The price index of agricultural products in the Xinfadi has become a barometer for the market price formation of agricultural products throughout China. It is more like a trans-shipment centre that collects from the whole country and distributes to the whole country.

The leading enterprise-centred model

The leading enterprise integrates the capital, technology, labour and other factors of production to promote the development of specialized, standardized, large-scale and intensive agri-food production. The Chinese government believes it plays an important role in building a modern agricultural industry and promoting industrial management of agriculture through fastening the systematization of agriculture, accelerating the transformation of agricultural development mode, facilitating the construction of modern agriculture and increasing farmers' income. According to Ma (2011) on Hebei province's leading enterprises, farmers involved in this model are provided with easy-to-follow guidance on how to produce safe products so that they can overcome their productivity problem that otherwise cannot be improved in the short term. Meanwhile, for the peasants who belong to farmers' cooperatives, the profit becomes predictable and stable and therefore inspires their confidence to continue. On the other hand, the leading enterprises function as a coordinator to balance the planned supply and the real market demand through their production activities on their own production bases. The supply of agricultural products account for over 30 per cent of the national supply and 80 per cent of the national agricultural exports in the same year. Each enterprise creates more than 1,000 jobs on average (China Association of Agricultural Leading Enterprises 2012).[16] In 2015, there were 1,191 certified national leading enterprises (see Figure 8.3).

Leading enterprises focus on the production, processing and marketing of agri-food products, in cooperation with their production bases or contract farmers to form a coalition and share risks and benefits based on the premise of orders. In this model, leading enterprises play a dominant role in applying the industrialized management scheme to modern logistics system and combining other market actors in the supply system, by which the planning and flexibility of production and supply can be improved. The actors include contract farmers who operate large-scale farmland, farmers' cooperatives, leading enterprises and downstream wholesale markets and retailers.[17] There are two ways of cooperation between leading enterprises and farmers (see Figure 8.4). The first is through employment. Leading enterprises rent farmland from peasants to build their own production bases for technical experiments and general production. Peasant smallholders are hired as full-time or part-time farm workers to help cultivation. Those enterprises are usually large scale and originated from

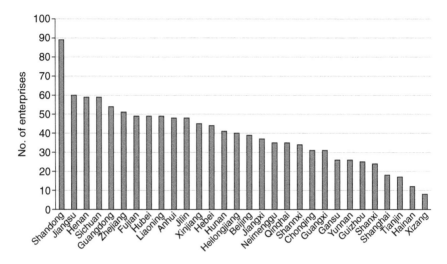

Figure 8.3 The national leading enterprises in each province.

Source: authors' elaboration according to MOA (2014).

agricultural technology promotion institutions or "Science and Technology Demonstration Parks" to promote agricultural technology, production and marketing. The other way is through production contracts. In the case that leading enterprises have no access to large-scale production bases but possess integrated sales network and fixed costumers, they make contracts with individual farms as well as farmers' cooperatives. Agricultural production by contract farmers or cooperatives is based on the orders signed with the leading enterprises, and their agri-food products are sold to the enterprises according to the required quality, negotiated prices and amount. The leading enterprises take charge of all the

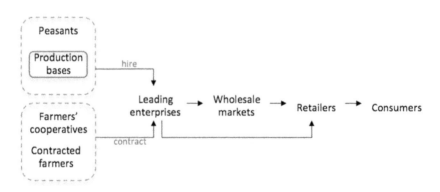

Figure 8.4 The leading enterprise-centred model.

Source: authors' elaboration.

work of processing, packaging and fresh keeping. They deliver the products to the wholesale markets or directly to retail markets through their own sales network and logistics system. In this way, leading enterprises help to achieve the efficient division of labour and make full use of all resources among producers and market operators. For example, Shouguang county of Shandong province is famous for its vegetable industry. About 95 per cent of its local vegetables are sold to nationwide retailers via Shouguang Vegetable Industry Group (He 2014). It is a representative leading enterprise established in 1998, engaged in fruit and seed breeding, vegetable production, wholesale market management, logistics and distribution, deep processing and export, and agricultural technology research and development. It owns 15 subsidiary companies, covering almost the whole county and all households.

The farming-supermarket docking model

The farming-supermarket docking model is most widely accepted in the agri-food supply system in developed countries. Unlike the former two models, the "farming-supermarkets docking" model is a new approach to skip the intermediate links and shorten the supply chains. It builds a platform extending from the farmland to the supermarket, which allows smallholders to enter into the market. The connection of supermarkets and farmers is in essence the direct connection of business and agriculture. It is conducive to two-way feedback between producers and the market so as to lessen market risks and protect the interests of producers.

In the Asia-Pacific region, more than 70 per cent of agri-food products are supplied to consumers through this model: the proportion is 80 per cent in the United States, while it is only about 15 per cent in China (Ren and Pan 2010). In 2007, Carrefour first introduced the "farming-supermarket docking" model to China, aiming to bypass dealers and reduce the involvement of intermediaries and procurement cost.[18] In 2008, the Ministry of Agriculture and the Ministry of Commerce in China officially launched the farming-supermarket docking trial by assigning some chain supermarkets as the pilot enterprises, and putting forward support policies to relax the financing regulation for related enterprises (Ministry of Commerce 2008).[19] In 2009, the government invested 400 million yuan in funds in 15 provinces to support the pilot implementation. In 2010 and 2011, this was raised to 680 million yuan and 640 million yuan respectively (Liu and Hu 2013).

This model mainly contains the following three types of cooperation among market actors (see Figure 8.5). The first is the "supermarkets + agents + farmers" type. Agents here include middlemen and wholesalers. They are entrusted to purchase and distribute the products based on the standards set by the supermarkets regarding packaging, transportation and storage. They take the risk of in-transit loss caused by unstable temperature or humidity and take the responsibility of production quality during the distribution. The second is the "supermarkets + production bases" type. Supermarkets create their private brands and authorize farmers to produce according to their requirements for seed selection, production structure and quality standard. This type offers the shortest and fastest channel to distribute the products to supermarket shelves. The third is the "supermarkets + farmers' cooperatives + farmers" type. Farmers' cooperatives act as an agency to connect supermarkets and smallholders, while they have to rely on supermarkets to distribute their products.

Taking Beijing as an example, there have been ten brands of chain supermarkets engaging in this model since 2012. They are large transnational retailers: Walmart, Carrefour and Ito-Yokado, as well as domestic enterprises: Wumei, Jingkelong, Chaoshifa, Huaguan, Yonghui, Hualian and Huarun (He 2014). They have been collaborating with 120 farmers' cooperatives. The products are usually collected in multiple ways: not only by direct purchase from their own production bases (the second type), but also from wholesale markets (the first type). For instance, in Chaoshifa, 70 per cent of the agri-food products are sourced from wholesale markets, and 30 per cent are from production bases. In Jingkelong, 90 per cent are from production bases while 10 per cent are from wholesale markets. Walmart, Carrefour, Wumei, etc. also stock from wholesale markets due to the limitation of quantity and variety available from their own production bases. However, there is an exception: Yonghui does not rely on any vendors. Yonghui Supermarket is a prominent example of the second "supermarkets + production bases" type. It is the first local chain supermarket that introduced fresh agri-food products into the modern supermarket system in China, established in Fujian province in 2001. It has expanded to be the biggest chain supermarket that deals with both processed food and fresh agri-food products. It operates 580 shops across 19 provinces.[20] Agri-food products account for over 45 per cent of its entire business. It has built 20 production bases to involve local famers in production. A good example of the "supermarkets + farmers' cooperatives" type is Carrefour. Carrefour has made contracts with 584 farmers' cooperatives, benefiting 1.29 million farmers as of 2016.[21] By reducing the involvement of intermediary vendors, Carrefour manages to shorten the distribution period by 3–5 days and save 20–30 per cent of the procurement cost. Even so, it still cannot compete with Yonghui in the fresh agri-food sector.

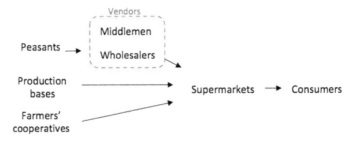

Figure 8.5 Farming-supermarket docking model.

Source: authors' elaboration.

Data collections

This section will look at the role and status of Chinese peasants and other actors in the agri-food supply system with evidence from our fieldwork. The details of the evidence will be first presented.

The empirical evidences were collected from our field surveys in Henan province. Henan is a big agricultural province, located in Central China. It has more than 49 million farmers, accounting for half of its population in 2016.[22] Most of the farmers are small-scale peasants. The arable land per capita was only 1.23 *mu*[23] in 2009. It is considered an influential region in China's agri-food supply. In 2016, its grain yield was 59.466 million tonnes, accounting for about 10 per cent of the national grain yield; its vegetable and fruit yield was 97.561 million tonnes, accounting for approximately 9 per cent of the national total yield (National Bureau of Statistics of Henan 2017). Its agri-food produce is distributed to all over the country. We assume that peasants in Henan province are typical and represent most of the peasants in Central China, and therefore our field surveys can factually reflect the reality of peasants in the region. We will demonstrate that, in whichever conventional models of agri-food supply, peasants are dependent on and subordinated to other actors in the agri-food supply system.

The surveys were conducted in 16 villages[24] from four regions, namely Muye township, Yanjin county, Fengqiu county and Weihui city. Collectively we have conducted more than 155 interviews in four consecutive fieldwork trips in September 2013, June and July 2014, May 2015 and October and November 2016. Our interviewees were largely peasant households from the above-mentioned four regions, but also covered a broad range from village leaders, officers of county governments, employees and owners of agricultural material stores, vendors and owners of wholesale markets, managers of local supermarkets, vendors of local wet markets,[25] owners of local leading enterprises, middlemen, and leaders and members of farmers' cooperatives. The data were collected through five methods: semi-structured interview, questionnaire interviews, participatory interviews, telephone interviews and online interviews by Wechat.[26] The interview questions were designed to obtain information of peasants' demographic characteristics, agri-food production structure and distribution channels, behaviour of purchasing and using chemical input, awareness and cognition regarding pesticide residue, peasants' knowledge and ordinary behaviour related to pesticide use, access and training of production technique, administrative service from local government, farmers' involvement in cooperatives, and peasants' attitude towards society and agricultural policies nowadays. We randomly visited their houses and/or met them at the farms, wholesale markets or in the streets. Given that some peasants are not able to speak Mandarin Chinese, read written Chinese or understand some terminologies regarding chemical usage and policies, we hired one local peasant (sometimes two) who could speak fluent Mandarin Chinese and help us with communication and explanation. Small peasant families living in these regions normally produce vegetables, eggs, maize and other agri-food produce for self-consumption as well as for selling to the market, with approximately an average of 4 *mu* cultivated area. Their demographic characteristics are shown in Table 8.2. Needless to say, these peasants cannot absolutely represent the current rural China as a whole due to China's huge size and heterogeneity of different regions. However, we assume that those peasants more or less reflect current realities occurring in Central China, and tell us some of the main issues and challenges in the development of agriculture and rural economy.

The peasant niche in the conventional agri-food supply system

As a whole, the supply chain is shortened in the order from the "wholesale market-centred" model and the "leading enterprise-centred" model to the "farming-supermarket docking" model. In the downstream stage of the supply chain, wholesalers, leading enterprises and supermarkets in each model consistently keep their profit margin no matter how the supply forms are structurally

Table 8.2 Demographic characteristics of the interviewed peasants

Item	Basic definition	Number	Percent of all respondents
Sex	Male	98	63
	Female	57	37
Age	30~39 years old	47	30
	40~49 years old	62	40
	50~59 years old	46	30
Education level	Primary school	39	25
	Middle school	74	48
	High school	42	27
Main income source	Agri-food production	130	84
	Others (migrant work, etc.)	25	16
Family number	3~4 people	89	57
	5~6 people	66	43
Cultivation area	Less than 1 *mu*	13	8
	1.1~3 *mu*	34	22
	3.1~5 *mu*	73	47
	More than 5 *mu*	35	23
Cultivated years	Less than 3 years	21	14
	3~8 years	54	35
	9~14 years	55	35
	More than 15 years	25	16
Where to purchase chemical input	Agricultural material stores	118	76
	Maker	15	10
	Others (farmers' cooperatives)	22	14

Source: authors' field surveys.

changed. Consumers are getting closer to farmland. Yet, in the upstream stage, the situation of peasants has not been improved a lot in spite of the progress of the agri-food supply system.

The peasant niche in the "wholesale market-centred" model

In the "wholesale markets-centred" model, first, agri-food products are collected from scattered smallholders and packed in trucks to enter in wholesale markets. The inspection conducted by the wholesale markets cannot ensure the safety of the products since the sampling rate is low and small-lot transactions are unchecked. The wholesalers do not examine the safety sufficiently due to the cost, with the results that the supply chain becomes open-ended and unable to achieve all-sided supervision and traceability. Consumers can only identify the products by appearance, and therefore the wholesalers tend to concentrate on the superficial value of products. Then, peasants are driven to protect their crops from insect damage to meet the demand for good appearance. The only possible way for them is to intensify the usage of chemical fertilizers and pesticides. Consequently, less chemically polluted but insect-eaten products are disliked and removed from the market. Safe produce with a bad appearance is eliminated and replaced by chemically polluted produce with a seemingly fresh appearance. The problem is that the more chemical inputs, the more cost for peasants. To control the cost, peasants buy affordable fertilizers and pesticides at agricultural material stores close to where they sell produce, usually around the local wholesale markets. In these agricultural material stores, inferiors or counterfeits are often sold at a lower price than the standard products. These inferiors are highly toxic pesticides or unqualified pesticides that were not up to the national standard. They can have fast effect to reduce pests, which is an efficient and pragmatic way for saving time and labour for peasants. Compared to investing intensive labour, applying these pesticides seems more cost-efficient. In general, peasants can get even bigger daily wages from working in cities as builders, waiters or taxi drivers than working on farms. Therefore, using chemical inputs to save time and labour seems rational for peasants to reduce their opportunity cost. In this way, peasants become more and more dependent on low-price pesticides. In our field surveys, 118 households (51 per cent of all the interviewed peasants) accessed chemical inputs through local agricultural material stores. Among them, 13 interviewees (about 8 per cent of all respondents) have seen highly toxic pesticides sold in the stores.

Although chemical inputs' prices have not been increased so much in the past five years,[27] the growth rate of the producer price of agri-food products also remains low. This indicates that the profit for peasants is squeezed by both the wholesale and retailing industries, as well as the agricultural input industry. The low income impels them to further chase the productivity and appearance by applying synthetic chemicals, which leads to a vicious circle. Second, the cooperative relationship among peasants, middlemen and wholesalers in this model is too loose to form an alliance that can share the risks and profit. There is no contract among those different actors, and therefore they are not vertically integrated. The only connection among them occurs at wholesale markets, where wholesalers exchange and gain market information and complete the transactions based on self-interest. Wholesalers look for the cheapest products with good superficial values no matter who, in what way, produces the products. Middlemen and wholesalers may change their suppliers (peasant smallholders) at any time. Thus, the peasants have no fixed contacts with middlemen and wholesalers, and therefore no stable sales channels. Third, the current wholesale markets still have limitations in preservation, transportation and information disclosure. One reason is that there are a huge number of individuals and enterprises involved in the wholesale market system. That may affect the information distribution and price formation. Even though peasants are at the upstream of the supply chain, they actually may be the last to get the market demand information. This inevitably leads to the slow reaction of peasants to the market with the result of a big loss of products.

Under the situation of being squeezed, peasants unavoidably place their hope on the use of chemical inputs to increase their sales and income. In our field surveys, 76 peasant households (49 per cent of all respondents) were involved in the "wholesale markets-centred" model. They basically bring and sell the produce at wholesale markets by themselves or via middlemen. Of the respondents, 96 per cent considered insecticidal effects, other than toxicity of pesticides, as a determinant reason to buy (see Table 8.3). Of the respondents, 99 per cent increased their usage of chemical inputs by over 30 per cent in the past five years. Tomato, for instance, generally needs to be sprayed with pesticides 3–4 times every month according to the national standard, but the respondents on average spray pesticides six times every month. When using pesticides on vegetables, they ought to follow the instruction labelled on the container that records the ingredient, instructions, dispersion method, preparation (dilution) method, preservation method, expiration date, target (noxious insects) and so on. However, few of the interviewed peasants actually used the pesticides as instructed. They instead applied the chemical inputs based on their experience and observation of the growth conditions of vegetables. A total of 85 per cent of them said they did not pay attention to the safety of agri-food and did not even think it would cause a problem. Among the respondents who answered that they know pesticides may damage quality, 80 per cent of them did not care about pesticide residues.

The peasant niche in the "leading enterprise-centred" model

In the "leading enterprise-centred" model, leading enterprises often selectively cooperate with producers. The capacity of leading enterprises to involve farmers as symbiotic counterparts is limited. They prefer farmers who manage large-scale farmland rather than small-scale peasants. For enterprises, leading a large number of scattered peasants to collectively produce uniform agri-food and ensure the quality is not easy. It will increase "coordination cost" (Becker and

Table 8.3 Peasants' behaviour and cognition regarding pesticide use

Questions about the behaviour and cognition of peasants	Response	Respondents' per cent		
		Wholesale market-centred model	Leading enterprise-centred model	Farm-supermarket docking model
Which factor is most important when purchasing pesticides?	Insecticidal effect	96	75	73
What is your usage amount of pesticides in the past five years	Increased over 30%	99	79	75
Do you follow the instructions to prepare and apply chemical inputs?	No	92	72	69
Are you concerned with the food safety issue?	No	85	71	58
Do you know your usage of chemical inputs may lead to pesticide residual?	Yes	90	96	98
Do you care about the safety of your produce, as regards the public?	No, I also eat	85	64	52

Source: authors' field surveys.

Murphy 1992). On the contrary, it is easier to manage and integrate large-scale farmers, because they can quickly realize economies of scale and meanwhile seek deeper collaboration with enterprises. Therefore, it might be a rational choice for peasants to draw support from intermediaries such as farmers' cooperatives to collaborate with enterprises. However, on the one hand, not all smallholders are able to join in farmers' cooperatives. Those who want to have membership must gain the consensus of the leaders of cooperatives (Law of the People's Republic of China on Specialized Farmers Cooperatives 2006), and are required to invest in the cooperatives at a certain quota.[28] On the other hand, even if peasants could be the members of farmers' cooperatives, they might not necessarily benefit from that. In our fieldwork, we found that there are "empty" cooperatives that do not function at all in five villages of Henan province. Although there are a number of farmers' cooperatives nationwide, it is doubtful whether they are farmers' cooperatives in the real sense. Due to the low threshold for registration and relevant support policies, many cooperatives have been established by merchants and village cadres. These leaders gain the greatest benefit, whereas most peasant members hardly benefit, because few cooperatives can achieve the "return of surplus" to their peasant members. Therefore, peasants have two choices: one is to be left out to continue their own ruleless production, and the other is to receive unequal distribution of the benefit by joining in farmers' cooperatives. As a whole, although the leading enterprise-centred model is actively promoted by the government, it is not realistic to expect it to fully benefit most peasants.

In our fieldwork, 39 peasant households were involved in the "leading enterprise-centred" model through the membership of farmers' cooperatives. Of them 79 per cent increased the use of chemical inputs by more than 30 per cent in the past five years (see Table 8.3). More than half of them were concerned about the safety issue and pesticide residues. Although they had better cognition of the issue than those involved in the "wholesale market-centred" model, still 72 per cent of them applied chemical inputs without following the instructions. The reason is that, although 31 households held the membership of farmers' cooperatives, only eight households who were relatively affluent with bigger scale farmlands could benefit from well-functioning cooperatives. They can receive chemical inputs and technical guidance from the cooperatives, and collectively sell their products through the fixed channel to enterprises. It is an important point that peasants can shift their focus on to the quality without worrying about the sales channel. However, the other 23 households joined the cooperatives that were not worth the name. The remaining eight households were unable to participate in any cooperatives. They still acted as a "one-man army" to hunt for channels to sell their produce, usually waiting for middlemen to come and collect their produce and sell to enterprises. In such a case, peasants have to accept the discounted producer price and give up part of the profit to the middlemen.

The peasant niche in the "farming-supermarket docking" model

In the "farming-supermarket docking" model, it seems difficult for scattered peasants to benefit as well. On the one hand, supermarkets are not likely to purchase directly from peasants, which is same with leading enterprises, because with tenuous understanding of legal procedures and liability, peasants may have opportunistic behaviours such as suddenly breaching contracts. Even though the unified distribution of the farming-supermarket docking model stimulates the integration of peasant smallholders and encourages the expansion of farmers' cooperatives, it is still difficult for most peasants to access the market via cooperatives as just discussed above. Besides, there are some additional requirements such as the quality standard applied when supermarkets select suppliers, which takes many cooperatives away from the supermarkets' doors (Ren and Pan 2010). On the other hand, in this model, the supermarkets dominate the whole supply chain and control the price. What supermarkets care about is not the peasants' livelihood, but their own profit. At present, China's agri-food market is still a buyers' market. Compared with the influence of large supermarkets, the economic capability of peasant smallholders is limited and inferior. This is particularly obvious in deal negotiations. Once they get into trouble, they do not even know how to defend their interests and rights.

In the field surveys, 40 peasant households were involved in the "farming-supermarket docking" model. However, only five households directly made contracts with supermarkets, and the remaining 35 households were in cooperation with supermarkets through agents. Due to the composition of the respondents, the result of the interviews shows a high proportion of improper behaviour and cognition. Of the respondents, 75 per cent increased the usage amount of pesticides in the past five years (see Table 8.3); 69 per cent prepared and applied chemical inputs by self-decision without following the instructions; and 58 per cent expressed concern about the food safety issue. But the five households that directly connect to supermarkets showed higher safety awareness and 100 per cent proper behaviour in terms of chemical use. There is a question as to why the safety risks are bigger if the stock is sourced through agents. On the one hand, the supermarkets were the local supermarkets. They stock from multiple agents who can offer them produce at a cheaper price through comparison. For supermarkets, it is difficult to inspect various agri-food produce every day, and even if they find out about substandard produce, they can hardly (basically will not) track the origins and call agents to be accountable. Consequently, this leads to a loophole for the substandard produce to enter supermarkets, and this loophole inevitably reflects the unsound administration of government on the supermarkets, the loose management of the supermarkets themselves and the chaotic market inundated with commercial competition. Ironically, all of the supermarkets here have an organic corner nearby the ordinary produce, where the organic vegetables, crops and soya products are stocked from specialized channels such as certain food enterprises producing "pollution-free" products. That seems to say, if consumers happen to be discomforted by the ordinary produce, it is not up to the supermarkets to take responsibility, because the supermarkets have provided choices and by choosing expensive organic produce, consumers should have evaded the risk of poisoning. On the other hand, the agents helped collect produce from the farmland to supermarkets, but in order to maximize the price difference, they seek the cheapest produce among the peasants. Catering to the agents, peasants can only depend on chemical inputs to ensure the short-term output and profit, because they were not empowered to negotiate the price with agents. Thus, those who cannot directly connect to supermarkets are almost as equally unassisted as those who are in the "wholesale market-centred model".

Conclusion

In this chapter, we have explored the Chinese peasant niche in the domestic agri-food supply system, and have demonstrated how the peasant niche is associated with peasant behaviour and cognition in three supply models respectively.

In the "wholesale market-centred" model, peasants sell their produce basically through wholesalers, however, without fixed wholesaler counterparts. Although they seem physically free to sell their produce to whichever wholesale markets, they sometimes cannot find any wholesalers to purchase their produce. Peasants carry a heavy economic burden. Consumers can only judge the products by appearance. The only possible way for peasants to protect their produce from insects and maintain a better price is to intensify the usage of chemical inputs. Only by doing so can they relieve the insecurity of subsistence. The sale, for peasants, is not just a number, but the hope of themselves and their families improving livelihood. In the "leading enterprise-centred" model and the "farming-supermarket docking" model, peasants are confronted with a dilemma: by joining farmers' cooperatives, they would be able to gain more profit through the collective production and distribution, but at the same time, they must pay a membership fee beforehand and take a risk that their cooperatives may become out-of-operation; without joining in cooperatives, there still is a possibility that they could cooperate with leading enterprises or supermarkets, but it is almost impossible unless they relinquish the nature and autonomy of peasant farming and become employees of those enterprises or supermarkets in some form, meaning that they would accept being proletarianized. Finally, small-scale peasants have no choice but to seek markets by themselves. They either carry products to wholesale markets, where they do not have to pay booth fees but have no stable trading counterparts and only moderate price is available, or else they wait at home for middlemen to come and collect their produce. The peasants in the "leading enterprise-centred" model and the "farming-supermarket docking" model act as individuals and face the same predicament as the peasants involved in the "wholesale market-centred" model. In fact, most of the peasants can only rely on themselves without the possibility of benefiting from any other actors. Therefore, even though the peasants engaged in these two models have a bit better cognition in terms of food safety, their overall production behaviour has not been improved by much.

In sum, peasants are situated in the upstream of the supply system, but are subordinated to other strong actors: wholesalers, leading enterprises and supermarkets. They do not have a "free passport" into the market. Peasants represent a vulnerable group with extremely limited economic and political autonomy. They are marginalized in the conventional agri-food supply system, serving other actors. This is the current peasant niche in the agri-food supply system in China. It is not a suitable position chosen by peasants on their own initiative; rather, it is a passive position decided by the market and other actors in the agri-food supply system. Therefore, Schulz's (1964) assertion of leaving the small farm structure intact and providing them with modern factors of production including fertilizers and pesticides at reasonable prices does not seem suitable for the current Chinese peasants. When lacking capital, labour and access to the market in the modernized supply system, peasants may act as reckless producers under the unbearable economic pressure. Their seemingly improper behaviour is actually their individual strategy to reflect their niche and survive in the specific dilemma. It is meaningless to judge that peasants are rational or not. Every decision they make is to struggle for survival, facing their economic difficulties and social and political status. Put another way, the factors that affect peasant behaviour may exist in various ways, such as education, family formation and farmland, but the niche of peasants in the market structure is so significant and determinant that it cannot be overlooked. The chains centred by leading enterprises and supermarkets are expected to lead peasants to behave more correctly and safely than the chain centred by wholesale markets, however, due to intricate supply mechanism, unstable market structure (Augustin-Jean 2015) and the insufficient administrative management, they seem unable to function as expected. Therefore, the pesticide poisonings are not happening by accident. They are the product of risks created by the current agri-food supply system. The entities involved in the three supply models are in fact extending the risks of agri-food safety under the poor governance. The chief culprit of the safety risks is not the peasant, but the system itself and the governance. These arguments here precisely provide a complementary perspective and evidence to support Schneider's (2015) notion that Chinese peasants have been considered to be "problems" for political and economic elites in developing industrial agriculture.

Having said that, our understanding of peasant behaviour could (and should) be enriched by looking at social and cultural aspects of the peasant reality. For instance, the huge rural-urban disparity in education, medical services and house property are possibly affecting peasant behaviour. In order to allow their children to receive better education in cities, to support big medical expenses for their elderly families and to get a wife for young male siblings, peasant households have to carry heavy burdens regarding saving up. Given a possibility to get a certain level of income from migrant work, a way to relieve their economic pressure might be to abandon farming and focus on migrant working, which, however, is not likely to happen. We should not forget that peasants are not only economic actors, but also cultural actors. They have been embedded and attached to the rural social and cultural landscape and kin networks. If so, the current situation of their production behaviour and agri-food safety would hardly change in the short term.

Finally, it could also be necessary and important to explore alternative paths for peasants to solve their dilemma over how to farm and access the market and address the food safety issue. Various alternative agri-food initiatives among civil society actors have actually emerged. A growing number of consumers have been engaged in direct marketing channels together with uncertified producers (Scott *et al.* 2014), especially with small-scale peasants, through Community Supported Agriculture (CSA) schemes and farmers' markets. Although their scope at present is limited, they are courageous attempts to break peasants away from the conventional supply system and transform the problematic agri-food system. These initiatives to establish alternative food networks are worthy of further study.

Notes

1 Agri-food supply in this chapter refers to the production and distribution of agri-food products.
2 http://news.qq.com/a/20110306/000357.html [accessed 6 June 2017].
3 Pollution-free, or "green", food refers to produce processed with a high level of attention paid to quality standards. It is one standard of the quality certification scheme in China.
4 We employ the *Cambridge Dictionary*'s definition of "niche", namely "an area or position that is exactly suitable for a small group of the same type". We refer to the connotation of "niche" in the term "ecological niche". In ecology, the term "niche" describes the relational position of a species or population in an ecosystem (Hutchinson 1961). It includes how a population responds to its resources, the physical environment and other beings.
5 In this chapter, "peasant" refers to those who are described as small-scale farmers whose economic development relies on their own workforce, rather than hired labour, according to Chayanov (1926/1966). "Farmer" in this chapter includes peasants and big-scale farmers.
6 According to "Report of New Type of Agricultural Management Agent Development Survey", *Economic Daily*, August 2016, www.ce.cn/xwzx/gnsz/gdxw/201608/22/t20160822_15089476.shtml [accessed 6 March 2017].
7 They are also known as "dragon-head" enterprises.
8 http://theory.people.com.cn/n/2013/0808/c40531-22491484.html [accessed 7 March 2017].
9 www.moa.gov.cn/zwllm/zwdt/201410/t20141024_4115262.htm [accessed 7 March 2017].
10 The qualification of farmers to join in the four types of entities is interpreted in Table 8.1.
11 www.ccmb360.com/article/show.asp?id=445603 [accessed 7 May 2017].
12 Since the members of farmers' cooperatives also include some peasant households, specialized households and family farms, the overall production area of the four entities is only 30 per cent of the national production area. Here, the production area refers to the areas under contracted management. In farmers' cooperatives, the members can make capital contributions in cash or in the form of intellectual property rights, farmland-manage rights or other property rights. This was not explicitly regulated in "Laws on Farmers Professional Cooperative 2007", but has relevant

descriptions in regional regulation or laws on farmers' cooperatives such as in Heilongjiang, Zhejiang, Shanxi and so forth.

13 *Mu* is a Chinese unit of area; 1 *mu* approximately equals 0.067 hectare.

14 http://finance.ifeng.com/a/20140807/12877565_0.shtm [accessed 5 January 5017].

15 According to the "Report on the Development of Agricultural Wholesale Market in China", 2014.

16 www.caale.org.cn/newshtml/13.html [accessed 12 January 2017].

17 In this chapter, retailers include supermarkets, wet markets, traditional groceries, individual restaurants and organizational canteens, and street hawkers.

18 www.carrefour.com.cn/other/ncdj.aspx [accessed 29 April 2017].

19 http://scjss.mofcom.gov.cn/aarticle/cx/200902/20090206042174.html [accessed 27 April 2017].

20 www.yonghui.com.cn/2008_model.asp?menu_level_a=1&menu_level_b=1&menu_level_c=2 [accessed 30 April 2017].

21 www.morningpost.com.cn/2017/0116/1588636.shtml [accessed 7 May 2017].

22 According to "Statistical Bulletin of National Economic and Social Development of Henan Province 2016", Henan Provincial Bureau of Statistics (NBS), http://hn.chinaso.com/qbxw/detail/20170302/1000200033030061488410876697419423_1.html [accessed 5 June 2017].

23 http://finance.ifeng.com/a/20140610/12512811_0.shtml [accessed 5 June 2017].

24 During the fieldworks, we were requested by the village leaders and peasant households to keep their anonymity, so in this chapter we will not disclose the names of villages or peasants.

25 Wet market is a retailing market in which fresh vegetables, fruits, meat, seafood and some processed food are sold to consumers by vendors, owned by the local government.

26 We also did complementary interviews via Wechat, which is a popular online communication application.

27 This is probably because they only buy the low-price goods.

28 This is according to the interviewed peasants and farmers' cooperatives in authors' field surveys in Henan province.

References

Augustin-Jean, L. (2015) "When Risks Turn to Uncertainties: Insights from the Food Markets in China and in Japan", *Journal of Social Work*, 8(3): 247–268.

Becker, G. S. and K. M. Murphy (1992) "The Division of Labor, Coordination Costs, and Knowledge", *The Quarterly Journal of Economics*, 107(4): 1137–1160.

Burch, D. and G. Lawrence (2009) "Towards a Third Food Regime: Behind the Transformation", *Agriculture and Human Values*, 26(4): 267–279.

Chayanov, A. V. (1926/1966) *Theory of Peasant Economy*, Homewood, IL: The American Economic Association/Richard D. Irwin.

Chen, J. 陈建青 and G. Ren 任国良 (2012) "Development of Agricultural Products Wholesale Market: Concentration, Diffusion and Disintegration – and the Development Stage of Wholesale Trade" 农产品批发市场的发展演进:集聚、扩散与瓦解 – 兼论中国农产品批发贸易发展阶段, *The Economist* 经济学家, 12: 74–84.

China Association of Agricultural Leading Enterprises (2012) "协会简介" (Introduction of Association), www.caale.org.cn/Index/index/menu/menu_id/7.html [accessed 12 January 2017].

Day, A. (2008) "The End of the Peasant? New Rural Reconstruction in China", *Boundary 2*, 35(2): 49–73.

Day, A. (2013) *The Peasant in Post-socialist China: History, Politics, and Capitalism*, Cambridge: Cambridge University Press.

Giddens, A. (1986) *The Constitution of Society: Outline of the Theory of Structuration* (Vol. 349), Berkeley: University of California Press.

Gong, P., S. Liang, E. J. Carlton, Q. Jiang, J. Wu, L. Wang and J. V. Remais (2012) "Urbanisation and Health in China", *The Lancet*, 379(9818): 843–852.

Han, J. (2014) "韩俊：要让农民感受到自己是土地的主人" (Han Jun: Make Peasants Feel that They are the Owners of the Land), 25 May 2014, http://finance.sina.com.cn/hy/20140525/094119217568.shtml [accessed 10 May 2017].

He, M. L. 何美丽 (2014) "Study on the Discursive Right in Vegetable Supply Chain in China" 蔬菜供应链中的话语权问题研究, unpublished PhD thesis, China Agricultural University 中国农业大学.

Hisano, S. 久野秀二 (2014) "Transnational Agribusiness Corporations" 多国籍アグリビジネス, in T. Masugata 桝形俊子, Y. Taniguchi 谷口吉光 and M. Tachikawa 立川雅司 (eds), *Sociology of Food and Agriculture* 食と農の社会学：生命と地域の視点から, Kyoto: Minerva-Shobo, 41–67.

Hofs, J. L., M. Fok and M. Vaissayre (2006) "Impact of Bt Cotton Adoption on Pesticide Use by Smallholders: A 2-year Survey in Makhatini Flats (South Africa)", *Crop Protection*, 25(9): 984–988.

Huang, P. C. C. (1985) *The Peasant Economy and Social Change in North China*, Stanford, CA: Stanford University Press.

Hutchinson, G. E. (1961) "The Paradox of the Plankton", *The American Naturalist*, 95(882): 137–145.

Ji, C. 季崇威 (1984) "The Theory and Practice of China's Opening to the Outside World Policy" 我国实行对外开放政策的理论和实践, *Economic Research Journal* 经济研究, 11: 34–42.

Jiang, J. Y. 江激宇, M. Ke 柯木飞, S. Y. Zhang 张士云 and C. B. Yin 尹昌斌 (2012) "An Analysis on the Influencing Factors of Farmers' Awareness of Vegetable Safety: An Evidence of 151 Farmer Households in Hebei Province" "农户蔬菜质量安全控制意愿的影响因素分析 – 基于河北省藁城市151份农户的调查", *Journal of Agrotechnical Economics* 农业技术经济, 5: 35–42.

Kloppenburg, J., J. Hendrickson and G. W. Stevenson (1996) "Coming in to the Foodshed", *Agriculture and Human Values*, 13(3): 33–42.

Lichtenberg, E. and R. Zimmerman (1999) "Adverse Health Experiences, Environmental Attitudes, and Pesticide Usage Behavior of Farm Operators", *Risk Analysis*, 19(2): 283–294.

Ling, N. B. 凌宁波 and F. Zhu 朱凤荣 (2006) "Constructing Supply Chain of Fresh Agricultural Products Dominated by Supermarkets" 构建由超市主导的生鲜农产品供应, *Rural Economy* 农村经济, 7: 116–118.

Liu, B. 刘兵 and D. Hu 胡定寰 (2013) "Summary on the Practices of Farming-Supermarket Docking" 我国"农超对接"实践总结与再思考, *Rural Economy* 农村经济, 2: 109–112.

Liu, E. M. and J. K. Huang (2013) "Risk Preferences and Pesticide Use by Cotton Farmers in China", *Journal of Development Economics*, 103: 202–215.

Liu, J. and J. Diamond (2005) "China's Environment in a Globalizing World", *Nature*, 435(7046): 1179–1186.

Ma, J. 马进军 (2011) "Study on the Development of Rural Leading Enterprises in Hebei Province" 河北省农村龙头企业发展研究, *Agricultural Economy* 农业经济, 8: 27–28.

Ma, Y. 马颖 and B. Chen 陈波 (2009) "Chinese Economic System Reform, Financial Development and Economic Growth since Reform and Opening up" 改革开放以来中国经济体制改革、金融发展与经济增长, *Economic Review* 经济评论, 1: 12–18, 25.

Maye, D. and J. Kirwan (2010) "Alternative Food Networks", *Sociology of Agriculture and Food*, Sociopedia.isa.

Ministry of Agriculture (2015) "中国农产品批发市场发展研究报告2014" (Report on the Development of Agricultural Wholesale Market in China 2014), June 2015, www.scagri.gov.cn/zwgk/zcfg/dzfz/201506/t20150623_346261.html [accessed 25 July 2017].

Ministry of Commerce (2008) "商务部农业部关于开展农超对接试点工作的通知" (The Notification of the Implementation of Farmer-Supermarket Docking Pilot Projects from Ministry of Commerce and Ministry of Agriculture), 20 December 2008, http://scjss.mofcom.gov.cn/aarticle/cx/200902/20090206042174.html [accessed 27 April 2017].

MOA (2014) "农业部关于公布第六次监测合格农业产业化国家重点龙头企业名单的通知" (The Notification of the Sixth Monitoring Result of Qualified National Leading Enterprise of Agricultural Industrialization), 18 September 2014, www.moa.gov.cn/nybgb/2014/shi/201712/t20171219_6111539.htm [accessed 8 May 2017].

National Bureau of Statistics of Henan (2017) "2016年河南省国民经济和社会发展统计公报" (The Statistical Bulletin of National Economic and Social Development of Henan Province 2016), 1 March 2017, www.ha.stats.gov.cn/sitesources/hntj/page_pc/tjfw/zxfb/article1c436c26b024460eb08177a6a1c6f7cd.html [accessed 15 February 2017].

National Bureau of Statistics of the People's Republic of China (2015) "中国统计年鉴2015" (*China Statistical Yearbook 2015*), www.stats.gov.cn/tjsj/ndsj/ [accessed 5 May 2017].

Netting, R. M. C. (1993) *Smallholders, Householders: Farm Families and the Ecology of Intensive, Sustainable Agriculture*, Stanford, CA: Stanford University Press.

Peng, W. (2001) "Pesticide Poisoning Accidents and Control Management", *Profession Health*, 17(1): 13.

Phipps, R. H. and J. R. Park (2002) "Environmental Benefits of Genetically Modified Crops: Global and European Perspectives on Their Ability to Reduce Pesticide Use", *Journal of Animal and Feed Sciences*, 11(1): 1–18.

Popkin, S. (1979) *The Rational Peasant: The Political Economy of Rural Society in Vietnam*, Berkeley: University of California Press.

Ren, X. 任学军 and L. Pan 潘灯 (2010) "Farming-Supermarkets Docking Reconstructs Retail Value Chain" 农超对接重构零售业价值链, *China Marketing (Management Edition)* 销售与市场 (管理版), 9: 62–65.

Roumasset, J. A. (1971) "Risk and Choice of Technique for Peasant Agriculture: Safety First and Rice Production in the Philippines", PhD thesis, Social Systems Research Institute, University of Wisconsin.

Schneider, M. (2015) "What, Then, Is a Chinese Peasant? Nongmin Discourses and Agroindustrialization in Contemporary China", *Agriculture and Human Values*, 32(2): 331–346.

Schultz, T. W. (1964) *Transforming Traditional Agriculture*, New Haven, CT: Yale University Press.

Scott, J. C. (1976) *The Moral Economy of the Peasant: Rebellion and Subsistence in Southeast Asia*, New Haven, CT and London: Yale University Press.

Scott, S., Z. Si, T. Schumilas and A. Chen (2014) "Contradictions in State- and Civil Society-Driven Developments in China's Ecological Agriculture Sector", *Food Policy*, 45: 158–166.

Thiers, P. (2005) "Using Global Organic Markets to Pay for Ecologically Based Agricultural Development in China", *Agriculture and Human Values*, 22: 3–15.

van der Ploeg, J. D. (2010) "The Peasantries of the Twenty-first Century: The Commoditisation Debate Revisited", *The Journal of Peasant Studies*, 37(1): 1–30.

van der Ploeg, J. D. (2013) *Peasants and the Art of Farming: A Chayanovian Manifesto*, Winnipeg: Fernwood Books Ltd.

van der Ploeg, J. D. and J. Ye (2016) "The Conundrum of Chinese Agriculture", in J. D. van der Ploeg and J. Ye (eds), *China's Peasant Agriculture and Rural Society: Changing Paradigms of Farming*, New York: Routledge.

van der Ploeg, J. D., J. Ye, H. Wu and C. Wang (2014) "Peasant-Managed Agricultural Growth in China: Mechanisms of Labour-driven Intensification", *International Journal of Sociology of Agriculture and Food*, 21(1): 155–171.

Wang, Q. 王清 (2005) "Study on Ecological Security Assessment of Shandong Province" 山东省生态安全评价研究, unpublished PhD thesis, Shandong University 山东大学.

Wasim, A., S. Dwaipayan and C. Ashim (2009) "Impact of Pesticides Use in Agriculture: Their Benefits and Hazards", *Interdiscip Toxicol.*, 2(1): 1–12.

Wei, L. 卫龙宝 and G. M. Lu 卢光明 (2004) "The Mechanism of Quality Control in Agricultural Specialized Cooperative Organizations: A Case Study of Zhejiang Province" 农业专业合作组织实施农产品质量控制的运作机制探析 – 以浙江省部分农业专业合作组织为例, *Chinese Rural Economy* 中国农村经济, 7: 36–40, 45.

Wu, L. 武力 (2008) "Analysis of the 30 Years of the CCP's Leading Economic Reform" 中国共产党领导经济改革三十年的阶段分析, *Journal of Chinese Communist Party History Studies* 中共党史研究, 4: 76–84.

Wunder, T. A. (2012) "Income Distribution and Consumption Driven Growth: How Consumption Behaviors of the Top Two Income Quintiles Help to Explain the Economy", *Journal of Economic Issues*, 46(1): 173–192.

Xu, R., R. Kuang, P. Even, D. Hong and R. Geert (2008) "Factors Contributing to Overuse of Pesticides in Western China", *Environmental Sciences*, 5(4): 235–249.

Yang, S. 杨叔进 (2001) "China's Economic Reform and Development: Review and Prospect at the Turn of the Century" 中国的经济改革与发展:世纪之交的回顾与展望, *Open Times* 开放时代, 1: 17–28.

Yang, W. 杨为民 (2007) "A Study on the Integration Mode of Agricultural Product Supply Chain" 农产品供应链一体化模式初探, *Rural Economy* 农村经济, 7: 33–35.

Yang, X., F. Wang, L. Meng, W. Zhang, L. Fan, V. Geissen and C. J. Ritsema (2014) "Farmer and Retailer Knowledge and Awareness of the Risks from Pesticide Use: A Case Study in the Wei River Catchment, China", *Science of The Total Environment*, 497: 172–179.

Ye, J. (2015) "Land Transfer and the Pursuit of Agricultural Modernization in China", *Journal of Agrarian Change*, 15(3): 314–337.

Zhang, H. and Y. Lu (2007) "End-Users' Knowledge, Attitude, and Behavior Towards Safe Use of Pesticides: A Case Study in the Guanting Reservoir Area, China", *Environmental Geochemistry and Health*, 29(6): 513–520.

Zhang S. 张素勤 (2016) "Overcoming the Difficulties of Supply Chain Integration from the Narrow Perspective of Agricultural Products Supply Chain" 论狭义农产品供应链视角下的供应链整合困境突破, *Agricultural Economy* 农业经济, 10: 143–144.

Zhou, J. H. and S. Jin (2009) "Safety of Vegetables and the Use of Pesticides by Farmers in China: Evidence from Zhejiang Province", *Food Control*, 20(11): 1043–1048.

9 Food risks? What food risks?

Gaps between perception and practice in Chinese food consumption

David Kurt Herold

Over the past decade a number of high-profile food-related scandals have taken place in China that have shaken consumer confidence in food produced in China. One announcement by China's largest search engine, Baidu, demonstrated in 2014 just how serious the situation is. In September 2014, Baidu presented a pair of internet-connected "smart chopsticks" to the media that were meant to test the safety of food items being consumed (Jie 2014). People were meant to swirl around the chopsticks in their food and after consultation of an online database the chopsticks delivered their verdict on whether the food was safe to eat or not.

While never widely available to consumers, the chopsticks still symbolize a number of issues involved in discourses on food safety in China. These range from the pervasiveness of food-related problems to customer insecurities about potential dangers to the widely announced but never quite delivered technological solution to all difficulties. This is combined with the perception that the government, while trusted in a generic sense on food safety, is not doing enough to protect Chinese consumers while individual government officials care more about their career and less about doing their duty – hence the necessity of relying on business entities to solve China's food-related problems.

The size of China and the numbers of companies and regulatory agencies and officials involved weaken the implementation of food-related laws, regulations and control systems (Lam *et al.* 2013). This is exacerbated by the overlapping responsibilities of competing government authorities (see similar points made by Mertha 2005), mistrust in official sources of information and widespread ignorance about food safety among both producers and consumers in China (Augustin-Jean and Alpermann 2014).

Another layer of complexity is that the discourse on food safety is situated within larger discourses on standards for a better quality of life in China driven by the expectations of the emerging middle class (Wu *et al.* 2017). Large numbers of people in China have become more affluent and more interested in the consumption of goods appropriate to their level of disposable income. This includes holidays abroad, larger living spaces, modern furniture and appliances, as well as food of better and more reliable quality (Chen and Qin 2014; Tsang 2014). The newly affluent want everything in their life to improve and are willing to spend money to do so. This has (re-)created a link between money and quality of life in China that was absent for much of the twentieth century and one that is in two important ways different from the earlier link: more people have enough money to afford better things in life and their aim is not a luxurious but rather a good life – widespread change, not small-group-led revolution (Chen and Goodman 2013; Nathan 2016). By implication this raises the notion that to have a good life in China, one needs to spend money, or put differently: the poor do not have the right to a decent life or decent food (see, for a similar argument, Yu *et al.* 2014).

In the context of the above expectations of the Chinese middle class it is no surprise that they still place their trust in the Chinese government and its officials. Chinese authorities made them comparatively rich, so why not trust them to keep them safe? As a result, the default expectation among Chinese consumers is that government authorities are hard at work to ensure their safety from food risks and will get there eventually (Wu *et al.* 2013). This belief is supported by evidence that shows that in China it is the government rather than news media or concerned citizens who uncover and publicize most food-related scandals and incidents (Liu *et al.* 2015).

Despite the many problems the Chinese middle class in particular have with the current system of government in China, they nevertheless still hold fast to the belief that the government is more reliable than any of the other stakeholders in the production, sale and consumption of food. Most consumers thus display a marked preference for stricter government controls over the food chain rather than for a relaxation of controls in favour of a more competitive market (Ortega *et al.* 2011; Zhang *et al.* 2016).

Middle-class consumers buy food certified – by the government – as safe, preferably imported from outside of China, without much knowledge about different certification systems and safety standards for the production and transport of perishable food items (Chen *et al.* 2014). Ironically, with many middle-class Chinese their twenty-first-century attitudes towards food safety clash with a nineteenth-century admiration for modern, industrial animal husbandry and food production processes – again betraying a lack of knowledge about the advantages and drawbacks of the different systems, forcing them to instead trust government authorities (de Barcellos *et al.* 2012).

Many Chinese people are aware of safe food and its identifying labels, mostly via information obtained online, but are not very knowledgeable about them (MacArthur *et al.* 2016). This contributes to their anxieties and wariness of food labelled safe and prevents them from experimenting to a meaningful degree with new food sources outside the supervision of the authorities (Liu *et al.* 2013; Si *et al.* 2014).

The distrust and lack of knowledge of Chinese consumers about food-related production, transportation and certification systems also means that they are very willing to trust internet rumours about products and their problems or about companies and their mismanagement or even criminal activities. Anonymous (and often uninformed) posters on the Internet, especially on microblogging platforms, have more credibility than the producers of food themselves (Peng *et al.* 2015), which means decisions about food are rarely made based on solid and verifiable data but instead merely based on unsubstantiated but widely shared online gossip.

Although very few people admit to blindly following online advice about food, most people state that the Internet is their primary source of information about food scares and scandals and related risks, even if they insist that they do not trust the Internet far enough to believe the solutions offered online. Research has shown that people expect solutions to come from properly certified authorities, meaning online posters offering advice need to back up their posts with evidence from medical research – even if nobody seems to follow up to check those sources (Liu *et al.* 2014).

Another source of anxiety and uncertainty is the growth of fake, misleading or paid-for posts on the Internet (Chen *et al.* 2011; Jin and Herold 2014). Fake news stories are spread via the Internet and online gossip, thus damaging people's willingness to believe anything posted online (Huang 2017). Many Chinese internet users claim not to rely on the Internet for information about food problems any more, while still trying to learn from the personal stories about "prevention actions" taken by other internet users (Mou and Lin 2014: 609). This demonstrates a worrying trend to distrust or reject information unless it is tied to a personalizing narrative of a "real" person of questionable credentials – anecdotes of personal experience rather than hard data about the ingredients of food items and their effect on human bodies (Chen 2013; Liu *et al.* 2014).

Looking at the actual food consumption by Chinese people, research into motivating factors for food choices shows that Chinese consumers care more about the sensory appeal of food and its integral status in Chinese culture and tradition – often tied to specific localities – than any underlying food safety issues (Oxfeld 2017). As long as the food looks, smells and tastes good, food safety becomes secondary (Wang *et al.* 2015), which is the starting point for this chapter.

This chapter wants to take a closer look at the confused food-related behaviour of Chinese consumers whose culinary habits often contradict their expressed opinions about food safety. First, the next section will provide an overview about some of the major food scandals of the past decade, with an emphasis on consumer reactions to each scandal. This will be followed by an overview of a few of the larger flare-ups caused by food scandals with a view on how Chinese consumers talk about food safety and observations of food-related everyday behaviour of Chinese consumers based on ethnographic encounters over the past 20 years. The final section will attempt to discuss some of the contradictions in Chinese attitudes towards food and what they could mean for the development of food safety standards in China.

Scandals, scandals everywhere

The paper by Liu and others (Liu *et al*. 2015) reports on a study based on a database of 295 "food safety incidents" between 2001 and early 2014, which translates into an average of over 22 publicly known food-related incidents each year in China. The abstract to their paper ends rather cynically with the statement: "A little fortunately, the number of food safety incidents caused by fraud is less than those caused by un-intentional human errors. Otherwise, one would have been exceedingly depressed" (Liu *et al*. 2015: 206). Even if the researchers – as researchers – may not be depressed by their findings, the sheer volume of known food-related problems is staggering, in particular as it has to be assumed that far more cases of unsafe food entering the food markets exist than have been discovered. For the average Chinese consumer, who worried more about their own health than about the state of morality of their fellow citizens, the situation has become frightening. As the selection below of the more famous Chinese food scandals of the past decade will show, Chinese consumers have little reason any longer to trust the food they eat, or the companies that are involved in its production and sale, or the government authorities that are supposed to control and certify safe food while preventing unsafe food items from reaching the market. With an average of about two food scandals each month, where would the trust come from?

In 2007, a reporter for Beijing Television secretly filmed a food vendor replacing the meat in pork buns with cardboard. Lard was added to provide consumers with a pork-like taste, which allowed the vendor to sell buns that consisted up to 60 per cent of cardboard (Kwok 2007). After much outrage about the story online and increased worries of consumers about the safety of food bought from food stalls in Beijing, the *China Daily* published an article claiming the reporter had made up the story and paid someone to pretend to make cardboard buns while being filmed doing so (Pennay 2007). This calmed people down, although many internet users speculated that the *China Daily* report was written on government orders to defuse the situation and to maintain societal harmony – a major policy goal of the Chinese government at the time (Klortho 2007).

China's most famous food-related scandal happened in 2008: the Sanlu melamine milk powder scandal. Affecting close to 300,000 babies and resulting in multiple deaths and hundreds of hospitalized babies, the scandal was made worse when it emerged that the Sanlu company producing the tainted milk had known about the problem for months without doing anything about it and without informing either the authorities or the general public (Branigan 2008a). Primarily individual small farmers were blamed for introducing the dangerous chemical into the raw milk they sold to large companies – mainly Sanlu, although other Chinese dairy companies were affected as well. The companies and government authorities were blamed for their unwillingness to publicize and solve the problem, though, which led to an unwillingness of consumers to purchase Chinese-made milk products and to an increase in distrust of government or business communications (Branigan 2008b).

The distrust was made worse when two of the largest dairy companies, Mengniu and Yili, began a war of smear campaigns against each other in 2010, which lasted until 2013 and included adversarial advertising, the running of professional online PR campaigns against each other, and even court cases (Wu et al. 2014). Not surprisingly, consumer confidence in Chinese milk products was damaged even more in the process leading to the mass purchases of milk powder from abroad (Chung 2015), which in turn prompted foreign governments to restrict the purchase of milk powder by Chinese consumers (Tsang and Nip 2013), thus creating a market for fake foreign milk powder in China (Wong 2013).

In May 2011, several Chinese media outlets reported on government efforts to curb the practice of many Chinese farmers to inject their watermelons with growth-promoting chemicals. The chemicals used were only mildly poisonous to humans, but caused watermelons to explode – some in transport, some in the face of consumers trying to cut them open (Burkitt 2011). Interestingly, the scandal was brought to the attention of the general public by government officials, rather than by outraged consumers or investigative journalists, thus it was largely seen as an attempt by the government to demonstrate their efforts on behalf of the people rather than a real problem for consumers. Nevertheless, it contributed to growing uncertainty and anxiety about the safety of food produced in China.

In September 2011, Chinese authorities cracked down on businesses selling so-called "gutter oil" for human consumption. A university professor had published research results and caught the public's attention showing that as many as 10 per cent of the restaurants in China were using cooking oil unfit for human consumption. The report led to "a six-month investigation across 14 provinces" and the closing down of "six illicit oil recyclers" (Ramzy 2011). Many of the companies involved in this scandal were ostensibly repurposing used oils and fats for use as bio-fuels, but diverted their products into the food markets as they could earn more money there (*Global Times* 2011). Despite the widely publicized government crackdown and multiple arrests, Chinese consumers were not reassured. However, as they did not know what else to do, the only published solution to the anxieties of consumers was to "choose more expensive restaurants in future to minimize the risk" (Cao and Luo 2012).

Between 2011 and 2016, authorities inside and outside China, including countries like Nigeria or Greece, as well as many reporters claimed that companies producing fake rice for display purposes out of plastic materials had in fact been selling this toxic rice for human consumption. The story gained such wide play in the international media that the fact-checking site Snopes decided to follow up on the claims in an effort to verify the stories; however, they failed to do so (LaCapria 2016). Despite numerous statements from government authorities and even confessions from managers admitting partial responsibility for allowing plastic rice to enter the food chain, the stories have as yet neither been proven nor disproved, thus contributing to consumer insecurity and a lessening of trust in both the authorities and the media.

In 2013, people living along tributaries of the Huangpu River, the main source of tap water for Shanghai, were shocked to see pig carcasses floating in the water. In the end, over 16,000 pig carcasses were fished out of the water, all displaying signs of disease. The back story that emerged was even worse. Apparently, several black market butchers and dealers had been buying diseased, unfit-for-consumption pigs for years ostensibly for disposal and then sold their meat illegally on Chinese food markets. After a crackdown on the practice by government authorities in late 2012, pig farmers not wanting to pay for the disposal of their sick animals began dumping them in nearby rivers (Davison 2013). The flood of dead pigs was thus a positive sign rather than an ominous one – at least these pigs were not sold for human consumption. Not surprisingly, Chinese consumers were shocked and shaken in their trust in meat produced and controlled in China and began to worry what else might be swimming in their tap water (Duggan 2014).

In 2014, a cook working at a fancy restaurant was put on trial for improving the looks of the dishes served at his restaurant by painting abalones and goose feet – local delicacies – in bright and appetizing colours. The downside of his improvement measures was that the colours he used contained toxic materials, which poisoned a number of guests. In a similar manner cooks across China were found guilty of prettying food using "dye, bleach" and other materials – in particular in more expensive restaurants (Chen 2014). The chilling effect of this scandal was that China's middle-class consumers had in the past reassured themselves that by avoiding cheap restaurants they could ensure the safety and quality of the food items they consumed, which now proved to be a fallacy. No Chinese restaurants were safe, not even the ones frequented by China's elites.

In 2015, the American company Yum, owners of KFC and Pizza Hut, decided to give up and terminate their long struggle with food safety and consumer trust issues in China by franchising out their existing restaurants in China (Riley 2015). Their decision was the end-point of a three-year-long fight to win back the trust of Chinese consumers amidst emerging scandals around the safety of the meat served in their restaurants and the cleanliness of the ice-cubes added to all the drinks served on their premises. Despite their repeated attempts to reassure consumers through improved hygiene and safety protocols and an increase in transparency about suppliers and food-processing procedures, they continued losing customers as people trusted neither the company's statements nor supporting certifications and statements issued by government authorities (Baertlein and Jourdan 2012; Chen 2012; China Economic Net 2012; Li 2012).

Internet riots

Chinese internet users are infamous for running riot and causing the downfall of politicians or of companies, as well as creating problems for commercial brands or individuals misbehaving in public (for detailed discussions, see e.g. Herold 2008, 2011a, 2011b, 2012, 2016).

Large multinational companies, like the above-mentioned Yum, or its main competitor McDonald's have had enormous trouble with the fast transmission of food safety stories online. A TV report on unsanitary practices at a McDonald's restaurant in Beijing (*Beijing Times* 2012) turned very quickly into a major topic for online discussion and sharing with over 30,000 people participating on just one of China's many internet portals (Netease BBS 2012) that the restaurant chain found hard to counter (for more on this and similar events, see Herold 2015).

However, even local food scandals made national news and attracted the attention of international media outlets because of online interest in the stories. In one example, a story reported that a noodle restaurant in Xi'an in northern China had used a food additive to make (cheap) pork meat taste and look like (more expensive) beef (*Anhui News* 2011). This story was also shared by large numbers of people (24,000) on the same internet portal (Netease BBS 2011), although it did not have any direct implications for people not living in Xi'an. Internet users nevertheless discussed the story endlessly and contributed to anxieties about beef sold all over China.

Over the years, websites tracking popular Chinese internet stories have posted summaries of and links to large numbers of food scandals that attracted heated online debates. Just searching for a term like "food scandal" on the Shanghaiist (http://shanghaiist.com/), chinaSMACK (www.chinasmack.com/) or on WhatsonWeibo (www.whatsonweibo.com/) leads to long lists of food scandals discussed on the Chinese Internet over the past ten years. The discussions have in common that the posts display very little actual knowledge about food production in China, while also betraying high levels of distrust for all types of communication or information made available by government authorities or commercial entities as well as displaying a lot of anger and frustration about life in China today.

A food scandal about genetically modified corn imports is thus transformed into a complaint about the treatment of people in China in general by the authorities and businesses. They are accused of using people to experiment with unsafe foods, while consuming safe foods themselves:

> 1.3 billion people are being used as lab mice for the world. Well, no, out of those 1.3 billion people, there is a group that doesn't eat it, they have specially produced food, even specially provided air....
> (Comment by an internet user from Anhui on Phoenix online
> as quoted in Knotts 2014)

> Discarded and re-used cooking oil, genetically modified food, can people die from eating these things? Experts and academics just say it's fine while not practicing what they preach, simultaneously saying [it's safe] and avoiding [such things], secretly eating their specially supplied food!
> (Comment by an internet user from Beijing on Phoenix online
> as quoted in Knotts 2014)

Posts like these, or the fact that a post about a potential problem with an orange juice produced by Coca-Cola is "forwarded over 77,000 times within 15 hours of being posted" (Fauna 2011) are contributing not only to better flows of information about food crises in China, but are demolishing the remaining trust people have in food items produced in China and increasing people's anxiety levels. Each new scandal refreshes people's memories of scandals past while reinforcing the notion that government authorities and businesses are not to be trusted and are seemingly not doing enough to prevent the ever increasing numbers of scandals related to food.

Even traditional media outlets in China, heavily controlled and censored by the authorities, admit that food safety has become the most talked about issue in China and that it constitutes the biggest worry for Chinese consumers (*Xinhua News Agency* 2015). Chinese people talk about food safety online, they complain about food safety online – to such an extent that both foreign media and Chinese authorities cannot help but notice and respond to it, which raises the question how this online performance of concern and outrage over food safety is reflected in the daily (offline) life of people in China.

What's for dinner?

As Michel de Certeau (2000) insisted, human behaviour only makes sense when seen through the lens of large-scale statistics and from a great distance. Once a researcher begins to look more closely at the everyday lives led by individual people certainties disappear and it becomes largely impossible to predict human behaviour or to find a reliable connection between a person's statements of opinion and their daily activities. Real life does not follow nicely formulated rules. Large numbers of individual (human) trees only turn into a regular (people) forest if their observed behaviour is cleaned up, regularized and differences are averaged out.

Based on the evidence presented above, it would be reasonable to assume that Chinese consumers would increase their efforts to obtain safe food and constantly protest against government ineptitude, corruption, apathy, etc. in food-related matters. They should be wary of all food not prepared by themselves and try to source their food very carefully so as to ensure the best possible supply of food items for their families. Yet, as the Chinese celebrity blogger Han Han put it in an interview once (talking about the high-speed train crash in 2011):

> "You feel everyone's really angry, you feel like you could go open the window and you would see protesters on the street," Mr Han said. "But once you open the window, you realise that there's nothing there at all."
>
> (*The Economist* 2011)

Chinese people do not protest enough about the quality or safety of the food they eat, nor have there been large movements towards verifiably safe foods such as imported organic food. While China has become the largest market for iPhones or VW cars or even international beer and is of crucial importance to many international businesses, Chinese are not consuming organic foods in large quantities, nor has the volume of food imports grown explosively. The question is why not?

In what follows, two ethnographic accounts will be presented of food-related choices by Chinese consumers. The two accounts were chosen because the people involved display above average concern about food safety – one for business, the other for personal reasons – while also being representative for many of China's so-called emerging middle class. The accounts are based on the author's repeated encounters with the people involved between 2000 and 2016.

Organic status symbols

A and B are an upper middle-class couple in their early fifties. They have one daughter in her mid-thirties. Over the past 25 years, they have been involved in various business ventures from shops to factories, some of which were successful and some of which failed. They are very well connected and though maybe not quite rich still financially secure.

When their daughter left home five years ago, A decided she wanted to open her own restaurant while her husband kept running their other businesses. She opened a three-storey restaurant serving local cuisine on three floors with an open space on the ground floor and niches as well as private rooms on the two upper floors.

The restaurant is not a huge success, but it is not losing money either and seems to serve mostly as both an outlet for A's creativity and management skills as well as a space to take friends or family to whenever there is something to celebrate. Hired managers oversee the day-to-day running of the restaurant while A drops in frequently to check on things and to eat at the restaurant with guests.

On several occasions during the past few years, the author had the chance to talk to A about safe food, whether it was important, and where to obtain it in town for our children. Interestingly, her opinion changed over the years. She used to recommend getting vegetables and meat from one of the special farms run for high party officials through one of her connections. Beginning in 2014 she recommended a newly opened supermarket instead that – among other imported goods – specialized in organic foods. The imported, organic food sold by this supermarket was more trustworthy than the food produced even for China's elite. The irony is that the latter is only available through connections, while the former can be freely purchased.

An interesting characteristic of these exchanges on food safety was that A did not actually know very much about food safety or about the actual produce she was recommending. Formerly, she merely trusted her contacts to supply the required items from the foodstuffs produced for the party elite. Now she trusted the reputation of this one supermarket selling imported goods, without knowing anything about different organic food labels or certification schemes. These purchases thus represented status symbols rather than actual safe food choices. Being able to obtain produce meant for the elites demonstrated the quality of A's connections, while the purchase of organic food showed that she was able to afford the products sold in this one supermarket.

Looking at her own food choices confirms this interpretation of her consumption of safe food as a symbol of wealth and connections. On several occasions, she expressed her surprise that we would insist on purchasing only organic food for our children from this one supermarket. In her opinion, the food from there was far too expensive for everyday use and not fresh enough to be desirable. Buying such expensive food from abroad for oneself when not observed by others appeared senseless to her as food bought at a local market was far cheaper and much fresher.

Another aspect of obtaining food via connections are gifts from friends or relatives. On several occasions A served us sausages and meat that had been cured by her sister's husband. This was a great honour and could not be refused by us, nor did the notion of food safety ever come up in connection with these items, although I tried to raise the issue a few times. The origin of the meat to be cured was irrelevant – it had been bought by her sister's husband, which put its quality and safety beyond question. Similarly, the curing of the meat – similar to the process of air-drying sausages – was not to be questioned as it had been done by her brother-in-law, a connection, and was thus *of course* safe. Air-pollution levels or the busy road choked with exhaust fumes outside the sister's home were also irrelevant. Connections surpassed science or knowledge (see also Gong and Jackson 2012). The food items were safe to eat because of who had supplied them, not because of what they might contain.

A study by Veeck and others confirmed similar attitudes for people from Nanjing (Veeck and Burns 2005), with Chinese people valuing freshness in food above all else. Just like A, the people in Nanjing typically expected the fruit or vegetables they ate to have been harvested that very same day, and they expected the animals their meat came from to have been slaughtered on that day. Before the central government did away with them for hygienic reasons, many restaurants in China were surrounded by cages and tanks holding live animals and fish that were only slaughtered after a customer had selected them for his or her meal. In many places it is still expected practice that a live fish is brought to the table for the customer to approve before it is taken to the kitchen.

In her restaurant, neither A nor any of her staff ever even considered purchasing safe food items for the consumption of their guests. Her staff purchased fresh, cheap and good-looking items daily on the local markets to ensure the best possible flavours in the dishes served at the largest profit margins. Serving comparatively old produce transported halfway around the world was not a desirable option, especially when this came with a higher price tag. Additionally, it has been shown that Chinese consumers are suspicious of change and "new" things – at least where food is concerned (Grunert *et al.* 2011), and are unwilling to experiment, be it with new, organic food items, or unconventional methods of preparation, or with non-traditional recipes.

Online order uncertainty

C is a single woman in her early thirties, living in Shanghai. She is earning a good salary, which allows her to rent a small apartment that she has furnished largely with items purchased from IKEA. She owns an iPhone, an iPad, a Macbook Pro and a fashionable wardrobe that demonstrate her affluent status. She loves going out with friends, but also enjoys cooking at home – she and her friends have formed an informal cooking club, taking turns to prepare nice meals for the group.

C worries about food safety and therefore tries to only purchase safe food items for her own consumption. For her, this means a preference for slightly more expensive restaurants if she does not cook herself, and the purchase of food items from safe sources if she does. Based on information she obtained online while surfing through Chinese forum discussions on food safety, she prefers food produced in Europe to food produced in the US (genetically modified) or Australia/New Zealand (less reliable certification). This again demonstrates a lot of trust in online sources in combination with only rudimentary knowledge about food safety issues or certification systems. Despite C's often expressed worry about food safety she is thus not taking active steps either to educate herself about safe food or to reliably obtain safe food items for her own consumption. Instead, she trusts vague information provided by other internet users and bases her food-related decisions on these.

When purchasing food items for her kitchen, C prefers to do her shopping either in a supermarket that offers certified (European) produce or on Taobao, a Chinese online auction site comparable to eBay. Similar to A, C does not know much about the European certification systems for organic or green or safe or … food or about the difference between these systems and others. She trusts the European certificates because they are European and thus reliable as other internet users have assured her. As many studies have shown (for food-related studies, see e.g. Xu-Priour *et al.* 2014; Zhang and Gu 2015), Chinese people born after 1980 – the so-called "After-80" (*Bashihou*) generation – trust the comments of internet users more than government authorities or businesses and rely on them even as a replacement of hard data.

A simple search (in Chinese) on Taobao for "vegetables" or "meat", or for more specific items like "spinach" or "mutton" yields large numbers of results. C evaluates the offers in a similar manner to her other online purchases – she looks at the reputation of the sellers, comments left by others, accessible chat records, and then starts communicating directly with the seller to verify that her purchased items will be exactly what she wants. Additionally, similar to what has been reported by Klein whose study (2013) also mentions the importance of connections and their opinions about food sources, C prefers to purchase produce or meat from regions famous for them, e.g. mutton from Xinjiang.

It should be noted that C's purchase decisions online are not based on certification schemes or verifiable proof of food safety, but solely on the reputation of the sellers and their products. This means C trusts anonymous (to her) buyers of food items online to guide her to safe choices about the food she consumes. Her concern about food safety, while more pronounced than that of many of the people around her, is thus not fully expressed in her food-related practices, which are more a result of the general trust she displays in the truthfulness of online communities than in verifiably safe food purchases. Chinese consumers can thus again be shown to prefer connectivity to science or knowledge in the certification of food items as safe (see similar points made by Lu et al. 2010; Hung et al. 2011), although research has shown that trust in Chinese online communities, particularly on Taobao, may be misplaced as the feedback mechanisms are anything but reliable (Li et al. 2016).

Living with uncertainties?

Food choices and related behaviour in China do not seem to make a lot of sense when seen from the outside. Despite having justified, grave concerns about the quality and safety of the food available for consumption in China, and despite the constant reminder of food risks provided by the endless stream of food scandals, Chinese consumers often act as if completely unaware of any food-related problems. In their daily lives, they habitually consume foods that they (must) know to be unsafe without reflecting on it.

People in China in general, even in the so-called middle class, continue to consume food from non-verifiable sources and in unsafe environments and do not actively demand better practices from government authorities or businesses involved in the food economy in China. They do not "vote with their feet" by purchasing certified or imported food to encourage other businesses to improve their food production processes, nor do they attempt to obtain more information about certification systems, sources of safe food, etc. beyond consultation of online forums of internet users discussing such issues.

Despite a lot of noise about the lack of food safety in China, it thus makes little sense for either government authorities or for businesses to genuinely pursue stricter food safety laws or to ensure closer adherence to existing laws and regulations. Whenever the authorities do decide to act against places selling unhygienic food, there is usually an outcry demanding protection for traditional Chinese foods by Chinese consumers as well as by others (Koetse and Myers 2016). Cultural ideas about food in China demand retention of traditional sources and methods of preparation of food items while other sources of food are regarded as new and thus unreliable, strange, foreign, especially when Chinese preferences for freshness are taken into account as well (Deng et al. 2017; Wang et al. 2016).

Food consumption in China remains trapped in larger cultural logics of the reliability of connections and a distrust for impersonal knowledge (Yang 2013) that is combined with food-specific preferences for the freshness of ingredients and a distrust of anything new in relation to food sourcing or preparation. To push this conclusion to an extreme, while frozen spinach from certified organic sources may be objectively safer and healthier than fresh spinach sourced from a farm situated between a factory and a highway, Chinese consumers will choose freshness over certification – or over anxieties about pollution.

References

Anhui News (2011) "Noodle Restaurant Uses a 'Beef Paste' Food Additive to Turn Pork into Beef in 90 Minutes" 面馆用"牛肉膏"添加剂90分钟让猪肉变牛肉 [Online]. Available at: http://news.163.com/11/0413/08/71GPSGM600011229.html [accessed 5 May 2017].

Augustin-Jean, L. and B. Alpermann, eds. (2014). *The Political Economy of Agro-Food Markets in China: The Social Construction of the Markets in an Era of Globalization*, Houndsmill and New York: Palgrave Macmillan.

Baertlein, L. and A. Jourdan (2012) "Diners Not Biting on KFC's China Revival Campaign" [Online]. Available at: www.reuters.com/article/2013/12/04/us-yum-china-safety-idUSBRE9B306L20131204 [accessed 9 April 2017].

Beijing Times (2012) "CCTV 315 Party: McDonald's Expired Food" 央视315晚会：麦当劳售过期食品 [Online]. Available at: http://news.163.com/12/0316/02/7SMELD2S00014AED.html [accessed 5 May 2017].

Branigan, T. (2008a) "Chinese Figures Show Fivefold Rise in Babies Sick from Contaminated Milk" [Online]. Available at: www.theguardian.com/world/2008/dec/02/china [accessed 30 April 2017].

Branigan, T. (2008b) "Q&A: China's Contaminated Milk Scandal" [Online]. Available at: www.theguardian.com/world/2008/sep/23/china.milk.scandal [accessed 30 April 2017].

Burkitt, L. (2011) "Watermelon Scandal Bursts in China" [Online]. Available at: https://blogs.wsj.com/chinarealtime/2011/05/17/chinas-latest-food-scandal-explodin-watermelons/ [accessed 30 April 2017].

Cao, Y. and W. Luo (2012) "Rotting Meat Used to Make Illegal Oil" [Online]. Available at: www.chinadaily.com.cn/china/2012-04/04/content_14975475.htm [accessed 30 April 2017].

Chen, C. and B. Qin (2014) "The Emergence of China's Middle Class: Social Mobility in a Rapidly Urbanizing Economy", *Habitat International*, 44: 528–535.

Chen, C., K. Wu, V. Srinivasan and X. Zhang (2011) "Battling the Internet Water Army: Detection of Hidden Paid Posters", *Management*, 10.

Chen, J. (2012) "KFC Replies on the Accelerated Growth Chickens: Suhai Corporation Supplies Less Than 1% of Our Chicken Meat", *China Securities Journal Online*.

Chen, J., A. Lobo and N. Rajendran (2014) "Drivers of Organic Food Purchase Intentions in Mainland China – Evaluating Potential Customers' Attitudes, Demographics and Segmentation", *International Journal of Consumer Studies*, 38: 346–356.

Chen, M. and D. S. G. Goodman, eds. (2013) *Middle Class China: Identity and Behaviour*, Cheltenham and Northampton, MA: Edward Elgar.

Chen, T.-P. (2014) "From Tainted Food to Painted Food: China's Latest Food Scandal" [Online]. Available at: https://blogs.wsj.com/chinarealtime/2014/08/25/from-tainted-food-to-painted-food-chinas-latest-food-scandal/ [accessed 30 April 2017].

Chen, W. (2013) "The Effects of Different Types of Trust on Consumer Perceptions of Food Safety", *China Agricultural Economic Review*, 5: 43–65.

China Economic Net (2012) "Suhai Corporation Is Providing KFC with Chickens Grown in Accelerated 45 Day Processes with Chicken Feed That Can Poison Flies"

粟海集团供，*KFC* 原料鸡 45 天速成饲料能毒死苍蝇 [Online]. Available at: http://health.sohu.com/20121123/n358470558.shtml [accessed 14 June 2018].

Chung, F. (2015) "Outrage as Chemist Warehouse Buys into Chinese Baby Formula Racket" [Online]. Available at: www.news.com.au/finance/business/retail/parents-outraged-as-chemist-warehouse-buys-into-chinese-baby-formula-racket/news-story/45a8d54dd88ae7bc1fa9f780ff3549aa [accessed 30 April 2017].

Davison, N. (2013) "Rivers of Blood: The Dead Pigs Rotting in China's Water Supply" [Online]. Available at: www.theguardian.com/world/2013/mar/29/dead-pigs-china-water-supply [accessed 30 April 2017].

De Barcellos, M. D., K. G. Grunert, Y. Zhou, W. Verbeke, F. J. A. Perez-Cueto and A. Krystallis (2012) "Consumer Attitudes to Different Pig Production Systems: A Study from Mainland China", *Agriculture and Human Values*, 30: 443–455.

De Certeau, M. (2000) "Walking in the City", in G. Ward (ed.), *The Certeau Reader*, Oxford and Malden, MA: Blackwell.

Deng, X., Y. Qu, H. Zheng, Y. Lu, X. Zhong, A. Ward and Z. Li (2017) "Metaphorical Mapping between Raw-Cooked Food and Strangeness-Familiarity in Chinese Culture", *Cogn Process*, 18: 39–45.

Duggan, J. (2014) "Dead Pigs Floating in Chinese River" [Online]. Available at: www.theguardian.com/environment/chinas-choice/2014/apr/17/china-water [accessed 30 April 2017].

The Economist (2011) "China: Han on a Minute" [Online]. Available at: www.economist.com/node/21537011 [accessed 6 December 2016].

Fauna (2011) "Fear of Carbendazim in Coca-Cola's Orange Juice Spreads Online" [Online]. Available at: www.chinasmack.com/fear-of-carbendazim-in-coca-colas-orange-juice-spreads-online [accessed 12 May 2017].

Global Times (2011) "Our Kitchens Must Be Freed from Gutter Oil" [Online]. Available at: http://news.xinhuanet.com/english2010/indepth/2011-09/14/c_131138019.htm [accessed 30 April 2017].

Gong, Q. and P. Jackson (2012) "Consuming Anxiety?: Parenting Practices in China after the Infant Formula Scandal", *Food, Culture and Society: An International Journal of Multidisciplinary Research*, 15: 557–578.

Grunert, K. G., T. Perrea, Y. Zhou, G. Huang, B. T. Sorensen and A. Krystallis (2011) "Is Food-Related Lifestyle (FRL) Able to Reveal Food Consumption Patterns in Non-Western Cultural Environments? Its Adaptation and Application in Urban China", *Appetite*, 56: 357–367.

Herold, D. K. (2008) "Development of a Civic Society Online? Internet Vigilantism and State Control in Chinese Cyberspace", *Asia Journal of Global Studies*, 2: 26–37.

Herold, D. K. (2011a) "Human Flesh Search Engines: Carnivalesque Riots as Components of a 'Chinese Democracy'", in D. K. Herold and P. Marolt (eds), *Online Society in China: Creating, Celebrating, and Instrumentalising the Online Carnival*, London and New York: Routledge.

Herold, D. K. (2011b) "Noise, Spectacle, Politics: Carnival in Chinese Cyberspace", in D. K. Herold and P. Marolt (eds), *Online Society in China: Creating, Celebrating, and Instrumentalising the Online Carnival*, London and New York: Routledge.

Herold, D. K. (2012) "Rage and Reflection – Chinese Nationalism Online between Emotional Venting and Measured Opinion", in P.-L. Law (ed.), *New Connectivities in China: Virtual, Actual, and Local Interactions*, Berlin and New York: Springer.

Herold, D. K. (2015) "Whisper Campaigns: Market Risks through Online Rumours on the Chinese Internet", *China Journal of Social Work*, 8: 269–283.

Herold, D. K. (2016) "Internet Vigilantism and Chinese Nationalism", in *The Wiley-Blackwell Encyclopedia of Race, Ethnicity and Nationalism*, Oxford: Wiley-Blackwell.

Huang, E. (2017) "In China, Consumers Have to Be on Guard Not Just Against Fake Food, But Also Fake News About Food" [Online]. Available at: https://qz.com/934038/in-china-fake-news-about-food-goes-viral-because-people-find-it-hard-to-trust-anyone/ [accessed 27 April 2017].

Hung, K., S. Y. Li and D. K. Tse (2011) "Interpersonal Trust and Platform Credibility in a Chinese Multibrand Online Community", *Journal of Advertising*, 40: 99–112.

Jie, Y. (2014). "Is Your Food Safe? New 'Smart Chopsticks' Can Tell" [Online]. Available at: https://blogs.wsj.com/chinarealtime/2014/09/03/is-your-food-safe-baidus-new-smart-chopsticks-can-tell/ [accessed 27 April 2017].

Jin, G. and D. K. Herold (2014) "Gold Farmers and Water Army: Digital Playbour with Chinese Characteristics", in P. Marolt and D. K. Herold (eds), *China Online: Locating Society in Online Spaces*, London and New York: Routledge.

Klein, J. A. (2013) "Everyday Approaches to Food Safety in Kunming", *The China Quarterly*, 214: 376–393.

Klortho (2007) "Cardboard Baozi" [Online]. Available at: http://klortho.livejournal.com/51581.html [accessed 30 April 2017].

Knotts, J. (2014) "Genetically Modified Corn Imports, Chinese Netizen Reactions" [Online]. Available at: www.chinasmack.com/genetically-modified-corn-imports-chinese-netizen-reactions [accessed 12 May 2017].

Koetse, M. and R. Myers (2016) "The Disappearance of Beijing Street Food" [Online]. Available at: www.whatsonweibo.com/the-disappearance-of-beijing-streetfood/ [accessed 12 May 2017].

Kwok, V. W.-Y. (2007) "Yum! Cardboard-Stuffed Buns" [Online]. Available at: www.forbes.com/2007/07/12/china-cardboard-buns-face-markets-cx_vk_0712autofacescan01.html [accessed 30 April 2017].

LaCapria, K. (2016) "Plastic Rice from China" [Online]. Available at: www.snopes.com/plastic-rice-from-china/ [accessed 30 April 2017].

Lam, H. M., J. Remais, M. C. Fung, L. Xu and S. S. Sun (2013) "Food Supply and Food Safety Issues in China", *Lancet*, 381: 2044–2053.

Li, J. (2012) "Too-Fast Food: Behind the Scene of YUM! Brand China Slump" [Online]. Available at: www.forbes.com/sites/junhli/2012/12/06/too-fast-food-behind-the-scene-of-yum-brand-china-slum/ [accessed 30 April 2017].

Li, X., X. Guo, C. Wang and S. Zhang (2016) "Do Buyers Express Their True Assessment? Antecedents and Consequences of Customer Praise Feedback Behaviour on Taobao", *Internet Research*, 26: 1112–1133.

Liu, R., Z. Pieniak and W. Verbeke (2013) "Consumers' Attitudes and Behaviour Towards Safe Food in China: A Review", *Food Control*, 33: 93–104.

Liu, R., Z. Pieniak and W. Verbeke (2014) "Food-Related Hazards in China: Consumers' Perceptions of Risk and Trust in Information Sources", *Food Control*, 46: 291–298.

Liu, Y., F. Liu, J. Zhang, J. and J. Gao (2015) "Insights into the Nature of Food Safety Issues in Beijing through Content Analysis of an Internet Database of Food Safety Incidents in China", *Food Control*, 51: 206–211.

Lu, Y., L. Zhao and B. Wang (2010) "From Virtual Community Members to C2C E-Commerce Buyers: Trust in Virtual Communities and Its Effect on Consumers' Purchase Intention", *Electronic Commerce Research and Applications*, 9: 346–360.

MacArthur, R. L., Y. H. Wang and X. Feng (2016) "Influence of Age and Education on Nutritional Knowledge and Dietary Choices Among Chinese Consumers in Shenyang, China", *Malaysian Journal of Nutrition*, 22: 17–28.

Mertha, A. C. (2005) *The Politics of Piracy: Intellectual Property in Contemporary China*, New York: Cornell University Press.

Mou, Y. and C. A. Lin (2014) "Communicating Food Safety via the Social Media: The Role of Knowledge and Emotions on Risk Perception and Prevention", *Science Communication*, 36: 593–616.

Nathan, A. J. (2016) "The Puzzle of the Chinese Middle Class", *Journal of Democracy*, 27: 5–19.

Netease BBS (2011) "Discussion: Noodle Restaurant Uses a 'Beef Paste' Food Additive to Turn Pork into Beef in 90 Minutes" 话题：面馆用"牛肉膏"添加剂90分钟让猪肉变牛肉 [Online]. Available at: http://comment.news.163.com/news_shehui_bbs/71GPSGM600011229.html [accessed 5 May 2017].

Netease BBS (2012) "McDonald's Expired Food Scandal Expose Blocked by the Media" 话题：麦当劳被曝销售过期食品遭媒体围堵 [Online]. Available at: http://comment.news.163.com/photoview_bbs/PHOT0L6C000100AP.html [accessed 5 May 2017].

Ortega, D. L., H. H. Wang, L. Wu and N. J. Olynk (2011) "Modeling Heterogeneity in Consumer Preferences for Select Food safety Attributes in China", *Food Policy*, 36: 318–324.

Oxfeld, E. (2017) *Bitter and Sweet: Food, Meaning, and Modernity in Rural China*, Oakland, CA: University of California Press.

Peng, Y. L., J. J. Li, H. Xia, S. Y. Qi and J. H. Li (2015) "The Effects of Food Safety Issues Released by We Media on Consumers' Awareness and Purchasing Behavior: A Case Study in China", *Food Policy*, 51: 44–52.

Pennay, P. (2007) "The Fake 'Fake Baozi' Report" [Online]. Available at: www.thebeijinger.com/blog/2007/07/19/fake-fake-baozi-report [accessed 30 April 2017].

Ramzy, A. (2011) "China Cracks Down on 'Gutter Oil', a Substance Even Worse Than Its Name" [Online]. Available at: http://world.time.com/2011/09/13/china-cracks-down-on-gutter-oil-a-substance-even-worse-than-its-name/ [accessed 30 April 2017].

Riley, C. (2015) "Yum Brands to Spin Off China Business After Food Scandals" [Online]. Available at: http://money.cnn.com/2015/10/20/investing/yum-brands-china-spinoff/ [accessed 30 April 2017].

Si, Z., T. Schumilas and S. Scott (2014) "Characterizing Alternative Food Networks in China", *Agriculture and Human Values*, 32: 299–313.

Tsang, E. and A. Nip (2013) "Milk Powder Limits to Start on March 1" [Online]. Available at: www.scmp.com/news/hong-kong/article/1156644/two-can-limit-milk-powder-start-march-1 [accessed 30 April 2017].

Tsang, E. Y.-H. (2014) *The New Middle Class in China: Consumption, Politics and the Market Economy*, London: Palgrave Macmillan.

Veeck, A. and A. C. Burns (2005) "Changing Tastes: The Adoption of New Food Choices in Post-Reform China", *Journal of Business Research*, 58: 644–652.

Wang, O., H. De Steur, X. Gellynck and W. Verbeke (2015) "Motives for Consumer Choice of Traditional Food and European Food in Mainland China", *Appetite*, 87: 143–151.

Wang, O., X. Gellynck and W. Verbeke (2016) "Perceptions of Chinese Traditional Food and European Food Among Chinese Consumers", *British Food Journal*, 118: 2855–2872.

Wong, E. (2013) "Chinese Search for Infant Formula Goes Global" [Online]. Available at: www.nytimes.com/2013/07/26/world/asia/chinas-search-for-infant-formula-goes-global.html [accessed 30 April 2017].

Wu, L., Y. Zhong, L. Shan and W. Qin (2013) "Public Risk Perception of Food Additives and Food Scares: The Case in Suzhou, China", *Appetite*, 70: 90–98.

Wu, M., P. Jakubowicz and C. Cao (2014) *Internet Mercenaries and Viral Marketing: The Case of Chinese Social Media*, Hershey, PA: IGI Global.

Wu, X., D. L. Yang and L. Chen (2017) "The Politics of Quality-of-Life Issues: Food Safety and Political Trust in China", *Journal of Contemporary China*, 1–15.

Xinhua News Agency (2015) "Food Safety Top Concern in China" [Online]. Available at: www.chinadaily.com.cn/bizchina/2015-06/19/content_21050938.htm [accessed 30 April 2017].

Xu-Priour, D.-L., Y. Truong and R. R. Klink (2014) "The Effects of Collectivism and Polychronic Time Orientation on Online Social Interaction and Shopping Behavior: A Comparative Study Between China and France", *Technological Forecasting and Social Change*, 88: 265–275.

Yang, S.-Y. (2013) "From Personal Striving to Positive Influence: Exploring Wisdom in Real-Life Contexts", in M. Ferrari and N. M. Weststrate (eds), *The Scientific Study of Personal Wisdom: From Contemplative Traditions to Neuroscience*, Dordrecht: Springer Netherlands.

Yu, X., Z. Gao and Y. Zeng (2014) "Willingness to Pay for the 'Green Food' in China", *Food Policy*, 45: 80–87.

Zhang, L., Y. Xu, P. Oosterveer and A. P. J. Mol (2016) "Consumer Trust in Different Food Provisioning Schemes: Evidence from Beijing, China", *Journal of Cleaner Production*, 134: 269–279.

Zhang, Z. and C. Gu (2015) "Effects of Consumer Social Interaction on Trust in Online Group-Buying Contexts: An Empirical Study in China", *Journal of Electronic Commerce Research*, 16: 1–21.

Conclusion

Jean-Pierre Poulain and Louis Augustin-Jean

This book brings together contributions from experts from different disciplines in the social sciences (sociology, economics, political science and law), as well as in food sciences, from production to consumption. Working for the most part in Europe and Asia, they have tried to identify the theoretical and practical challenges regarding the issue of food risks in Asia. Some contributors tackle this issue head on, while others approach it from the perspectives of related fields. As such, this book is a testimony of a dynamic cooperation between Japanese, Chinese, Malaysian and European universities. It features theoretical discussions and puts detailed case studies into perspectives, which often open interesting interdisciplinary dialogues. Several authors adopt critical standpoints that have evolved into new theoretical propositions under their hands.

Food crises or, more broadly, food-related – be they sanitary, economic, environmental or cultural – issues have entered into political and media agendas all over the world. But in Asia this phenomenon has taken a form and intensity that lay a foundation for further theorization. First of all, there are implications from the increased internationalization of food trade, which are coupled with the rapid modernization of some countries in the region, such as China, Malaysia and South Korea. Within the timeframe of two generations, urbanization, the size of households, the transformation of the means of communication and transportation, as well as the fall in self-production have revolutionized food lifestyles in the region.

The "compact modernity", described by Chang (2010), is a result of the combined socio-economic and demographic phenomena that have taken place for over a century and a half in the Western world. Extending this idea to the subject of food, Poulain shows that the compact modernity is accompanied by the juxtaposition of several issues likely to be at the origin of crises such as fraud control, the management of food security and food safety, as well as socio-technical controversies about technologies used in the production, processing and commercialization of food.

With the relationship between "food availability" and "population growth" introduced by Malthus (1798), food security has become one of the major issues in the history of the social sciences. From that point, quantitative and macro approaches became an effective analytical tool for the study of food security.

During the nineteenth century, scientific advancements in both microbiology (Louis Pasteur) and physics (Ferdinand Carré), on top of the explorative work by Nicolas Appert, Benjamin Delessert and Charles Tellier before them, have created the conditions for the technological development that slows down the natural decomposition process of food, for example, canning, refrigeration or freezing, and desiccation (Poulain and Neirinck 2012). All these processes have facilitated the spatial and temporal disconnection between food processing and its consumption. Hence, it is now possible to store and transport food on a scale unseen before. It indicates the birth of food processing industries and their internationalization. As a result, health risks have become more of an issue. It is thus imperative to have a better understanding and control over the agents that may cause food poisoning. Expertise has been developed and administrative controlling bodies and international trade law have been put in place, in order to monitor both the "integrity" of the trade and the quality of food. In the 1960s, the World Health Organization (WHO) and Food and Agriculture Organization (FAO) joined forces to establish the Codex Alimentarius, which brought together almost 200 nations, with a mission to develop "standards" and "definitions and requirements for food" to facilitate international exchanges. The shortage of food, as defined by the term "security", is still a concern, but the industrialization and internationalization of agri-food markets have intensified health and quality issues. The 2000s was marked by the bovine spongiform encephalopathy (BSE) crisis and the debates over Genetically Modified Organisms (GMOs) in Europe and, to a lesser extent, the United States. Science does not explain everything; debates and controversies that are emerging go beyond the mere issue of food to encompass societal choices. The BSE crisis – in terms of severity, of the gloomy projection by some epidemiologists whose models predicted hundreds of thousands of fatalities, and of the scientific enigma regarding the cross-species barrier – has made the problem of risk and its scientific and administrative management the dominant analytical framework. Other issues, such as the environmental impact and animal rights, have taken a back seat, even though they have not disappeared completely. Similarly, several crises, both in Europe (lasagnas with horsemeat) and in Asia (adulterated milk powder), have shown that the scientific and administrative framework, as indispensable as it is, must be enlarged to take into account the consumers' and citizens' "concerns", who so far have been left in the dark with regard to sanitary risks. Such "concerns" call for the development of new ways to detect weak signals during the handling of crises.

Under the context of modernization that transformed the traditional patterns of food risks, Asia is an empirical field that questions and renews the conceptualization of risks. As we have seen, China and Malaysia are examples of "compact modernity". On these empirical grounds, phonemes known in Europe, though developed separately and over much longer periods, aggregate and collide. In China, things are happening at an unprecedented scale. In addition, food sovereignty issues are on the agricultural policies agenda everywhere, in varying degrees depending on the products and countries, but especially prevalent in the case of animal products. In spite of this, there have been significant flows of food import; and, with that, normative systems of food quality and safety interpolate. The demand for safer food products and the increase in international trade, as seen earlier, have called for the use of more and more technology, the use of drugs at the level of livestock, etc. The utilization of chemicals at different stages of production, processing and preservation have created new elements of risks, such as dosage and handling errors. Therefore, the ambivalence of the technology – which on one hand provides a solution or rectification of the food and sanitary risks, and, on the other, gives rise to new potential risks and uncertainty – is a source of controversy.

In China, crises and scandals are multiplying. Almost no category of products seems to be spared. Sanitary crises, fraud, controversies and so on intertwine within a food system undergoing profound changes. Japan, a country with one of the highest levels of industrial expertise in the field of nuclear power, has experienced an unprecedented nuclear disaster in Fukushima: the technological mastery was not sufficient to prevent the accident, nor to smooth the crisis management of its aftermath. This event has given substance to the awareness of the risk of nuclear contamination of food, whether it is seafood, which is so important in the Japanese food model, or other plant or animal products (Augustin-Jean). This "awareness" goes well beyond the national boundaries and has had implications at the international level. At the same time, it contributed to an enlargement of the portfolio of food risks and to an intensified perception of risks. In an analysis of the perception of the risks, Niiyama shows how the history of Japan and the first use of the atomic bombs at the end of the Second World War, along with the "manga culture", weigh in on the consumers' modes of perception of the nuclear risks in food (personal communication).

For about thirty years, the theorization on the issues of risk and food crises has intensified. These Asian settings provide empirical materials for both contextualized thinking and a revisit of theories of risk in general. They enable one to assess the consequences of the compact modernity in which various regional and international food cultures are colliding and weakening the food models and the apparatuses of social norms. These norms and models, in turn, have led to anxiety and the feeling of uncertainty, but at the same time generated a social demand for the explicitation of risks (Poulain 2017). Because of the undermining of traditional knowledge on which exchanges and food consumption were based, these norms and models engage us to reflect on what a new "food pact" could be (Champy). The advancement of technology in food production revamps the conditions of the food pact, i.e. the set of assumptions that underpin confidence. Under an environment of proximity, the pact is based on social interactions, on the mutual familiarity among individuals and on well-established techniques which have stood the trial of time. How can this food pact be redefined in modern societies under the multiplication of new technology applied to food but also within the framework of the administrative management of risks? Under the Asian settings, this analysis leads to the issue of the governance systems and makes it possible to contemplate a typology of the crises, from the point of view of public action (Simoulin). They relaunch the debate of rationality that has traversed the social sciences since their origins and encouraged us to reconsider the relations between individuals, actors and distribution systems. What matters here may be less the dichotomy between rationality and irrationality, but rather the *process* through which people make contextualized decisions in the presence of risks. The economic motivations linked to individuals' "greed" are not sufficient to explain fraud; nor does it fully explain risk taking. The lengthened value chains are constraining at different levels the behaviours of the participants who are pushed to search for "solutions" that are cheaper but possibly riskier. In this context, economic sociology reframes the issue of rationality by taking into account the role of the economic systems and organizational systems in which individuals make their decisions (Augustin-Jean 2014, 2015).

What remains at the end of this Asian journey of food risks? First, a confirmation: the risk is not fully controllable and there always remains some uncertainty and unpredictability; this is the case even when a very high level of expertise is involved. It is essential to make every effort to bring the probability of danger arising close to zero, and, at the same time, to accept the idea that it is impossible to completely eliminate risks and share this insight with all the actors involved. The second contribution lies in the multi-dimensionality of the food risk: food security, food safety, fraud, and controversies in technological use constitute some of the dimensions that sometimes intertwined. The result is a complexity that goes far beyond the traditional technical-scientific approach. It is therefore necessary to improve the system to detect "weak signals" in order to anticipate and be prepared for the onset of crises. To do so, Poulain proposes to explore the sources of anxiety that originate from the hierarchy of risks established by classical scientific expertise. On one hand, there are "real" risks that affect the health of the populations and are measured in terms of mortality or morbidity; on the other hand, there are the "other" risks, which are more qualitative and cannot be mediated by science. This intrinsic impossibility for mediation is therefore related to ethical issues or societal choices; or it might be temporary only and could be resolved once scientific or technological advancements are made. To take into account, within the risk management, the issue of anxiety is to accept the idea that the views of the citizens and consumers cannot be reduced to the problem of perception. It is to acknowledge the social dimensions of risk as legitimate and recognize the eaters' ability in making responsible decisions. Finally, it is to accept the idea that public action has the objectives of not only risk management but also of laying the foundation for the (re)construction of a food pact. Risk management is based on a tripod consisting of risk assessment expertise, the analysis of perceptions and evaluation of anxiety.

The epistemology of contemporary social sciences invites us to take an interest in the impact of the transformations of modern societies on the imaginary infrastructure of crises. This perspective creates the conditions for a new way to reframe scientific problematization. In this respect, Asia is a particularly fertile ground for studies. Half a century ago, Jurgen Habermas (1962/1991) pointed out that for each cultural domain that has become autonomous and whose relations can be analysed immanently based on the presupposed finality of a system, it develops, so to speak, a new discipline within the social sciences. More than a new discipline, it is in our case a socio-anthropological object, which calls for joint research projects within the social sciences and interdisciplinary dialogue.

References

Augustin-Jean, L. (2014) "An Approach to Food Quality in China: An Agenda for Future Research", in Louis Augustin-Jean and Bjorn Alpermann (eds), *The Political Economy of Agro-Food Markets in China: The Social Construction of the Markets in an Era of Globalization*, Houndmills, Basingstoke: Palgrave Macmillan, 47–74.

Augustin-Jean, L. (2015) "When Risks Turn to Uncertainties: Insights from the Food Market in China and Japan", *China Journal of Social Work*, 8(3): 247–267.

Chang, K.-S. (2010) "The Second Modern Condition? Compressed Modernity as Internalized Reflexive Cosmopolitization", *The British Journal of Sociology*, 61(3): 444–464.

Habermas, J. (1962/1991) *The Structural Transformation of the Public Sphere: An Enquiry into a Category of Bourgeois Society*, Cambridge, MA: MIT Press.

Malthus, T. R. (1798) *An Essay on the Principle of Population, as it Affects the Future Improvement of Society with Remarks on the Speculations of Mr. Godwin, M. Condorcet, and Other Writers*, London: Printed for J. Johnson, in St. Paul's Church-Yard. www.esp.org/books/malthus/population/malthus.pdf [accessed 18 June 2018].

Poulain J. P. (2017) *Sociology of Food: Eating and the Place of Food in Society*, London: Bloomsbury.

Poulain, J. P. and Neirinck, E. (2012) *Histoire de la cuisine et des cuisiniers: Techniques culinaires et manières de table en France, du moyen âge à nos jours*, Paris: Lanore.

Index

Page numbers in **bold** denote tables, those in *italics* denote figures.

For Product Safety Concerns and Information please contact our EU
representative GPSR@taylorandfrancis.com
Taylor & Francis Verlag GmbH, Kaufingerstraße 24, 80331 München, Germany

www.ingramcontent.com/pod-product-compliance
Ingram Content Group UK Ltd.
Pitfield, Milton Keynes, MK11 3LW, UK
UKHW020956180425
457613UK00019B/712